Please return this book to:

Books to You!

QUEST FOR THE GOLDEN CIRCLE

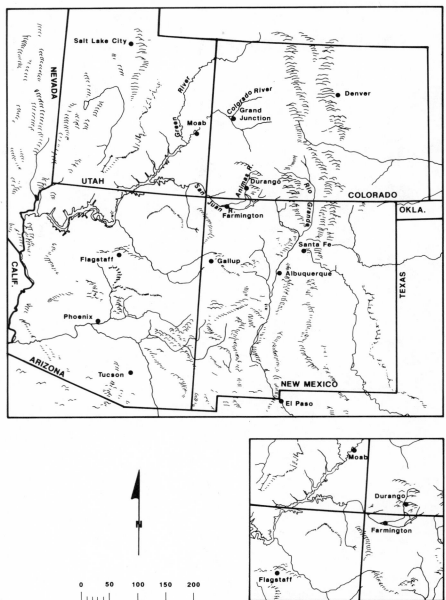

THE FOUR CORNERS STATES
(Map by Ernesto Martinez.)

ARTHUR R. GÓMEZ

Quest for the Golden Circle

THE FOUR CORNERS
AND THE METROPOLITAN WEST
1945– 1970

University of New Mexico Press • Albuquerque

Library of Congress Cataloging-in-Publication Data

Gómez, Arthur R.
    Quest for the golden circle : the Four Corners and the
metropolitan West, 1945–1970 / Arthur R. Gomez. — 1st ed.
        p.   cm.
    Includes bibliographical references and index.
    Contents: Prologue — The energy intensive West — The West
against itself — Urban imperialism in the hinterland West — That
ribbon of highways — The golden circle — Tourism and the
regional ethos — The inexhaustible resource — The fabulous
Four Corners.
    ISBN 0-8263-1540-2
    1. Four Corners Region—History.
    2. Four Corners Region—Economic conditions.
    I. Title.
    F788.5.G66   1991
    978—dc20   94-3212
                                                                          CIP

For Penny

loving wife

lifelong companion

and number one fan

Contents

Illustrations & Maps

ILLUSTRATIONS

Following page 70

Vanadium Corporation of America
AEC, Raw Materials Division
Main Street, Moab, Utah
Uranium Prospector
Charlie Steen's Mi Vida Mine
Barker Dome Field
James McNary
Oak Creek Lumber Company
San Juan Basin Pipeline
"Oil Progress Week" Parade
Charlie Steen (with glasses) and Rose Shumaker
Durango, Colorado
San Juan River Plant
Arizona Snowbowl
Navajo–Hopi Reservation
Interior Three-Band Sawmill
Signing of "Operation Gasbuggy" Agreement
Lowering Nuclear Device Near Gobernador, New Mexico
Construction of Colorado State Highway 160
Highway 550, North of Durango
Druid Arch Near Moab, Utah
Canyonlands Park Study Group
Governor John Love
Purgatory Ski Development Corporation
Uranium Mining Industry
Projected Interstate Highways, 1947

ix

MAPS

Acknowledgments

The idea for this book began quite innocuously with a trip to southwest Colorado in the spring of 1984. It was my intent to introduce Jack August, good friend and fellow graduate student at the University of New Mexico, to the Four Corners area. It is said that one never completely goes home. In this case, my return resulted in observing—with Jack's poignant and objective input—the familiar setting of Durango, Colorado, but in a much broader context than I had ever before imagined.

When my parents moved me to the Four Corners in 1956, local municipalities hummed with excitement, the result of a flurry of energy exploration activity initiated by the federal government and the private sector. Because my father owned and operated a small wood molding manufacturing plant east of town, our family benefited directly from record-breaking housing construction that typified not only Durango's growth but also that of its regional neighbors: Farmington, New Mexico; Moab, Utah; and Flagstaff, Arizona.

The decades of the 1950s and 1960s were the glory days of growth and prosperity in the Four Corners—development that mirrored the dynamic expansion of the postwar West. It was during these years that obscure, isolated hamlets like Durango were transformed into vibrant municipalities with widespread reputations as energy, scenic, and recreational meccas. My intent in undertaking this study, then, was to document the economic transformation that commenced with the termination of the Second World War.

By the 1970s, however, America's growing dependence upon foreign-produced oil reached its apex. The result was a dramatic alteration in the course of the nation's domestic petroleum industry. To adequately document the boom-to-bust drama of these historical events in the Four Corners (followed by a remarkable economic resurgence in recent years) would require a second full-length manuscript. Thus, the decade 1970 seemed to me to be an appropriate watershed as well as a convenient breaking point for this initial examination of subregional growth and change. Perhaps another trip home will inspire me to one day undertake the production of a much needed companion to this work.

The principal focus of the book is to examine economic change and urban expansionism among four small hinterland cities placed in the context of the postwar metropolitan West. In assuming this challenge, I made a conscientious decision to address Indian reservations only as they appeared germane to the main theme; therefore, they were not treated separately. It is not my intent to undermine the importance of Indian reservations as they pertain to regional growth. Indeed, the contribution of Indian lands and labor to energy resource development and scenic recreation in the Four Corners warrants a comprehensive but separate treatment. To have relegated this fascinating and complex story to one or more related chapters would have been futile. Therefore, references to the Navajo, Ute, and Apache Reservations throughout the following narrative are for the most part purposely incidental.

In writing this book I have imposed upon the personal time and professional expertise of numerous friends and colleagues. Still, there are always those who deserve special thanks for their invaluable suggestions and constructive criticism. First, I wish to thank Duane Smith, professor of history at Fort Lewis College, for his early influence and continued support. His professional example taught me the value of good local and regional history. A heartfelt thank you goes to Gerald D. Nash, the scion of twentieth-century western history, eminent scholar, mentor, and friend. He was tireless in his personal attention to my work and patient beyond any graduate student's expectations. He broadened my perspective and taught me to understand the national relevance of otherwise local events. I also want to thank Professor Richard Etulain, master wordsmith, whose persistent "tinkering" helped to make the manuscript readable.

I also owe a great deal to the remaining faculty and staff of the University of New Mexico Department of History, who nurtured me through the trials of an exceptionally demanding program. The department's generous award of the Woodward Fellowship funded most of the research for this project; I am forever grateful for your encouragement and support. Other experts read the manuscript and offered invaluable suggestions; I am especially indebted to Gene Gressley who made time within a hectic work schedule to offer his perceptive critique.

Among the myriad librarians, archivists, and local history enthusiasts who aided me in this work, I wish to recognize a handful individually: Bill Chenoweth, a former employee of the Atomic Energy Commission in Grand Junction, who guided me to the most pertinent unpublished sources—many of which he wrote; Dennis "Pete" Byrd, personal friend and pilot for Charlie Steen, who provided me with great insight to the boom town days in Moab; Emery Arnold and Tom Dugan, pioneer oilmen in the San Juan Basin, who unselfishly contributed time and postage to my cause; Leslie Gosling, Lee Byrd, James Dean, Rose Vaquera, and all of the helpful people at El Paso Natural Gas Company for their generous donation of many of the photos that embellish this manuscript; and finally, Ernesto Martinez of the National Park Service for his tremendous enthusiasm and painstaking care in producing the enclosed maps. Thank you all.

My deepest gratitude, however, is reserved for family and friends. To my parents, sisters, and two sons, Paul and Chris, for their unshakable faith that I would finish my doctoral program and publish this book. To Joanne, who endured with me through the worst of times, yet will never fully enjoy the benefit of the book's completion. Above all, to my beloved wife, Penny. She renewed my spirit and instilled in me the resolve to finish what I started. Finally, to the community of Durango for providing the amiable social atmosphere and quality learning environment that made my childhood a special experience.

Introduction

In early 1970 *Washington Post* columnist Neil R. Peirce traveled through the Rocky Mountain West in search of material to include in his book, *The Mountain States of America*. During the course of his research, Peirce, a former political editor for the *Congressional Quarterly*, noted in a conversation with Governor Forest Anderson of Montana that one of the most significant problems affecting the intermountain subregions of the West was their continued reliance upon "an almost purely extractive economy." Based on his findings, Peirce concluded that the Rocky Mountain states—virtually with the arrival of the earliest fur trappers and placer miners—had existed as natural resources colonies for the burgeoning urban-industrial segments of America. Beginning with the preindustrial development of the East in the latter half of the nineteenth century, and continuing through the post-World War II metropolitan expansion of the West, the less populated but resource-abundant intermountain states fulfilled their roles as suppliers, not processors, of raw materials for the region and the nation.[1]

In many respects, Peirce's general assessment about the state of the West in 1970 merely echoed the concerns of historians, journalists, economists, and sociologists of earlier decades who had examined the long-term consequences of rapid industrialization and urbanization on the hinterland subregions of the West.[2] With regard to studies undertaken after 1970, however, Peirce's work provided a useful model for attempting to understand the dynamics of the postwar period. Although the political development of the modern West was his main focus, Pierce advanced two ideas that have become central to the increasing body of research published in the field of twentieth-century western history since that time. First, his work on the intermountain states, together with companion books on the Pacific states and the Great Plains region, underscored the importance of subregional differentiation as a key to a better understanding of the western region as a whole. Second, Peirce's observations—along with those of earlier writers—about the seemingly irreversible colonial status of the hinterland subregions in juxtaposition to the explosive growth of the metropolitan capitals of the American West has emerged as one of the most persistent themes of western urban and economic history since World War II.[3]

It is within the context of these two predominant western themes that this study of the Four Corners, a distinct economic and cultural subregion incorporating portions of the Rocky Mountain states as well as those of the desert Southwest, is presented. In response to tremendous economic activity in the West after the Second World War, remote hinterland subregions such as the Four Corners contributed markedly to the "metropolitanization" of the larger, more dominant region. Endowed with abundant natural resources—minerals, petroleum, natural gas, and timber—hinterland communities became the principal source of energy commodities required for the protracted urbanization and modernization of the West. In the process, intraregional colonialism, in which influential metropolitan centers exploited raw materials supplied to them from the interior subregions, became the pervading economic trend in western growth during the early postwar decades.[4]

Recent scholarship has produced a number of western urban biographies that provide keener insight into the postwar growth of the region's most dynamic cities. With a few notable exceptions, these studies focus on a single entity and, in most cases, fall short in placing the subject city into the broader context of regional growth. The number of works dealing with communities of fewer than 50,000 people is even less impressive. With the exception of Duane Vandenbusche's and Duane Smith's examination of Western Slope communities in Colorado, and Roger M. Olien's and Diana Davids Olien's investigation of five oil-boom towns in West Texas, there are surprisingly few works available that analyze subregional development in the West. It is the intent of this work, therefore, to fill an historiographic gap with an in-depth examination of the urban–economic growth of four separate municipalities located in four different states within the West. In doing so, this work places the postwar expansion of the so-called Four Corners subregion into the context of regional and national development since 1945.[5]

In his introduction to Ray B. West's *Rocky Mountain Cities*, written more than forty years ago, Los Angeles journalist Carey McWilliams commented on the importance in the West of hinterland communities with populations ranging from 20,000 to 30,000 people. These cities, McWilliams observed, are "big in relation to the territories they serve, big in relation to total state population, big in relation to the functions they discharge."[6] No words are more descriptive of the Four Corners for the years 1945–1970. When compared with their respective sister cities of Denver, Salt Lake City, Phoenix, and Albuquerque, the hinterland municipalities of the Four Corners—Durango, Moab, Flagstaff, and Farmington—appear relatively insignificant in terms of size and population. But, as the following presentation argues, there is ample documented evidence to prove that the Four Corners subregion made an enduring contribution to the postwar economic expansion of not only the West but the entire nation.

QUEST FOR THE GOLDEN CIRCLE

PROLOGUE

The Frontier in Transition

In the heart of the American Southwest one encounters a peculiar phenomenon: the only spot in the United States where the borders of four contiguous states converge at a single point. The Four Corners, as this region is known, is a topographic wonderland whose convoluted features vary in elevation from the depths of the Grand Canyon to the cathedral-like spires of the Rocky Mountains. Geographers call this southwestern subregion the Colorado Plateau. Diverse landscapes, visible throughout its semiarid domain, acutely define its natural boundaries.

Beginning on the west, the Grand Canyon of the Colorado River abruptly punctuates a seemingly endless stretch of Arizona desert. Continuing clockwise, the brilliant vermilion cliffs of southeast Utah's canyon lands, which tower in dramatic relief over the monotonous desert terrain, form part of the Colorado Plateau's northern perimeter. Approximately 100 miles northeast, volcanic domes rise up to form a portion of the southern Rocky Mountains. The Abajo, La Sal, and Henry Mountains of Utah enclose the Colorado River in a natural protective envelope as it meanders southward toward the Gulf of California. Farther southwest lie the imposing silhouettes of the rugged San Juan Mountains of Colorado. These snow-capped peaks, many reaching elevations in excess of 14,000 feet, comprise the western slope of the Great Continental Divide.

Continuing clockwise, the Colorado Plateau extends across the wind-swept domain of the Navajo nation into northwestern New Mexico, until reaching its easternmost boundary at the base of the Jemez and Nacimiento Mountains. Finally, there is a southward continuum across the Arizona portion of the Navajo Reservation toward the White Moun-

3

tains and the Mogollon Rim, which most geographers accept as the south-ernmost edge of the Colorado Plateau.[1]

Contained within a nearly 50,000-square-mile area is a diverse land-scape that wields a mysterious appeal over most observers. Dr. Laurence M. Gould, one early visitor to the canyon country of southeastern Utah and northeastern Arizona, commented in 1926: "One's first impression of this plateau country is deceptive. It seems to be a relatively flat surface possessing no marked features of relief." Upon further exploration, the eminent geologist found the area to be "dissected by a veritable maze of canyons."[2] Topographic maps validate elevations varying from more than 14,000 feet in Colorado's San Juan Mountains to less than 2,000 feet in the Grand Canyon. Land forms are equally disparate, ranging from the broad valleys and mesa tops of the desert to the heavily wooded and mountainous formations common to the eastern and western extremities.

The Colorado River and its tributaries bring cohesiveness to this oth-erwise disjointed topography. According to one writer, the Colorado River drainage system resembles a "splayed left hand, palm facing away and the thumb (representing the 800-mile main stem of the river) pointing down." The Green River, whose headwaters pour forth from the glacial terraces of northern Wyoming, winds its way through Utah until it joins the upper Colorado in present Canyonlands National Park. Originating high in the Continental Divide, the San Juan River—and its arterial-like tributaries—links southwestern Colorado to northwestern New Mexico and southeast-ern Utah before it flows into the mighty Colorado a few miles upstream from present Glen Canyon Dam. Finally, the Little Colorado River curves gracefully toward the southeast, connecting with other, smaller streams to form a nebulous web that separates the mountain regions of northern Arizona from the barren Navajo Reservation farther south.[3]

Although scholars readily acknowledge the Colorado Plateau as a dis-tinct geographic area, the term "Four Corners" remains somewhat more obscure. There appears to be no conclusive agreement on its meaning. In recent years, geographers have associated the term more closely with po-litical and cultural identification rather than physiographic definition. His-torically, however, the inhabitants of this land—from its earliest arrivals to its current occupants—have acknowledged the same natural landmarks familiar to this unique landscape. For this reason, Four Corners as refer-enced in this study refers to a subregion contained within the parameters of the Colorado Plateau, a larger, more broadly defined landmass. Refer-ences to its physical boundaries more or less conform to those recognized over centuries of human migration and habitation.

Some of the most imposing evidence of prehistoric culture in the Southwest is common throughout the Four Corners. The Anasazi were among the most advanced people to settle along the northern plateau of the Colorado River.[4] Comparative latecomers, the Anasazi settled in the heartland of the Four Corners region around 200 B.C.[5] Between A.D. 1100 and 1300 this great civilization reached its zenith, having demonstrated tremendous advances in agriculture as well as architecture.

Closer examination of the abandoned remains of the Anasazi suggests that they may have established the earliest physical delineation of what today approximates the Four Corners. In Canyonlands National Park near Moab, Utah, for example, panels of extraordinarily well-preserved rock art indicate that the Anasazi hunted and farmed this northern extreme for nearly three centuries. Located about 300 miles southwest of Canyonlands, near Flagstaff, Arizona, is Wupatki National Monument. The Wupatki Basin, a spacious but isolated area with little annual rainfall, was the home of the Kayenta Anasazi, who migrated from the northeast during the twelfth century A.D. The ruins of apartment-like complexes, typical of Anasazi—and later Pueblo—architectural styles remain standing to this day.[6]

The magnificently preserved masonry structures of Chaco Culture National Historical Park are found on the eastern fringe of the Four Corners, 70 miles southeast of Farmington, New Mexico. These multistoried clusters represent perhaps the highest architectural achievements of the Anasazi builders. A veritable desert metropolis that housed some 5,000 residents, Chaco was likely a major religious center for the entire region. Mesa Verde National Park, located 50 miles southwest of Durango, Colorado, is probably the best-known example of Anasazi culture in the Four Corners. "The Mesa Verde development is among the finest and most appropriate in the National Park system," remarked landscape architect and conservationist, Frederick Law Olmstead, Jr., when he visited there in 1945. Indeed, one breathtaking view of the Cliff Palace, a consolidation of one to two hundred rooms into a sprawling, apartment-style complex, leaves little doubt as to the achievements of the Anasazi during their relatively brief inhabitation of the American Southwest.[7]

By the early 1700s Athapaskan- and Uto–Aztecan-speaking nomads had invaded the Southwest. In time Navajos, Hopis, and Apaches claimed the southern half of the Four Corners, while Utes, Navajos, and Pueblos occupied the north. In defining the boundaries of their ancestral home, modern Navajos attach spiritual significance to a set of fixed geographic points that closely parallel earlier Anasazi population centers. Moving counterclockwise from Window Rock, Arizona, capital of the Navajo nation, the northernmost landmark is Naatsis'aan (Navajo Shell Woman). The modern name is Navajo Mountain, and it is situated on the Utah–Arizona border approximately 100 miles southwest of Canyonlands National Park. Southwest of Window Rock looms Dook'o' oos'liid (Shining Top). Geographers refer to this sacred Navajo mountain as Humphrey's Peak; it is the most prominent topographic feature of the San Francisco Mountains, located only a short distance from Wupatki National Monument. Rising to an altitude of 12,670 feet, Humphrey's Peak is the highest point in the state of Arizona.[8]

Looking southeast from Window Rock, Tsoodził (Meadow Mountain) ascends more than 11,000 feet above the New Mexico plains. This spiritual landmark is Mt. Taylor. Located about 75 miles southeast of Chaco Canyon, Mt. Taylor is one of the highest elevations in New Mexico. Continuing counterclockwise from Mt. Taylor stands Dibe Ntsaa (Big Sheep), another of the sacred mountains. The more common name for this summit is Hesperus Peak, and it is part of Southwest Colorado's La Plata range. Less than 30 miles east of Mesa Verde, this seasonally white-capped citadel towers above the Animas-La Plata valley like a mute sentinel in watch over the crumbling ruins of an ancient culture.[9]

The first white visitors to the region were similarly impressed with its spectacular topography. Vivid descriptions of the canyon and plateau country of the Colorado River first appeared during the surge of Spanish explorations in the Southwest. While the existence of the Grand Canyon had been known to Spain since the encounters of García López de Cárdenas in 1540, more than two centuries elapsed before the significance of his find was fully appreciated. Franciscan friars, charged with establishing a direct route to the Pacific from remote outposts located in New Mexico and Arizona, became the first accomplished cartographers of the Four Corners.

Sometime in 1776 Fray Francisco Tomás Gárces approached the Grand Canyon from the south, while his monastic brethren Francisco Atanasio Domínguez and Silvestre Vélez de Escalante, made similar excursions from the north. Reportedly, it was Fray Garcés who sighted the lofty peaks near present Flagstaff, naming them *La Sierra de San Francisco* in honor of the patron saint of his religious order. In the narrative account of his epic journey through the rugged woodlands of northern Arizona, Fray Garcés alluded to the Grand Canyon as "the barrier which nature had fixed, a prison of cliffs and canyons."[10]

The first white men to enjoy an uninterrupted view of Mt. Taylor were the soldiers of the Francisco Vásquez de Coronado expedition who in 1540 traveled south of present Grants, New Mexico, en route to their winter encampment near Albuquerque. Two hundred and thirty-six years later, the Franciscans—Domínquez and Escalante—departed Santa Fe on a daring but unsuccessful attempt to establish an overland link to California. Their explorations took the adventurous missionaries to the foot of the La Plata Mountains, so named because of the silver-like appearance of their snow-covered peaks. Setting a course to the northwest, the Spaniards skirted the canyon country of southeastern Utah, no doubt in full view of the La Sal and Abajo Mountains near present Moab. After nearly a year and a half, the trail-weary friars traversed the Colorado River near present Lake Powell just south of Navajo Mountain, before recrossing the Arizona desert on their return home.[11]

More illuminating than the accounts of the early Spanish explorers are the official journals of the members of the U.S. Army Corps of Topographical Engineers. Commissioned to survey the most practical wagon and railroad routes to the Pacific, this elite group of army officers provided detailed and colorfully illustrated reports of the hitherto unknown geography of the Four Corners. In the summer of 1849 Lt. James H. Simpson led the earliest army reconnaissance into the Four Corners. Simpson and his staff, including brothers Richard and Edward Kern, who produced a pictorial account of the journey, were the first non-Indians to document the ruins at Chaco Canyon.[12]

From 1852 to 1858, the army commissioned a flurry of explorations into the valley of the Little Colorado. These included the overland expeditions of Capt. Lorenzo Sitgreaves (1852), Lt. Amiel Weeks Whipple (1853), and Capt. Edward Fitzgerald Beale (1857). In addition, there were the navigational exploits of Lt. Joseph C. Ives (1858), who upon sighting Humphrey's Peak near present Flagstaff, referred to the massive sentinel as "a rocky island rising from the surface of the sea visible from all parts of a circle drawn around it for a radius of 100 miles."[13]

Not all topographical officers were successful in mapping a suitable transportation route across the Southwest. In his failure to determine such a course through the Four Corners, however, Capt. John N. Macomb recorded stirring visual descriptions of the land he reconnoitered. The Macomb expedition departed Santa Fe in the summer of 1859, roughly following the trail that Domínguez and Escalante had forged nearly a century before. As the expedition penetrated the southwest corner of Colorado into the Animas River valley, Captain Macomb described what would become the future site of Durango: "a basin-like space, lying between the mountains on the north and the tablelands south; a depressed area, completely inclosed in high lands except where these were cut by the narrow gorges through which the Animas and the Pinos [Rivers] have forced their way to join the San Juan."[14]

Continuing his journey through Colorado into southeastern Utah, Macomb dutifully noted the less impressive landscape between the La Plata Mountains of Colorado and the Abajo Mountains of Utah. "The surrounding country is hopelessly sterile," Macomb concluded. "The region is a series of table lands in which its broad eroded valleys are scored by canons [sic]." As he struggled across the cavernous gorges of what today comprises Canyonlands National Park, however, Macomb detailed the remarkable land forms. "Between the Sierras Abajo and La Sal lies a lateral canyon, its walls are precipitous, generally almost perpendicular, the lower half is composed of strata which are bright red, green, yellow, or white." Obviously impressed with these visual wonders, the officer depicted them as "soft but massive beds, weathering into arches, domes, spires, towers and a thousand other imitations of human architecture, all on a colossal scale."[15] Though Macomb expressed his personal fondness for the natural beauty of the region, he judged its rugged terrain to be ill-suited for railroad construction.

While the army engineer failed to accomplish his military objective, Captain Macomb's animated accounts of the Four Corners region had a long-term impact. His eloquent, lavishly illustrated narrative lured countless others to the American Southwest. Printed nearly two decades after the expedition, Macomb's report read like a booster publication that heralded the land he christened "a region rich and beautiful." His treatment of the mountainous areas of southwestern Colorado have an alluring appeal to this day. For example, he described the area as "a region of green and flowery mountain valleys, of clear, cold and copious streams; of magnificent forests with an atmosphere of unrivalled purity, and a climate delightfully temperate." Anticipating the importance of natural resources to future growth in the West, Macomb predicted, "Here, too, are the mineral treasures, and here will congregate the mining population whose business it will be through future ages to extract for our use the mineral wealth. . . ."[16]

Not surprisingly, when Anglo-American settlers began moving west in the nineteenth century, many were attracted to the astringent yet captivating ambiance of the Four Corners. Not unlike earlier arrivals, Anglo settlers who entered the fertile valleys of the Colorado drainage system located their townsites near the most prominent landmarks. The Mormons were among the first to settle in the valleys of southeastern Utah and northern Arizona. While church officials planned their expansion into the

Moab area shortly after arriving in the Wasatch Valley in 1847, colonization was delayed until the 1870s. Mormon pioneers found the grassy plateaus near Moab—biblical term meaning "far country"—superlative cattle country. Thus, from its founding until well into the mid-1900s, Moab flourished as a ranching community.

Concurrent with the desire of the Mormon Church to extend a corridor of settlements to the Pacific, the Latter-day Saints asserted an early influence in northern Arizona. In the summer of 1874 Brigham Young dispatched a Mormon mission into the Arizona timberlands to cut lumber for the temple at St. George, Utah. Two years later, he ordered the establishment of two permanent settlements just west of present Winslow, Arizona. By 1880 the first non-Mormons homesteaded the valley of the Little Colorado River. Attracted to the lush, heavily timbered meadows near the San Francisco Mountains, the colonists founded the community of Flagstaff.[17]

As the economic enticements of cattle raising and timber production lured early settlers into Utah and Arizona, mineral riches and the fertile valleys of the San Juan River attracted the first Anglo residents to southwest Colorado and northwest New Mexico. The prospect of instant wealth from gold and silver summoned thousands of miners to the San Juan Basin between 1859 and 1879. Ramshackle mining camps that riddled the Colorado countryside created a ready market for farm and garden products, which flourished in the milder climates of the low-lying valleys. In August 1876 a group of speculators founded Animas City (Durango's precursor) as an agricultural community. That same summer, near the confluence of the Animas and San Juan Rivers in the territory of New Mexico, William and Simeon Hendrickson of Animas City established Farmington (originally named Farmingtown).[18]

By the turn of the century, each of the pioneer communities harbored populations ranging from 500 to 2,000 people. For the most part, they developed in the tradition of most frontier towns in the West. With the exception of Moab, all enjoyed the commercial advantages of a railroad. Flagstaff, situated on the main line of the Atchison, Topeka & Santa Fe Railroad, instantly thrived as a cattle and lumber town. Coconino County officials projected an early self-image of the town as "a business center of vast grazing, lumbering, and agricultural resources, peopled by energetic, progressive Americans." Farmington and Durango, economically bonded in 1880 by the narrow-gauge rails of General William Jackson Palmer's Denver and Rio Grande Western Railroad, also boasted early successes. Farmington's 500+ residents demonstrated outward pride in the town's agricultural diversity. Durangoans, too, had cause for great expectations, as their town supported not only a railroad but two smelting and refining companies.[19]

More important to the future of these frontier communities than their early commercial success were indications of the region's potential to produce energy-rich resources. Ironically, the dawn of resource exploitation in the Four Corners began innocuously in the pastoral surroundings of southeast Utah, where an amateur archeologist made an intriguing discovery. The unidentified yellow substance John Wetherill found in a shallow cave near Moab in 1898 was, in fact, uranium. While the pre–World War I era established a market for radium, a radioactive byproduct used for medical purposes, uranium had no other known value at the time. Nevertheless, National Forest Service employee Howard W. Balsley, who came to Moab in 1912, grubstaked local prospectors in exchange for deposits of the yellow cake. Balsley stored sackfuls of uranium-bearing ore in anticipation that future commercial uses might result in substantial profits.

Howard Balsley was not disappointed. In the 1930s American steel producers demanded huge deposits of vanadium, a steel-hardening element derived from the same carnotite and roscoelite ores as uranium. Up to this time, the most important sources for the exotic mineral were Peru and South Africa. Discovery of the ore in the Four Corners attracted the attention of American mining companies who were always mindful of developing a domestic source for the product. Balsley, meanwhile, became the first Moab resident to benefit from a sudden national interest in radioactive material. In 1934 he sold his stockpile to the Vitro Manufacturing Company of Pittsburgh.

In addition to encouraging independent contractors like Balsley, rising demands for vanadium stimulated a spirited competition between the Vanadium Corporation of America (VCA) and the United States Vanadium Company (USVC), a subsidiary of Union Carbide, to process the element. In 1930 the VCA subsidized construction of the first vanadium processing mill on the Colorado Plateau near Naturita, Colorado. Less than a decade later, the USVC responded by placing a second smelter into operation near present Monticello, Utah.

America's entry into the Second World War accelerated the demand for the steel-hardening agent. In May 1942 the U.S. government awarded the USVC a federal contract designating that company as the official wartime agent for the production and sale of vanadium. Later that year, the USVC reactivated the American Smelting & Refining Company (ASARCO) plant at Durango, dormant after several years of operation as a lead and silver smelter, for conversion into a second vanadium processing mill.

The strong position of the USVC in Utah and Colorado, meanwhile, forced VCA officials to seek new sources of vanadium and uranium-bearing ores, which geologists believed were available in huge deposits throughout the desert regions of Arizona and New Mexico. As the American war effort heightened, scientists devised new and unusual technological applications for uranium. The presence of large, undeveloped deposits of the exotic material on the Colorado Plateau precipitated economic changes that would have a lasting impact on each of the Four Corners communities.[20]

While the discovery of uranium gave Durango renewed importance in the twentieth century, its reputation as a smelter town had been well established during the frontier period. In those days, coal rather than uranium distinguished southwest Colorado as an energy-producing region. In the early 1900s, American industrialists coveted the rich coal deposits buried in the heart of the so-called Durango–Gallup field. In 1907 Southern Pacific President Edward H. Harriman tried unsuccessfully to use his railroad to link the energy-rich communities of the Four Corners with industrial markets in the East. Harriman's death two years later reduced the grandiose scheme to no more than a fizzle.

Its proximity to huge coal deposits enabled Durango to emerge as a regional smelting center for mining operations in the Southwest. One enthusiast commented on Durango's natural setting for a smelter, saying, "God so ordained it by placing around it [Durango] on every side, coal fields of the best quality, and almost inexhaustible in quantity." Indeed, even the internationally famed Guggenheim family invested in the town's economic future when they established the ASARCO mill there in 1901. The Guggenheim facility remained operational until 1930, when the effects of the Great Depression forced a nationwide decline in the mining industry. The USVC's reactivation of the old mill just prior to World War II, therefore, promised to reinstate mining as the preeminent industry in the San Juan Basin, and to restore Durango to its former economic glory.[21]

Farmington, on the other hand, evolved at a more leisurely pace than its northern neighbor, though not for long. The New Mexico community seemed content to remain an agricultural center. Local boosters predicted, though somewhat unrealistically, that "San Juan County is destined to be a great agriculture region capable of supporting a half million people." It is important to note, however, that the town's success as a farming community was due in large measure to increased mining activity throughout Colorado.

The discovery of new sources of energy in the early 1920s did more to shape the direction of Farmington's growth than did either mining or agriculture. In August 1922, L. E. Teague, a Farmington engineer under contract to drill for the Midwest Refining Company of Odessa, Texas, brought in the area's first oil well twenty miles west of town. Two years later, Continental Oil and other top American producers invested in a flurry of explorations all over the San Juan Basin. Economic setbacks incurred during the Great Depression, however, hampered production until the beginning of the Second World War.

A related discovery in the spring of 1923—though not considered important at the time—also promised long-term benefits for Farmington. In its search for oil, the Producers and Refiners Company of West Texas discovered the largest natural gas well in America to date. "The gas blew tools weighing nearly ten tons right out of the hole when it came in; the roar of the gas could be heard for ten miles," reported the *Farmington Times Hustler*. While the discovery of the natural gas well proved interesting reading to local townspeople, oil company officials were unimpressed because there was as yet no commercial market for natural gas. Recalled J. A. "Harry" McWilliams, one of the early oil and gas producing pioneers in the San Juan Basin, "We were hoping to strike oil . . . At that time, nobody wanted to hit gas; there was no market for it, and it was just a bother."[22]

In contrast to the agrarian economies of Moab, Durango, and Farmington, Flagstaff was an industrial town from the onset. Early on, the Babbitt Brothers Trading Company, established in 1890, brought recognition to Flagstaff as a prominent cattle town. Still, the little sawmill operation that the Riordan family took over in 1887 provided greater long-term benefits to Flagstaff in future years. Denis Matthew Riordan, a five-foot, seven-inch Chicago Irishman with "impeccable manners and gentlemanly conduct," came to Arizona not as a sawmill operator, but as a federal appointee to the Navajo Indian Agency at Fort Defiance. At the behest of his good friend and former employer, Edward E. Ayer, Riordan quit his government post in 1884 to become the general manager of Ayer's Arizona Lumber & Timber Company (AL&T) sawmill at Flagstaff. Edward E. Ayer, a Chicago industrialist, had over the years built a lumbering empire in northern Arizona that included five sawmills and a chain of lumber yards from Flagstaff to Los Angeles. When fire destroyed the company's original Flagstaff mill in 1887, Denis Riordan assumed

ownership and rebuilt the plant into an efficient, fully mechanized operation.

The Riordan family sawmill was just one of several that accounted for
Flagstaff's stable growth in the early 1900s. "If Flagstaff was fathered by
the railroad, then its mother was the lumber industry," declared one local
historian. Indeed, in the first decades of the twentieth century lumber and
timber production dominated the Flagstaff economy as three major producers operated simultaneously. In addition to AT&L, the Flagstaff Lumber & Manufacturing Company, capitalized by California investors, and
Cady & McNary Lumber Company of southeastern Louisiana also established mills in Flagstaff. Company owners introduced modernized processing techniques to make the Arizona lumber town competitive with
industrial giants located in the Midwest, Southeast, and the Pacific Northwest. Despite an economic slump in the lumber industry on a national
scale during the 1930s, wartime demands for wood products used for
shipping and construction caused the resurgence of the industry. Cognizant of the changes that could result from rapid industrialization, Flagstaff
appeared better prepared than other Four Corners municipalities to cope
with the incomparable demands of an energy-intensive West in the years
immediately following the Second World War.[23]

That the interior communities of the West, not unlike their urban
counterparts in the late nineteenth and early twentieth century, were
marked by continuity of growth and change is clearly evidenced in the
Four Corners. If, as historian Earl Pomeroy suggested, the urban frontier
of the West was simply an "imitation" of the older, more established
eastern cities, one can argue that the hinterland communities of the western frontier closely emulated their metropolitan neighbors.[24] As in the
case of the larger western communities, these remote municipalities ad-
hered to the age-old pattern of western economic dependency upon eastern industrialism as their chief source of livelihood. In the image of the
great cattle towns of the Plains region, the mining capitals of the Rocky
Mountains, and the lumbering empires of the Pacific Coast, the Four
Corners, a little-known subregion of the American Southwest, struggled
to gain acceptance into the social and economic mainstream of a developing West. In the process, these communities hastened the exploitation
of their natural and mineral resources in exchange for economic prosperity
and subregional self-esteem.

Just as there were similarities in the growth patterns between the metropolitan West and its hinterlands, there were also sharp differences. With
the exception of Flagstaff, the Four Corners municipalities did not enjoy

the benefits of an interstate transportation link to the larger regional and national community. Unlike Denver, San Francisco, Salt Lake City, Seattle, Albuquerque, and El Paso, there were no transcontinental railroads, natural harbors, or well-traveled public highways to stimulate the economic expansion of the Four Corners. An evolving urban rivalry among sister cities in the West to monopolize the extraction of mineral resources from the interior subregions beginning in the late 1880s, confirmed the colonial status of the hinterland communities. Thus the absence of an adequate transportation network and the inability to establish a nonextractive economy—fundamental requirements for independent growth—resulted in the prolonged geographic isolation and economic retardation of subregions like the Four Corners until the advent of World War II.

As the world plunged deeper into the abyss of global war, a new dawn of energy resource exploitation in the West hastened the transformation of the interior subregions. American economic expansion in the previous century dictated the terms of a colonial relationship in which the hinterland West supplied natural and mineral resources for industrial use in the East and in the Midwest. Just as the Industrial Revolution of the 1800s broke down the geographic isolation endemic to the American frontier, scientific advances and technological innovation in the twentieth century drew the interior West deeper into the mainstream of the regional and national milieu.[25]

In contrast to earlier years, variations of the traditional East–West colonialism pattern emerged. Aided by an enormous infusion of federal subsidies, beginning with the national recovery effort of the New Deal, the West terminated its colonial subservience to the industrialized East. Exhilarating growth during the war years, moreover, enabled the West to forge a viable economy and regional identity of its own. As the size and population of the region's urban centers increased during the postwar era, the energy-laden subregions of Colorado, New Mexico, Arizona, and Utah became increasingly important to federal and state planners as factors for sustained regional and national development. In effect, colonialism did not cease to exist in the West. Rather, inter-regional demands gave way to intraregional priorities dictated by unprecedented change in the postwar metropolitan West.

By the end of World War II, visitors to the Four Corners no longer viewed the area as mysterious and uninhabitable. Some were intrigued with the region's undeveloped economic potential; others were enamored with its matchless beauty. Soldiers returning home from Europe and the Pacific to their once-secluded southwest desert and mountain communities no doubt realized that the Four Corners stood on the brink of a major social and economic transformation. More importantly, these future civic leaders perceived that the Four Corners, in the wake of unrestricted resource exploitation, would one day emerge as a distinctive economic and cultural subregion within the West. As each of the four hinterland cities anticipated the impact of postwar industrial expansion, they appeared willing—for the moment at least—to risk the "total liquidation" of their natural and energy resources in order to ensure direct participation in the overall explosive development of an increasingly urban West.

ONE

The Energy Intensive West

On August 6, 1945, just sixteen hours after the detonation of the world's first atomic weapon, President Harry S. Truman informed Americans that the Japanese city of Hiroshima had been devastated. This dramatic statement, in preparation since the president's departure from the world conference in Potsdam, Germany, announced the dawn of the nuclear age. "It is an atomic bomb," the president advised, "the force from which the sun draws its power has been loosed against those who brought war to the Far East." In this brief but important radio message, President Truman praised America's outstanding scientific achievements during wartime. In addition, he heralded a new era in man's understanding and use of nature's forces. "Atomic energy may in the future supplement the power that now comes from coal, oil, and falling water," Truman predicted. Noting further that the commercial uses of nuclear power were still unknown, the chief executive pledged America's scientific community to an intensive research program.[1]

American development of the atomic bomb was one of the most dramatic and influential events of the twentieth century. First, the bomb hastened the conclusion of World War II, while it marked the beginning of a new era that one historian labeled the "energy intensive society."[2] The war taxed both the human and natural resources of the entire world as no other global conflict had. The exhilarating pace with which America mobilized its natural resources in response to wartime demands set the standard for postwar economic recovery in the decades following the surrender of Germany and Japan.

Second, the introduction of nuclear energy as a weapon for war significantly restructured the international diplomatic order that had existed before 1945. From that moment in August, global power became synonymous with harnessing atomic energy; the result was a competitive race between nations to assert world preeminence. With "national security" their watchword, Americans viewed scientific understanding of the atom—in addition to the broader application of more traditional forms of energy—as vital to the achievement of peace and prosperity.

President Truman was the foremost proponent of the new postwar energy policy. The nation's chief executive exuded the confidence of a victorious world leader in his first State of the Union message to Congress on January 21, 1946. In this address, the president challenged the United States to live up to its responsibilities as an international power. Advances in science, communications, and transportation had virtually compressed the nations of the world into a single community. The economic and political health of that world community, Truman declared, was the responsibility of its individual members. Americans had no choice but to acknowledge that a "new era" of complexity and promise was upon them. The fulfillment of this commitment was possible only through continued exploration and increased use of the nation's exploitable energy resources.[3]

Truman's pledge in 1946 to increase America's supply of petroleum and fissionable materials had a profound impact on the growth of the American West. The exigencies of the war had already precipitated a massive infusion of federal money into the West under the auspices of the Reconstruction Finance Corporation (RFC), the Defense Plant Corporation (DPC), as well as other government agencies.[4] Immediately after the war, private industry and a host of newly created federal administrations exerted a similarly profound effort to meet the energy needs of a postwar industrial society. One positive result of this endeavor was the unparalleled growth of the Four Corners subregion and other hitherto inaccessible areas of the West.

In October 1945 Truman established the broad principles his administration would follow in its quest for domestic control of atomic energy. In a special message before Congress, which extolled the potentially revolutionary uses of nuclear power, he called for the conversion of wartime weapons development to peacetime research under the aegis of a joint military and civilian advisory board. Truman planned, with the consent of the Senate, to appoint a nine-member commission for this purpose. While the commission would be vested with the power to control all sources of atomic energy, production, and research activity, the president stressed that supervision should be with "the minimum practical interference" to private enterprise. Thus, it was Truman's intent to assure continued production of fissionable material for military purposes while promoting utilization of atomic energy for peaceful application.[5]

Following the president's message, Senator Edwin C. Johnson (D–Colo.), the ranking member of the Military Affairs Committee, and Congressman Andrew Jackson May (D–Ky.), chairman of the committee's counterpart in the House, cosponsored a bill designed to implement the president's request for a joint supervisory commission. The implication that atomic energy research be removed from the exclusive supervision of the military prompted a full investigative hearing on the matter. Surprisingly, the Army proposed that it no longer be vested with sole control over atomic energy "because the problems we now face go far beyond the purely military sphere." Maj. Gen. Leslie R. Groves, the acerbic director of the Manhattan Project, concurred with the War Department's position. General Groves concluded that a committee comprised of knowledgeable civilian and military advisors would better facilitate the proper management of the United States atomic energy program.[6]

Meanwhile, on the international front, President Truman espoused a policy of "cooperation rather than rivalry in the field of atomic power." The guidelines for such a program were formally set down in November 1945 in a Washington meeting with the prime ministers of Great Britain and Canada. At that time, the three world leaders recognized the need to promote atomic power not only as a weapon for war, but as a humanitarian contribution to the entire civilized world. They prefaced their signing of a joint declaration with a mutual agreement to exchange fundamental scientific knowledge for the expressed purpose of developing industrial uses for the atom. Careful to link the idea of a new atomic supervisory commission to the postwar planning concept of a united nations organization, President Truman stressed the plan as essential "for [the] control of atomic energy to the extent necessary to ensure its use only for peaceful purposes." Notably, the Russians were not mentioned in this mutual agreement.[7]

As the May–Johnson bill moved from the Military Affairs Committee onto the floor of Congress, it encountered unforeseen opposition from America's scientific community. Many of the physicists who had worked on the Manhattan Project feared that the restrictions imposed during wartime would carry over to postwar research. In effect, they desired that administrative control over future atomic development rest exclusively in civilian rather than military hands. J. Robert Oppenheimer, director of the

Los Alamos project, testified in defense of the May–Johnson measure. He argued that the explicit purpose of the atomic commission was to delimit the power of the War Department over future scientific research. Despite these assurances, the obdurate scientific community maintained their position until the May–Johnson bill was amended to make absolutely clear that "private research would be carried on without interference from the Commission."[8]

Opponents, like Secretary of Commerce Henry A. Wallace, believed that the May–Johnson bill was ill-conceived from the beginning. Its emphasis on secrecy and military application ran counter to the president's desire for industrial development of nuclear power. In a letter to President Truman, Wallace advised placing emphasis on peaceful uses of nuclear material. The secretary noted, "We must recognize that the development of atomic energy for industrial purposes may soon be of much greater concern to the nation and have greater effect on the economy and our way of life than the atomic bomb." Taking Wallace's letter under advisement, Truman withdrew his support for the May–Johnson bill and ordered that a counterproposal be reintroduced.[9]

In response, freshman senator Brien McMahon (D–Conn.), introduced S. 1717 as an alternative measure. The McMahon bill differed from the May–Johnson proposal in three ways. First, it deemphasized the military role in regulating future atomic research. Second, the bill stressed the potential for civilian applications of nuclear power. Third, the proposal reduced the size of the so-called Atomic Energy Commission (AEC) from nine members to five. In effect, under the terms of the McMahon bill, the newly established supervisory board held a monopoly over the procurement, production, and utilization of all domestic fissionable materials.

To offset this seemingly limitless control, the McMahon bill also provided for a Joint Committee on Atomic Energy (JCAE). This eighteen-member panel had the power as a regular standing congressional committee to ensure that the AEC be held accountable to both the executive and the legislative branches. The primary function of the JCAE was to maintain legislative authority over all atomic energy matters. In an effort to gain recognition for introducing one of the nation's earliest bills on atomic energy, Senator McMahon solicited his colleagues to select him as the logical choice to chair the JCAE, a rare opportunity for a freshman legislator. On August 1, 1946, less than one year after his State of the Union appeal to the nation to increase the search for new energy sources, President Truman signed the Atomic Energy Act of 1946 into law.[10]

Passage of the Atomic Energy Act of 1946 initiated a new episode in energy resource exploration in the West. Reports filed toward the end of World War II indicated that most of the domestic supply of radioactive material lay in the remote hinterlands of the Four Corners. The new law enabled the federal government to establish a legal basis for the procurement of all available fissionable material. According to the legislative mandate, "all land and mineral deposits owned by the United States which constitute sources of atomic energy, and all stock piles of materials from which such energy may be derived should be transferred to the supervision and control of the Commission." On April 27, 1946, Truman appointed David Lilienthal, the able but outspoken director of the Tennessee Valley Authority, the first chairman of the AEC. At midnight, on December 31, Executive Order 9816 transferred all functions of the Manhattan Engineer District (MED), the wartime agency responsible for the development of the atomic bomb, to the AEC. Eight months later, Lilienthal ordered the establishment of the Division of Raw Materials to supervise uranium procurement.[11]

Washington wasted no time in turning its attention to the arid regions of the Southwest as a principal source of nuclear material. Federal administrators long recognized the potential of the Four Corners to produce uranium. During World War II, the Metals Reserve Corporation, a subsidiary of the Reconstruction Finance Corporation (RFC) charged with the procurement of industrial ores for war production, directed vanadium mining activities in that area. Used as an alloy for hardening steel, vanadium was a critical element for defense production plants near Provo, Utah, and other western localities. From 1941 to 1943 the Defense Plant Corporation, another wartime subsidiary of the RFC, funded the construction of five vanadium processing mills in the Four Corners. The facilities, located at Durango, Colorado (1941), and Monticello, Utah (1942), were the most active during these years. By 1945, as the war ebbed and demands for vanadium declined, these plants ceased to operate.[12]

With the creation of the Manhattan Engineer District (MED) in August 1942, the War Department ordered the stockpiling of uranium, a byproduct of vanadium, for use in atomic weapons research. At that time, the Metal Reserves Corporation enlisted the services of the Vanadium Corporation of America (VCA), a private mining company with interests in South America, to act as a buying agent for the federal government. In January 1943 the VCA began processing uranium from tailings piles left over from the wartime production of vanadium. While the sludge produced from these tailings contained up to 50 percent uranium, the scientists at Los Alamos considered the radioactive quality of the material inferior for weapons research. Increased availability of high quality uranium ore from the Shinkolobwe Mine in the Belgian Congo, moreover, greatly reduced the market for the lower-grade carnotite ores found on the Colorado Plateau.

Nevertheless, in anticipation of future demands for domestic uranium, the MED ordered a geologic survey of all known reserves located in the Four Corners area. In the spring of 1943 the Metals Reserve Corporation subcontracted the Union Mines Development Corporation to conduct the federally sponsored field investigation. To ensure that the region was thoroughly surveyed, United Mines officials divided the area into fifty separate geologic districts. After careful exploration and mapping of each section, the company submitted a detailed summary report. While these investigations resulted in the discovery of more than one hundred new outcroppings of uranium-vanadium ore, most of the exposures were reported as "relatively unimportant and poor in prospective value." Thus, while the government had known since 1943 that uranium deposits existed in the Four Corners, the substandard quality of these ores made them less desirable than those mined in Africa and Canada.[13]

When the AEC resumed its domestic uranium procurement program in December 1947, the Raw Materials Division established its regional headquarters in Grand Junction, Colorado, in the heart of the Four Corners. The agency's first action was to provide monetary incentives for the exploration and production of uranium. With the approval of the AEC, the Raw Materials Division released its first Domestic Uranium Program Circular, dated April 11, 1948, which guaranteed a minimum base price of $3.50 per pound for high-grade uranium ore during the next ten years. In addition, the federal government offered a bonus incentive of $10,000 for delivery of uranium-bearing ores containing 20 percent or more of the radioactive material from any single source. Finally, the government pledged to pay for the expense of hauling shipments of uranium ore from remote mining production sites to the agency's earliest designated ore-buying stations located at Moab and Monticello, Utah.

These additional bonuses for uranium exploration stimulated expansion into other regions of the American Southwest. By 1949 the AEC reported discoveries in the Monument Valley area near the Arizona–Utah border.[14] The announcement of the government's uranium incentive program promised not only renewed mining activity in Moab, but also growth and development in other similarly sized communities located within the subregion. The local newspaper in Durango, for example, featured an article on the role of the San Juan Basin in the nation's atomic energy program:

"The San Juan Basin stands at the beginning of a period during which its growth, prosperity and welfare may hit all-time highs." The article predicted further, "A period in which its progress may be measured not only in dollars and cents, jobs and homes, but in invaluable and lasting service to mankind for generations to come."

Apparently, the AEC's plans to reactivate the old vanadium mill located in Durango for uranium processing inspired enthusiastic accolades from local news writers. Less than one month after their announcement, the AEC ordered the remodification of the World War II facility. Optimistic over the prospect for new housing needed to accommodate incoming federal employees, Durangoans expressed approval of the city's new "atomic importance."[5] Once operational, the Durango plant would co-ordinate efforts with nearby ore-collection stations in southeastern Utah to manufacture uranium concentrate.

Other southwestern cities were less influenced by the government's domestic uranium procurement program. The tiny community of Farmington, New Mexico, for example, appeared comparatively unchanged in 1948. While local newspapers reported promising petroleum discoveries, the town remained—as it had since its founding—provincial and virtually dependent upon agriculture. While the flood of uranium prospectors who took on supplies en route to Colorado and Utah had some positive effects on the Farmington economy, it was petroleum exploration and development in the mid-1950s that accounted for the city's mercurial growth.[16]

Meanwhile, Flagstaff based most of its hopes for future growth on lumber-related industries rather than the AEC's uranium program. One local newspaper assured its readers that the community need never fear becoming a "ghost town" as long as postwar demands for lumber and timber continued at current levels. One manufacturer disclosed modernization plans that promised the "most up-to-date sawmill obtainable." Despite impressive discoveries of uranium in northern Arizona, most deposits were located on the Navajo Reservation, too far north to have a significant impact on the Flagstaff economy.[17]

Although Durango and Moab anticipated immediate economic growth, federally sponsored activity in the area was a disappointment in the early years. The AEC exploration and production program developed slowly under the conservative leadership of AEC chairman, David Lilienthal. Lilienthal placed little faith in geological reports that cited the Four Corners as a principal source for domestic uranium. In his December 1948 speech presented in Denver, Lilienthal criticized U.S. reliance upon foreign sources of uranium to support nuclear research. While he stressed the importance of the domestic procurement program as a cure for American dependency, the AEC chief noted that production of Rocky Mountain resources for scientific use were "relatively unimportant in the overall atomic picture." Privately, Lilienthal believed that the low-grade carnotite ores now under production on the Colorado Plateau were no match for the premium raw materials supplied from Canada and the Belgian Congo. The AEC annual report for 1947–48, moreover, showed that the agency produced a paltry 54,000 tons of uranium ore valued at slightly more than $19 million.[18]

Lilienthal's skepticism about the quality and amount of domestic uranium in reserve in 1948 was clearly evident in the agency's initial purchasing practices. In one prospector's view, the $10,000 bonus was "nothing more than a token gesture." Indeed, the AEC guaranteed price of $3.50 per pound for uranium and the bonus for the discovery of new deposits applied only to high-grade uranium-bearing ores. The less concentrated carnotite and roscoelite formations most common to the Colorado Plateau were guaranteed at a much lower fixed rate of $2.00 per pound. Such discriminatory practices discouraged prospectors in the early years and, in some cases, production in the Four Corners ceased altogether. In the summer of 1949, Senators Eugene Milliken and Edwin Johnson of Colorado, both members of the influential Military Affairs Committee, responded to the "pinch-penny" attitude of the AEC with acrimony. In addition to demanding Lilienthal's resignation, the bellicose senators called for less stringent AEC purchase policies to stimulate the exploration program.[19]

While the initial phase of the domestic uranium industry was, on the whole, unimpressive, Senators Johnson and Milliken were determined to guarantee its eventual success. The uranium procurement program underscored the West's increasing dependency upon the federal government to provide the impetus for postwar regional growth. As noted earlier, the impact of national defense spending in the West during World War II greatly affected the expansion of Pacific coastal cities as well as a select number of intermountain urban areas.[20] In response to Truman's pledge in 1946 to step up national resource development, a steady stream of federal dollars poured into the western economy.

More important to the Four Corners, the president's decision to make the United States less dependent upon foreign supplies of nuclear material extended the influence of the federal government beyond the confines of the urban West. Increased national interest in the undeveloped energy resources of the southwestern hinterlands broke down the traditional geographic isolation of this energy-rich subregion, placing the Four Corners communities in step with the remainder of the nation.

Although the uranium industry experienced a sluggish start, international events toward the end of the decade accelerated America's domestic procurement program. In September 1949 the Soviet Union detonated its first atomic weapon. This historic event, which marked the end of the American monopoly on atomic energy, heightened diplomatic tension between the United States and Russia. From that moment, the race for nuclear superiority between two emerging world powers gained momentum. In response, President Truman called for increasing military expenditures, from 5 percent to 20 percent of the gross national product. In the interest of national defense, Truman approved the proposal to strengthen the American arsenal through the development of the hydrogen bomb.

Concurrent with Soviet–American arms competition, United States involvement in the Korean War in the fall of 1950 reaffirmed the need for a stronger military defense program. In a special message to Congress on December 1, 1950, the president authorized a $1 billion supplemental appropriation for the AEC to enable a "substantial increase in the production of fissionable materials, and the fabrication of such material into atomic weapons." In the ensuing months, the words "military preparedness" and "national security" became the driving force behind the AEC's accelerated uranium procurement program. Under the forceful direction of newly appointed Raw Materials Division Chief Jesse C. Johnson, former director of the Reconstruction Finance Corporation, the AEC intensified uranium explorations on the Colorado Plateau.[21]

By the summer of 1951 the "rush" to the Four Corners began in earnest as thousands of prospectors converged upon the remote desert communities of southeastern Utah and northeastern Arizona. "By comparison," noted one jubilant speculator, "the gold rush of '49 was an easter-egg hunt!" An estimated 10,000 prospectors had filed claims throughout the Four Corners. Unlike their frontier counterparts, who sought out their fortunes with a "grubstake" and a good mule, these latter-day fortune hunters employed geiger counters, four-wheel-drive vehicles, and the latest aerial detection equipment to make even the most remote areas no longer impervious to exploration.

In further contrast to the gold-seekers of the mid-1800s, uranium miners were not concentrated in one locality. Rather, they were spread out over the entire 200,000-square-mile radius of the desert Southwest. "There must be a prospector on every hill," noted one observer, "but the vast Four Corners area still has more hills than it has people." As a result

of this onslaught of prospectors to the Colorado Plateau, uranium production nearly quadrupled, from 143,000 tons produced in 1948–49 to
520,000 tons mined in 1950–51.[22]

The AEC's active participation in sponsoring the uranium procurement
program was vital to its overall success. AEC purchases of carnotite ore
increased from a meager $1.6 million in 1948 to more than $52 million in
1955. Notably, the average price for uranium in the mid-1950s was $8.52
per pound, enough to encourage hundreds of would-be millionaires to
abandon local businesses and take up prospecting. In addition, the Grand
Junction office paid an average of $200,000 per month in cash bonuses for
all significant discoveries of uranium ore during this period. As part of the
incentive package for new uranium recovery, the AEC authorized the
Defense Minerals Exploration Administration (DMEA) loan. Prospectors
assumed the loan to cover all exploration costs on highly promising claims.
If there was a major commercial strike, the federal government assumed
payment for 75 percent of the loan and the balance would be repaid from
production profits. If no discovery occurred, the AEC cancelled the loan.
Thus, unlike the lone forty-niner of yesteryear, in constant pursuit of
financial sponsorship, the uranium miner of the 1950s enjoyed monetary
benefits available through the auspices of the federal government.[23]

No less impressive was the AEC's commitment to processing the newly
discovered uranium. In January 1952 the *Moab Times Independent* published an announcement from the Raw Materials Division in Grand Junction that it was preparing to spend $3.8 million on an access roads program
in Colorado and Utah. The purpose of this program was to facilitate
transportation of radioactive material from the mines to ore-processing
stations at various locations throughout the Four Corners. Between 1952
and 1958 the AEC constructed nearly 1,200 miles of access roads at a cost
of $13.5 million. According to local news writers, the roads were a direct
result of the so-called "uranium rush," and were considered an important
contribution because they made "back country never before accessible
open to exploration." Most of the roads built originally for the transportation of uranium ore were incorporated in later years into the state highway systems of Colorado, Utah, Arizona, and New Mexico.[24]

In addition to transportation improvements, the AEC constructed nine
ore-processing mills in the Four Corners to meet government demands
for uranium concentrate. The earliest were located at Monticello, Utah
(April 1948), and Durango, Colorado (February 1949). While the Monticello plant operated longer, the Durango mill was by far more produc-
tive.

The government's decision to enlist the services of the Vanadium Corporation of America (VCA) was a sound one. Under the able leadership of Dennis Viles, the feisty vice president in charge of the corporation's western mining operations, the VCA broadened its mining interests beyond Latin America to include the American Southwest. Other domestic ventures included uranium mines at Marysvale, Utah, south of Moab, and Monument Valley, Arizona. These latter claims accounted for nearly 73 percent of all uranium concentrate produced in Arizona from 1948 to 1950. Clearly, the VCA's experience in uranium production and processing made it the logical choice for the newly acquired government operation in Durango. In the beginning, the Durango mill processed nearly all of the ore mined on the nearby Navajo Reservation. In time, however, increased production of fissionable material in the Four Corners justified additional mills at Tuba City, Arizona, ninety miles northwest of Flagstaff, and Shiprock, New Mexico, thirty miles east of Farmington.[25]

Durango residents reveled in the town's "atomic importance." The arrival of the VCA meant 200 new jobs and nationwide acknowledgement of the community as a world producer of uranium concentrate. It did not take long for Durango to realize its desire for national recognition. In a series of articles entitled "Through Uranium Land," the *Rocky Mountain News*, a leading western newspaper headquartered in Denver, heralded the little town as America's alternative to the rich uranium resources of the Belgian Congo and Canada. A government report published in 1953 through the Bureau of Economics and Business Research of the University of Colorado similarly underscored the importance of southwestern Colorado in the future of non-fuel mineral production in the West.

Enamored by its own remarkable transformation, Durango noted in a 1954 newspaper special that uranium was simply the latest gift in a long history of mineral contributions from the San Juan Basin. In August of that year, the *New York Herald Tribune* listed the VCA as one of the world's top producers of uranium. In effect, Durango residents were grateful for the opportunities that accompanied the arrival of the VCA. More importantly, they recognized the value of the government's uranium procurement program in linking this once-isolated frontier community to the rest of the nation.[26]

Not unlike their Colorado neighbors, residents of Moab were equally pleased with the attention derived from the uranium boom. Contrasted with the other Four Corners municipalities, Moab experienced more of the "boom town" effects brought on by the massive influx of get-rich-quick prospectors. One observer recalled the lines of people extending for

several blocks just to use the "only pay-telephone in town." Hopes for
continued prosperity ran high in southeastern Utah. One University of
Utah scholar declared, "I cannot see that in our lifetime the demand for
uranium will ever diminish, and because of this I am convinced that Moab
will continue to grow."

Mayor Jack Corbin, however, expressed ambivalence, noting that Moab's population had more than doubled from 1,272 "happy and contented
souls" in 1950 to upwards of 2,775 harried prospectors in 1953. Most
Moab residents, however, welcomed the idea that their sleepy desert community had undergone social and economic transformation. A 1967 study
revealed that the uranium industry produced a $1 billion impact on the
southeastern Utah economy during the first decade of the uranium rush.[27]

No episode of mining history in the American West would be complete
without a bona fide folk hero. In the case of the uranium boom of the
1950s, Charles Austin Steen is the uncontested champion of the Four
Corners. Locals dubbed him the "Cisco Kid," in honor of the ramshackle
8 x 16 foot mobile trailer at Cisco, Utah, where he lived with his wife and
four active little ones. The young geologist eyed the nuclear age with
professional curiosity and visions of instant gratification. He theorized an
imaginary triangle connecting Moab on the west, Dove Creek, Colorado,
near the Utah–Colorado border in the southeast, and Grand Junction to
the north, which promised the best opportunity for a major uranium
strike. With the few dollars remaining in his pocket from the loan his
mother gave him, and sustenance derived from his daily intake of bananas
and potato chips, Charlie steered his dilapidated jeep into the trackless
Utah desert to seek his fortune.

Steen's success exceeded his wildest dreams. In July 1952 Charlie Steen
uncovered the most significant uranium strike of the decade. Unlike hundreds of prospectors before him, Steen—a trained scientist—knew what to
look for. The eccentric but persistent Texas A & M graduate found his
fortune along the Lisbon Valley anticline forty miles southeast of Moab.
With estimated reserves totaling 1.3 million tons, Steen's Mi Vida Mine
produced nearly fifty times the amount of uranium ore discovered up to
that time. Of greater interest to the AEC, Steen unearthed uraninite, a
high-grade, radioactive substance that compared favorably to Canadian
and South African ores.[28]

"For the past fifty years Moab has been known only as a small cow town
on the Colorado River," clamored Mayor Jack Corbin. "Then along came
Charlie Steen." The discovery of the Mi Vida Mine and other significant
deposits of uranium ore in southeastern Utah assured Moab citizens of a

new era of prosperity. The "rush" to the Four Corners was in high gear by the spring of 1953. In April of that year, local newspapers reported that the federal government paid Charlie Steen's UTEX Mining Corporation an average of $9,000 per month to have ore shipped to various processing stations.

The level of productivity from Steen's mine warranted construction of a $5 million processing mill in Moab. Thus, local producers were no longer dependent upon ore shipments 160 miles to southwest Colorado for smelting. Reported to be the largest uranium production plant in the region, the Uranium Reduction Company processed four times more radioactive material than Durango's VCA mill during its peak years of operation. In a speech before the Moab Chamber of Commerce, Steen assured fellow businessmen, "Moab will never go back to what it was. Atomic bombs have saved more lives than they destroyed."[29]

Charlie Steen's discovery of uraninite was only one of the landmark events of the 1950s that hastened the social and economic transformation of the Four Corners. In the interest of national security, the federal government continued to underwrite the expense of postwar economic expansion in the West. For the next twenty years the AEC intensified its search for fissionable material in all of the Rocky Mountain states. By 1953, AEC-sponsored explorations had expanded to include New Mexico, Wyoming, Montana, and Idaho. Comparatively speaking, the Four Corners reigned supreme as the chief producer of domestic uranium. In his end-of-year report dated December 30, 1954, Jesse Johnson, Director of the Raw Materials Division, stated that mining activity on the Colorado Plateau had made the United States "one of the world's leading producers of uranium." He listed 795 mines in operation within the Four Corners subregion alone. When the uranium procurement program terminated in December 1971, the AEC had spent an astounding $2.9 billion dollars to purchase more than 348 million tons of radioactive material.[30]

The discovery of vast reserves of uranium and petroleum in the Four Corners signaled the beginning of a new era of resource exploitation in the West that reached unprecedented heights. To be sure, dependency upon the western natural resources to satisfy national growth needs was not new. Since the California gold rush, the West had established a tradition as an exporter of mineral resources to the industrial East and the Midwest. In effect, the West became a resource colony in which eastern bankers and industrialists maintained a financial stranglehold on the entire region. For the remainder of the nineteenth century, western economic growth was inextricably linked to the business and industrial whims of the East.

With the advent of the Great Depression, the federal government promoted western growth. While mass infusions of federal appropriations set the forces of regional expansion into motion, western dependency upon outside economic sources remained essentially unchanged—dependency upon eastern capitalists gave sway to dependency upon the federal government. Economic relief programs and New Deal conservation politics validated the colonial status of the West. By the late 1930s, 54 percent of all western lands fell under federal ownership.

Not until World War II did the transformation of the colonial West into a "pacesetting" region take effect. Military defense needs hastened the industrialization of the western economy; war production factories, aircraft assembly plants, and fully integrated steel mills were the response. As a result of these wartime advancements, the West emerged from World War II fully industrialized and financially prepared to assert its own economic importance.[31]

Continued government spending in the West during the postwar years promised a healthy economic future for the Four Corners. While on the one hand the hinterland communities were dependent upon the federal largess, in future years Durango, Moab, Farmington, and Flagstaff asserted a distinct social and economic importance within their own subregion. No longer the forgotten frontier outposts of the previous century, these burgeoning communities became active participants in the postwar urban-industrial expansion of the region and the nation. Local boosters welcomed the prospect of new housing starts, civic improvements, and national media attention. In the ensuing decades, the accelerated exploitation of undeveloped energy resources exerted greater pressure on these hinterland municipalities to keep pace with an emerging West.

TWO

The West Against Itself

As the hinterland communities readied themselves for unprecedented economic growth, not all westerners welcomed change. Bernard De Voto, a native of Utah and renowned author of western history, criticized the most recent variant of the economic colonialism model. In his provocative 1947 essay, "The West Against Itself," De Voto acknowledged the progress of the American West during and after the war. He agreed that the West stood on the brink of economic self-sufficiency. Nevertheless, the author, a long-time advocate of resource conservation, argued that one critical factor tempered the West's ambitions for regional independence. The high-level development of the region, he asserted, could only be accomplished if the West overcame its tendency toward "self-inflicted failure."

De Voto cautioned against the probability of a new form of intraregional colonialism in which the centers of resource exploitation shifted from Wall Street to San Francisco. In his view, a handful of westerners were aligning with eastern capitalists for the sole purpose of self-aggrandizement. The inevitable result, De Voto predicted, would not be economic self-sufficiency, but an open invitation for regional self-destruction. "While the West moves to build that kind of economy," he prophesied, "a part of the West is simultaneously moving to destroy the natural resources forever." The future of the West, the author concluded, hinged upon whether "the West could defend itself against itself."[1]

De Voto's criticism had particular relevance to postwar development of the Four Corner's subregion. During these years of rapid urbanization in the West, a pattern of intraregional colonialism had clearly emerged. The exigencies of urban and industrial growth forced western metropolitan capitals to look inward toward the abundant and exploitable energy commodities of the hinterlands. As De Voto had suspected, a variation of the old East–West dependency relationship took shape in the 1950s. This time it was not eastern capitalists hoping to benefit from resource exploitation on the western frontier; rather, it was a new corps of western entrepreneurs who used money and power to exploit the interior communities.

The shift from interregional to intraregional colonialism was most evident in the economic relationship between urban centers of the West and the rural communities of the Four Corners. Beginning with the energy resource booms of the postwar era, remote towns like Durango, Farmington, Moab, and Flagstaff became subcolonies of Los Angeles, San Diego, Dallas, Houston, Phoenix, Albuquerque, and other blossoming cities. Recently recovered deposits of uranium, oil, and natural gas, coupled with existing supplies of timber resources, made the Four Corners a priority target for western speculators. The inhabitants of the modern West, unlike frontier populists who protested the wanton exploitation of their native resources, welcomed the opportunity to service the demands of Pacific Coast, Rocky Mountain, and desert Southwest municipalities.

Concurrent with military defense requirements for energy resources were increased demands for heating fuels, gasoline, and lubricants resulting from a major population shift westward during the Second World War. At the height of the conflict, West Coast war industries proposed a manpower plan to lure 500,000 men and women not enlisted in the armed forces to new jobs. This mass migration of workers to Pacific Coast and Intermountain region defense plants did not abate after the war. One postwar expert notes that between 1945 and 1960 the number of people living west of the Mississippi River rose from 32 to 45 million.

California and the southwestern states registered the most impressive population increases. Golden State inhabitants tripled, while Arizona's quadrupled! The impact upon Utah, Colorado, Texas, and New Mexico, while less dramatic, was nonetheless significant. Air conditioning and other technological comforts made these arid regions more livable. Air transportation, which considerably reduced the amount of travel time required to traverse the blistering desert landscape, was another factor in increased travel to the West. The automobile, however, remained the principal means of transportation for millions of American families heading west. Once arrived, cross-country immigrants enjoyed the benefits of a seemingly endless flow of federal dollars into the western economy, which created good jobs, new housing, and other personal amenities.[2]

If mobility was the hallmark of affluent Americans in the early decades of the postwar era, the automobile was the undisputed symbol of the modern westward movement. As more people crossed the Mississippi, what appeared to be an inexhaustible market for petroleum products developed. Consumption of petroleum increased 80 percent on the national level between 1945 and 1959. While the conversion of railroads to diesel fuels and a shift to mechanized farming accounted in part for the increase, consumption of gasoline for automobiles and natural gas for home heating was even more profound. Los Angeles, which housed an estimated 3 million people in the greater metropolitan area, generated enormous demands for petroleum. In 1943, according to historian Gerald D. Nash, "One of every forty Americans in the United States lived in the Los Angeles area." The majority of them drove automobiles to and from work, which doubled the use and ownership of vehicles in the West. Indeed, the increasing number of shopping centers, freeways, motels, and supermarkets after the war were testimony to the westerner's passion not only for his car but also his suburban lifestyle.[3]

While Durango and Moab were the chief beneficiaries of the government's uranium procurement program in the late 1940s, Farmington reaped the rewards of America's growing dependency upon petroleum. Just as the arrival of the AEC to the Four Corners proved critical to the economic revitalization of Durango and Moab, private industry's decision to intensify exploration and production of oil and gas in the San Juan Basin promised an era of unequalled prosperity to the New Mexico community. On March 18, 1945, Southern Union Gas Company, a firm organized in 1927 near Wink, Texas—in the heart of the Permian Basin—discovered the first major natural gas producing well in the San Juan Basin. The "gasser" was brought in at Barker Dome field—10,000 acres of proven natural gas reserves located in northern San Juan County, New Mexico, and southern La Plata County, Colorado. This important recovery of natural gas marked the decline of the independent "wildcatters," as the Barker Dome find prompted a flurry of explorations in which no fewer than sixteen of the nation's top oil-producing companies converged upon Farmington from 1945 to 1950.

As petroleum engineers speculated on the potential for oil recovery, natural gas was a proven reality. In the early days of the petroleum industry, field workers, who considered natural gas an unwanted by-product of oil, burned off millions of cubic feet as waste. Only a limited market for natural gas existed before World War II. According to Emery Arnold, former geologist for the state of New Mexico, "People knew that there

was natural gas here for a number of years, but it was practically a worth-
less commodity until such time that someone developed a market."
Knowledge of the reserves at Barker Dome, in fact, had been known since
1924, but the product was unmarketable. When in 1945 Barker Dome
field was finally brought into production, the United States witnessed an
upsurge in consumption of this relatively unexploited energy fuel.

Several factors accounted for rising demands for natural gas. First, an
expanding postwar population led to increased use of gas heating for
domestic and industrial purposes. Second, serious gasoline and oil fuel
shortages in the years following the war necessitated the use of alternative
sources of energy. Third, and perhaps most important, natural gas came
into its own with the development of new and improved pipeline distribution systems. One scholar writes, "It was only after 1930 that engineers
perfected electric welding processes for the manufacture of pipes adequate
for long-range distances." During World War II, hydraulic-bending techniques aided in the development of large diameter pipelines. Coupled with
the production of natural gas fields in the Permian Basin of West Texas—
and later the San Juan Basin of New Mexico and Colorado—the product
could readily be transported to markets located midst the sprawling metropolitan centers of the Atlantic and Pacific coasts. Accordingly, demands
for natural gas rose from 2.6 billion cubic feet (BCF) in 1940 to 9.4 BCF
in 1955.[4]

Pipeline distribution was not a new concept in the 1950s, nor was the
proposal to develop a system in the San Juan Basin a novel idea. The
exigencies of World War II forced a surge in pipeline production to
transport crude oil from the Southwest to the nation's leading industrial
centers. Privately financed corporations such as Stanolind Oil Company
(later Amoco) and Magnolia Oil Company (later Mobil) aggregated nearly
10,000 miles of pipelines during the war years. Under the aegis of Secretary of the Interior Harold Ickes, whom President Roosevelt designated
Petroleum Coordinator for War, the federal government increased its
involvement in pipeline construction as part of the war effort. Ickes's
responsibility for improving national oil production led to the construction of the Big Inch and Little Inch Pipelines in 1942. Designed to link the
oil fields of the Permian Basin with industrial centers on the East Coast
and the Midwest, these two networks facilitated the transfer of 379,207,
208 barrels of domestic crude oil for wartime use between 1943 and 1945.[5]

In May 1944, near the conclusion of the war in Europe, American oil
producers submitted a proposal to Ickes for the construction of a pipeline
from West Texas to Los Angeles. Dubbed the Pacific War Emergency

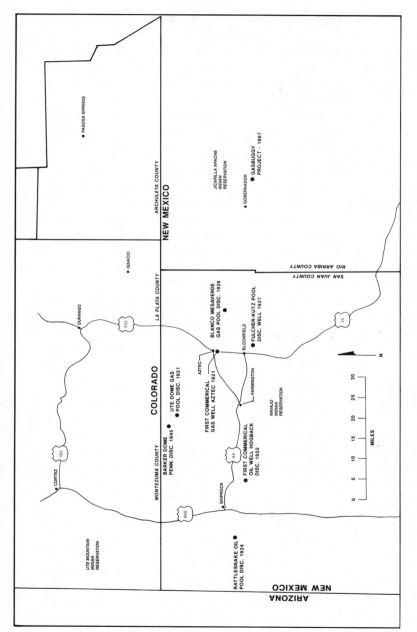

THE FOUR CORNERS OIL AND GAS PRODUCTION AREAS

(Map by Ernesto Martinez.)

Pipeline, the plan called for 986 miles of 20-inch line with the capacity to carry 175,000 barrels of crude to the West Coast daily. In the summer of 1945, petroleum czar Ickes turned down the request, arguing that there were insufficient reserves of crude oil in West Texas to support the project.[6] While the Pacific War Emergency Pipeline failed to win approval, the possibility of connecting California to West Texas had an alluring appeal to leading oil and gas producers at the close of the war.

The discovery of oil and natural gas reserves in the San Juan Basin just after the war made the dream of a transwestern pipeline a reality. The Southern Union Gas Company, which by now had located its headquarters in El Paso, Texas, was among the first distributors to capitalize on new markets for natural gas. On December 5, 1948, the *Durango Herald Democrat* printed a story announcing the company's plans for a multi-million dollar expansion program. The proposal promised to increase supplies of natural gas from the recently discovered Barker Dome fields to VCA operations in Durango as well as to other defense-related industries located in Albuquerque and Los Alamos.

Southern Union's announcement to expand its pipeline network, coupled with its discovery of new sources of natural gas, triggered a scramble to exploit the energy-rich resources of the San Juan Basin. Local newspapers featured the "battle of the giants" in the search for petroleum reserves. Col. Harold D. Byrd, president of the Dallas-based Byrd-Frost Corporation, was among those interested in Four Corners oil and gas reserves for growing western markets. Kenneth Wilson, resident geologist for Byrd-Frost, announced that his company's exploration efforts revealed enough gas in reserve along the Colorado–New Mexico border to produce 127 million cubic feet (MCF) of natural gas daily for the next twenty years.

In its effort to remain competitive with Southern Union Gas, the Byrd-Frost firm divulged its plan to lay a pipeline from southern Colorado to San Francisco via Salt Lake City, Utah. The Dallas company, already under contract with the Pacific Gas and Electric Company of California to redistribute the commodity, hoped to supply the bay area with 450 MCF of badly needed natural gas on a daily basis. Colonel Byrd also stressed the strategic importance of his proposed pipeline, noting that the system could be converted to transport crude oil and gasoline for aviation and defense installations "in the event of a war in the Pacific." Eventually, the plan called for an extension of the pipeline to Seattle and other metropolitan centers in the Pacific Northwest. Before undertaking the project, however, Colonel Byrd sold out his interest to a fast-rising petroleum producer. The El Paso Natural Gas Company, founded in Dallas in 1928, emerged onto the scene as principal supplier of Permian Basin gas to several Southwest communities. Shortly after its incorporation, the aggressive firm signed a contract to furnish El Paso, Texas, with all of that city's commercial gas needs. Prior to the war, El Paso Gas enjoyed limited expansion beyond West Texas when the company built a transmission pipeline to supply the copper-producing areas of southern Arizona. Bolstered by a $2.2 million loan secured from the Reconstruction Finance Corporation, the Texas firm completed a pipeline to Tucson and Phoenix in 1933. During the war, El Paso provided 42 percent of the natural gas requirements needed for the production of copper, an element considered critical to the war effort. In addition, the Dallas-based operation supplied crude oil and aviation fuel to the more than twenty military installations scattered throughout the Southwest. Thus, El Paso Natural Gas Company arrived to the Four Corners in 1948 fully prepared to capitalize on all prospective marketing opportunities.[7]

In August 1949 the Delhi Oil Corporation, an independent producer with leases in the San Juan Basin, revived the wartime idea of a transmission pipeline to the Pacific Coast in petitioning the Federal Power Commission (FPC) for permission to enter into a contract with El Paso to transport natural gas to California. "This project represents a portion of an overall effort on the part of these companies to relieve an imminent and potentially dangerous shortage of fuel in central and northern California," wrote President C. W. Merchison of Delhi Oil. Unlike the earlier proposal of 1944, however, the number of new recoveries in northwestern New Mexico and southwestern Colorado from 1947 to 1949 assured the feasibility of the transwestern pipeline. No longer would inadequate supplies of oil and natural gas suffice as a reason for denial of the proposed transmission of these essential products to the West Coast. A *Denver Post* editorial cited an estimated reserve of 3 trillion cubic feet of gas in the Four Corners.[8]

With access to a seemingly endless supply of natural gas and eager West Coast markets ready to consume as much as could be transported, El Paso formally petitioned the FPC to construct the transmission pipeline. El Paso Natural Gas Company, San Juan Pipeline Company, a subsidiary of the Texas-based firm, and California's Pacific Gas & Electric Company all filed their applications in the summer of 1949. The proposal called for a total delivery of 400 MCF of natural gas per day from the Farmington fields to Topock, Arizona (12 miles southeast of Needles, California). At this juncture on the Colorado River, the California utility company would redistribute the gas to consumers in central and northern California. Initially, the application called for delivery of 150 MCF of the total supply to San Francisco, Oakland, and Berkeley. In time, the companies anticipated building a 423-mile spur to provide an additional 100–150 MCF of gas to Los Angeles as well as other California cities.[9]

While Four Corners residents were for the most part enthusiastic about the prospect of a transwestern pipeline to California, Farmington citizens were ecstatic. A special editorial featured in the *Farmington Times Hustler* noted that only the actual flow of oil and gas could facilitate an industrial boom in the predominantly agrarian community. The proposed transmission of energy resources from the Four Corners region promised a lucrative future to its inhabitants. "Neither oil lease hounds nor newspaper writers can make a boom," the editor noted. "We just do our part and wait for someone to bring in the grease." Other writers expressed similar expectations in assuring readers that "1949 will be one of the most active years in San Juan Basin history."

More revealing, was a feature article published in the *Albuquerque Tribune* noting that Farmington's population had doubled to an estimated 5,000 inhabitants just two years after the first petroleum discoveries. Further, the three hundred new homes and a recently constructed $50,000 office building and hotel complex were directly attributable to the expanding oil and gas activities in the basin. In response, city officials expanded the corporate city limits from 1 square mile to 3.5 square miles in anticipation of population increases projected to reach 20,000 by 1960. The prospects for industrial development in Farmington were so great, one resident exclaimed, "Truly this area is at the threshold of a widespread drilling era that will see the expenditure of many millions of dollars."[10]

Despite local and regional support for the proposed pipeline, the FPC was reluctant to approve the application. There were strong arguments against the transmission of Four Corners resources to the West Coast. Colorado Attorney General, John W. Metzger, for example, tried to censure California's "secretive attempt" to drain vitally needed fuels from the San Juan Basin. In addition, some western politicians simply refused to acquiesce to the whims of the petroleum companies. Senator Dennis Chavez of New Mexico, chairman of the Senate Committee on Public Works and the Senate Subcommittee on Defense Appropriations, was the most ardent dissenter. Chavez believed that there should be some kind of regulatory safeguard to ensure the preservation of New Mexico gas in sufficient quantities for state consumption before shipment to California. Senator Clinton P. Anderson concurred with his senior colleague, arguing that atomic research facilities at Los Alamos demanded that local usage be given the highest priority. Concurrently, the AEC announced its plans on March 3, 1949, to build a natural gas pipeline from Kutz Canyon (southeast of Farmington) to Los Alamos to assure the research facility an uninterrupted supply of natural gas.

The Navy Department, on the other hand, countered that the proposed pipeline to California was more essential to "national security." Once completed, the line could be converted to transport oil and aviation fuel to West Coast military installations at the rate of 850,000 barrels per day "in the event of a war in Asia." Farmington's Mayor Tom Bolack, a self-made millionaire who had speculated in New Mexico's oil and gas industry in earlier years, led the assault for local supporters of the pipeline. First, Bolack refuted the standard argument that there was not enough gas in reserve in the San Juan Basin to supply both local and national needs. Of immediate concern, however, were the prospects for Farmington's economic future. If the pipeline application were denied, Bolack contended, the anticipated petroleum boom in the San Juan Basin would become an overnight bust.[11]

The arguments, in which local expectations were weighed against national priorities, were significant in that they illustrated the intraregional colonialism pattern endemic throughout the West during the early 1950s. Several pressing factors determined that the transference of energy resources from the hinterlands to the metropolitan centers of the West would take precedence over local growth ambitions. First, the population explosion along the California coast and in the Pacific Northwest resulted in an enormous consumption of public utilities. One decade after the Second World War, California housed nearly 60 percent of the nation's residential gas users. Four southwestern states—Texas, Oklahoma, Louisiana, and New Mexico—supplied more than 80 percent of all marketed production. New discoveries of natural gas in the San Juan Basin—and to a lesser degree some oil recoveries—contributed measurably to the national supply.

Further, United States involvement in Korea in June 1950 exacerbated demands for petroleum products on the West Coast. The probability of a major land war in Asia increased the strategic importance of the Pacific coastal states as never before. As California's own petroleum supplies dwindled, national attention focused upon the seemingly inexhaustible reserve of energy resources known to exist in the Four Corners. In the interest of national security, the imperatives of western coastal cities superseded local aspirations. Thus by 1950 the ominous predictions of Bernard De Voto had come true. Postwar urban and industrial expansion, coupled with the immediacy of strategic requirements for petroleum as the result of American military involvement in Asia, tightened the colonial bonds that existed between the metropolitan West and its interior subregions.

It was no coincidence that on July 14, 1950, less than one month after the Communist invasion of South Korea, the FPC authorized construction of the San Juan Basin Pipeline. In his inaugural address of January 1951, Governor-elect Edwin L. Mechem of New Mexico placed his state's oil and gas reserves at the disposal of the Pentagon, saying: "We must be in a position to take the fullest advantage of our resources, particularly those that are important to the maintenance of our independence and our system of government." By summer of that year, the first quantity of Four Corners gas passed through the transmission line en route to multiplying West Coast consumers.[12]

Meanwhile, on the local level, Four Corners residents were more interested in the growth of their respective cities than they were cognizant of larger regional priorities. Farmington welcomed the petroleum boom and eagerly hastened its success. By 1955 over 6,400 wells were in full operation in Blanco, Bloomfield, Kutz Canyon, Fulcher Basin, Ute Dome, and other gas-producing fields to meet deliveries promised to California. By mid-decade, Farmington boasted that it had earned the distinction as one of the fastest growing cities in the state. In testimony to that fact, Chamber of Commerce reports noted that housing construction in the southwestern desert community had doubled since the "wide open oil and gas boom."[13]

Not to be outdone by its southern neighbor, the *Durango Herald News* published its first booster magazine in May 1953, entitled "Durango, Colorado: A Region of Wealth." The Phillips Petroleum Company's discovery of natural gas reserves on the Southern Ute Reservation (20 miles southeast of Durango) expanded production activities in Colorado. Earlier that year, the Pacific Northwest Pipeline Corporation, a firm headquartered in Houston, Texas, announced its plans to seek approval from the FPC for a $130 million project to transport gas to Seattle, Spokane, Portland, Salt Lake, and other cities of the Pacific Northwest and the northern Rockies. The promise that the Houston firm would spend an estimated $60 million to locate its operation headquarters in Durango furthermore left local residents jubilant. The prospect of Durango becoming a petroleum capital in the Southwest, coupled with the arrival of the Vanadium Corporation a few years earlier, attracted a number of geologists, engineers, and other professionals to that city.[14]

Not all of the Four Corners municipalities experienced the profound impact from petroleum recoveries that Durango and Farmington enjoyed in the mid-1950s. Ironically, the first discovery of oil in the Four Corners was in 1908 at Mexican Hat, Utah (located on the Navajo Reservation 125 miles south of Moab). But because of larger petroleum strikes near the New Mexico–Colorado border in succeeding decades, the Utah oil industry floundered. After the Mexican Hat find, southeastern Utah saw no significant discoveries for thirty-eight years. Even then, there were only twenty-nine wells producing oil in that part of the state. Not until the Aneth discovery in 1956, the only "giant" oil field in the Four Corners, did southeastern Utah become a significant factor in the regional petroleum picture.[15] For the moment, uranium production reigned supreme as the leading energy-producing industry in southeastern Utah.

Northern Arizona, meantime, experienced no petroleum strikes of any kind until 1950. In fact, Flagstaff was virtually dependent upon natural gas from the San Juan Basin Pipeline to supply its commercial and industrial needs. In March 1951, when the Department of the Interior threatened not to allow El Paso Gas Company to cross the Navajo Reservation, one irate Flagstaff citizen requested assistance from Senator Carl Hayden. "Flagstaff and other northern Arizona cities have no natural gas service and badly need this fuel," he pleaded. "Many homes and business establishments have installed equipment for natural gas in anticipation of early gas service." A second disgruntled resident from the neighboring city of Holbrook reminded the state's senior senator of the political implications of the pipeline issue, saying, "If you gentlemen feel some of us are less than loyal Democrats don't strain us too far and make us downright Republicans." When the U.S. District Court finally ruled in favor of El Paso to proceed with the line in July of that year, northern Arizona relented in its barrage of complaints.[16]

In contrast to the other Four Corners municipalities, Flagstaff did not feel the effects of the boom town atmosphere generated during the "energy rush" years. Rather, consistency marked the growth pattern of this northern Arizona industrial town. Flagstaff's accessibility to a major railroad coupled with its location at the crossroads of U.S. Highway 66—one of the few existing cross-country thoroughfares in the postwar West—made this former frontier community a leading industrial producer in the Four Corners. Encircled by six designated national forests containing 20.6 million acres of Arizona's timbered lands, the production of wood products logically became the mainstay of the Flagstaff economy during and after the war.[17] While Moab, Durango, and Farmington speculated on the future of mineral resource development, the economy of Flagstaff was by comparison fixed upon a traditional industrial base.

Curiously, it was not the housing industry that provided the most lucrative market for Flagstaff lumber products during the early postwar years. Instead, it was the conversion of lumber into box shook used for crating and packaging. During the war, wooden crates were critical to the military mobilization effort. Nearly 60 percent of all lumber processed in the Southwest went into the manufacture of boxes used to transport war material, food, and medical supplies. Beginning in 1945, the task of reconverting the lumber industry from wartime utilization to a peacetime business fell principally to the Civilian Production Administration (CPA), the postwar counterpart of the War Production Board. At the Central Wooden Box Association annual meeting in Chicago in October 1945, President Oscar Z. Brewer expressed optimism for the reconversion program. New markets for packaging of furniture, enamel ware, refrigerators, and other household goods suggested a healthy outlook for the nation's wood products industry.

A second promising market for box shook was in the construction of wooden containers for shipment of West Coast produce, which had become a major national industry with the advent of World War II. A report published in November 1945 noted that the demand for fruit and vegetable crate material west of the Rocky Mountains had increased to "a level sufficient to absorb all available production from southwestern mills." The report concluded that 1946 would mark a new year in the development and production of wooden containers. Encouraged by these predictions, National Lumber Manufacturers Association (NLMA) members on the West Coast eagerly anticipated the impact on their industry. West Coast Regional President G. T. Gerlinger of Portland, Oregon, advised Jack Bedford, general manager of one of the Flagstaff sawmills, to prepare for a major upturn in the lumber business. "Because reconversion and postwar construction employment are so greatly dependent upon lumber supplies," the NLMA representative wrote, "it is very evident that [the] government is going to do something about lumber."[18]

Traditionally, the hinterland regions of the nation benefitted most directly from forest-based industries; the Four Corners was no exception. The remote communities of northern Arizona were almost entirely dependent upon the lumber industry for their livelihood beginning in the frontier days through the Second World War. Flagstaff, a lumber town since its founding in 1880, emerged from the war fully prepared to meet the rising construction needs of an urbanized West.

In 1945 three lumber mills operated within the city limits, the smallest of which belonged to the Babbitt Brothers Trading Company, a firm established in the 1890s specializing in cattle sales and the mercantile trade. A second sawmill was the Saginaw and Manistee Lumber Company, a Chicago-based operation that inherited the lumber-producing facilities of Flagstaff's pioneer lumbering enterprise, Arizona Lumber and Timber Company. Southwest Lumber Mills, Inc. was the third and largest producer in the city. The owners of this sawmill, established in 1928, moved their entire business from the clear cut forests of eastern Louisiana to the virgin stands of ponderosa pine abundant throughout northern Arizona. These three factories, combined with smaller independent operations that dotted the northern Arizona landscape, produced 241 million board feet (mbf) of lumber in 1946.[19]

The presence of a traditional industry assured Flagstaff, unlike its northern counterparts, a stable economy combined with steady population increases. When Southwest Lumber Mills built its Flagstaff plant in 1928, the town registered 6,000 inhabitants, nearly double the populations of either Farmington, Durango, or Moab. During the next two decades, the population of Coconino County rose from 14,064 in 1930 to 23,910 in 1950. More than half of that number lived in Flagstaff, Coconino County's largest community. Nearly 10 percent of the city's residents engaged in some form of lumber-related activity. In 1947 Mayor George Babbitt, patriarch of a pioneer Flagstaff family, predicted a population increase to more than 25,000 people within the decade. He cited the lumber industry and Flagstaff's location "at the crossroads of the northern section of the state" as reasons for optimism.[20]

While Babbitt's growth expectations proved to be exaggerated, he was correct in his evaluation about the growing importance of the lumber industry to Flagstaff's economic future. Lumbermen had anticipated an upturn in the industry after the war with good reason. The return of hundreds of thousands of war veterans, many of whom migrated west of the Mississippi River to find a new economic beginning, caused a major housing shortage in the West. In addition, President Truman's plans for reconversion, as outlined in his State of the Union message in 1946, closely linked the achievement of a stable, high-level economy to the maintenance of national security. The full utilization of national resources was fundamental to the success of America's conversion to a peacetime economy. For its part, the lumber and forest industry stood poised to make its contribution.

On February 7, 1946, President Truman announced the Veterans'

Emergency Housing Program, which was intended to alleviate the housing shortage through the construction of low-cost, affordable homes. Since most of the nation's lumber supplies had been diverted away from civilian construction during the war, the new legislation made materials available for new housing projects under the supervision of the Civilian Production Administration. In a letter written to all sawmill producers in the West, F. H. Brundage of the CPA anticipated the construction of 200,000 housing units in most of the principal western cities. Further, the agency requested that 40 percent of all lumber materials produced be set aside for the federal housing program. As a result, 1946 was a peak year for sawmill activity in northern Arizona, as sixty-six sawmills were reportedly in operation.[21]

Increased lumber production both nationally and in northern Arizona during these years was not without its consequences, however. The lumber industry suffered a dramatic slump at the end of the 1940s. A Department of Agriculture report entitled *Forests and National Prosperity*, which predicted the decline in 1948, cited the rise of sawmill production as the primary cause. In effect, the lumber market was glutted with wood products, causing prices to fall sharply because the supply of lumber far exceeded the demand. A second problem, according to the report, was that timber had become unaffordable since it could not be produced fast enough to keep pace with lumber mill capacities. Greater forestry development in the West was one solution to the latter problem. While the West held 65 percent of the nation's saw timber reserves, it accounted only for 35 percent of the national output.[22] The U.S. Forest Service determined, therefore, that greater accessibility of western timber through direct sales to private producers would become imperative as housing demands increased as expected in the 1950s.

Locally, producers expressed concern over the steady decline in commercial lumber prices contrasted with rising production costs because of the unavailability of good saw timber. In a letter to the U.S. Forest Service regional headquarters in Albuquerque, M. E. Kuhn, president of Saginaw and Manistee, warned that the lack of adequate timber supplies in Flagstaff threatened "the closing of additional small mills and some of the larger plants." The government's solution to this problem in 1949 was the establishment of the Flagstaff Federal Sustained-Yield Unit in the Coconino National Forest. The objective of this action was to provide permanent support to the Flagstaff community by ensuring forest product manufacturers a dependable supply of timber. Under the provisions of this policy, "eighty-five percent of the saw timber, excluding salvage, sold from the unit must be given primary manufacture within the City of Flagstaff or three miles thereof." In effect, the Flagstaff Federal Sustained-Yield Unit was one more example of government cooperation with private industry in the exploitation of Four Corners' resources.[23]

Increased availability of federal timber to private industry coincided with a greater concentration of sawmill ownership among a handful of lumber producers. The growth of Southwest Lumber Mills into a national corporation reflected the trend in the lumber industry toward the centralization of single-operator sawmills into modernized, fully integrated operations. Following the destruction of the company's original Flagstaff mill in 1947, Southwest Lumber built a completely automated facility with double the output capacity of the older sawmill. In 1952 company founder James McNary sold his interests in the Southwest Lumber Mills to James Ben Edens, a third-generation lumberman from Corrigan, Texas, who vowed to convert the local lumber company into a national forest products giant.

The promise of a virtually limitless supply of timber from Arizona's national forests assured the Flagstaff company an era of unparalleled prosperity. In November 1953 Saginaw and Manistee manager, Freeman Shultz, announced a merger between his company and Southwest Lumber Mills. The integration of Flagstaff's two major lumber producers meant year-round employment to local residents. That same year, the company reorganized under the name of Southwest Forest Industries and diverted all of Saginaw and Manistee's inventory to the more efficient, newly remodeled plant. The purchase of 87,000 acres of prime timberland from the Aztec Land and Cattle Company the following year made Southwest Forest Industries the largest private owner of commercial timber in the state of Arizona.[24]

The exertion of the federal government and private industry to exploit the abundant natural and energy resources of the Four Corners subregion in the early postwar decades initiated the West's active participation in intraregional colonialism. The rising energy needs of emerging metropolitan capitals in the "sunbelt" states, the Pacific Northwest, and the Intermountain West, accelerated the discovery and production of uranium, oil, natural gas, and timber reserves—found predominantly in the hinterland subregions—as never before. Urban expansion and economic security were the long-term benefits to Moab, Durango, Farmington, and Flagstaff. For the most part, the inhabitants of these Four Corners municipalities welcomed the monumental efforts of various federal agencies and western corporations. Their arrival to the Four Corners hastened the demise of geographic isolation and economic stagnation.

During the early years of frenetic exploration activity, the struggle to forge a distinct municipal identity obscured any semblance of regional cohesiveness in the Four Corners. Independent growth and economic rivalry marked the ensuing decade as the four communities competed to establish subregional preeminence. As the inertia of the energy "rush" years lost momentum, localism gave way to regionalism. In their effort to rejuvenate the economic vitality of the Four Corners, state executives and municipal leaders applied cooperative solutions to collective problems. In the aftermath of regional planning, coupled with the emergence of economic self-sufficiency in which the dependency relationship between the metropolitan West and the hinterlands more or less reversed, the concept of the Four Corners as a unique cultural and geographic subregion of the West crystallized.

THREE

Urban Imperialism in the Hinterland West

In the early 1950s the *Durango Herald News* printed the city's first annual booster magazine, entitled "A Region of Wealth, A Region of Health." The publication informed its readers that the keys to economic prosperity in the San Juan Basin were its vast undeveloped resources, especially uranium, coal, oil, and natural gas. Initially, the article applauded the success of the Vanadium Corporation of America (VCA), the only major uranium processing mill within two hundred miles. The VCA, journalists noted, employed 500 local residents while expending a monthly payroll of $200,000. Next, boosters cited the Durango region as having enough coal in reserve to "supply the United States for 337 years." An estimated 152 billion tons of reserve high-grade, bituminous coal made Durango one of the nation's formidable energy resource development areas.

No less promising was Durango's potential for oil and natural gas production. A follow-up booster publication released in October 1956 proclaimed the city's first "Oil Progress Week." After five years of seismographic mapping and exploration, oil companies were ready to convert the San Juan Basin into "the hottest oil reserve in the Rocky Mountains." Acknowledging the arrival to town of sixteen nationally known oil production firms, the *Durango Herald* staff credited exploration activities for the city's first notable population gains. The number of residents had risen from 7,500 in 1950 to nearly 10,000 in 1956. Finally, the newspaper gave details of a Federal Power Commission (FPC) decision to approve construction of a natural gas transmission pipeline from the San Juan Basin to the Pacific Northwest. The multimillion dollar proposal inspired one enthusiastic resident to exclaim, "It will be the closest thing to a boom that Durango has ever experienced. Our added prosperity is more likely to come from the royalty checks Basin residents will be getting."[1]

That Durangoans viewed their economic future with unqualified optimism mirrored an attitude common to each of the Four Corners municipalities by the mid-1950s. Since the frontier days, the San Juan Basin had confirmed its reputation as an excellent source for raw minerals. It came as no surprise that with the termination of World War II the area assumed similar importance in the development of a western industrial economy. As noted earlier, municipal growth in the postwar West heightened demands for energy commodities from Arizona, Colorado, New Mexico, and Utah. Insatiable markets, moreover, precipitated a subregional competition under which Durango, Farmington, Moab, and Flagstaff actively engaged in a form of "urban imperialism"[2] for regional and national recognition as the resource capital of the Four Corners.

One intriguing corollary related to the phenomenon of urban imperialism is energy resource exploitation. Since the late nineteenth century, small western towns, forced to exist in the shadow of larger urban communities, gauged local expansion upon their ability to maintain contact with a central economic system. The inevitable result was a classic colonialism relationship in which eastern industry nearly exhausted the West of its vital reserves. More significant was the dramatic impact of the Second World War on western industrial development. Technological change, combined with a continuous flow of federal subsidies, accelerated industrial growth in the West while creating new markets that demanded intraregional exploitation of natural and mineral resources. Meanwhile, interior communities, hoping to establish a broad-based trade network with national consumers, welcomed exploitation as a paramount need. As intraregional priorities superseded interregional demands, beginning about 1950, the Four Corners enjoyed a position of national as well as regional importance.[3]

Durango's acknowledgement of the VCA for its contribution to the economic well-being of the community was well founded. Scarcely one year after the company purchased the uranium processing facility from the Atomic Energy Commission (AEC), *Barron's Magazine* listed the firm as "the largest producer of uranium per share among the publicly owned companies in the United States." The magazine cited Dennis Viles, the feisty VCA executive who combined boundless energy with metallurgical knowhow, as largely responsible for the company's mercurial success. Viles, vice president in charge of the firm's western operations, pioneered the first uranium mine in Monument Valley, Arizona. "Mr. Viles was the first to take the Navajo reservation seriously as a source of uranium," the article read. Indeed, the VCA's Monument II mine accounted for 51 percent of the Durango smelter's total mill feed from 1953 to 1962. The VCA's reservation properties, moreover, enabled it to increase its output of processed ore from 175 tons per day in 1953 to 750 tons in just five years. As anticipated, the federal government acted as sole purchasing agent for all uranium produced in Durango. *Barron's* financial experts estimated the corporation's annual earnings to be $5.6 million.[4]

Rampant community growth underscored Durango's debut as a regional energy producer. The arrival of 150–200 geologists, engineers, mining experts, and other professionals with their families forced a rash of housing starts. In response, land developers built instant residential subdivisions on the western and eastern fringes of the city. Contractors built more than 800 new homes from 1955 to 1960. In addition, local businesses boasted a record $18 million in sales, making Durango the eleventh largest retail outlet in the state of Colorado. Like the hub of a wheel, Durango became one of the principal trade centers for small, neighboring, San Juan Basin towns. "The purchasing power of Durango changed," recalled one merchant, "Instead of making $4,000 or $5,000 a year, we had a group of people who were making $8,000 to $15,000." Clearly, the prospect for long-term employment through the VCA, coupled with the steady influx of highly trained professionals, transformed Durango from a rural hamlet into a thriving urban community.[5]

Hoping to compete with its southern neighbor, Moab anticipated its introduction to the uranium processing industry in the summer of 1955. In that year, Charlie Steen, president and chief geologist of the UTEX Exploration Company, appeared before a special Senate investigative committee to make a case for the construction of a processing plant in Moab. Inasmuch as there were already two mills in the vicinity, one sixty miles away near Monticello, Utah, and the VCA operation in Durango, the AEC questioned Steen's proposal to locate a third plant at Moab. Stressing the volume of productivity from his nationally famous Mi Vida Mine, Steen noted that his company produced 24,000 tons of uranium ore in a single production year. This rate of production equated to 120 times more than all other mining endeavors in Moab during the previous four years. In addition, Steen advised, his calculations indicated that 98 percent of his discovery was still under ground. The mineral richness of the Big Indian Mining District was so extensive, Steen declared, that four other mining companies had begun operations in 1954. Not including production from the Mi Vida Mine, the combined efforts of these other mines averaged more than 1,000 tons of ore daily. Impressed with these statistics, the AEC approved construction of the UTEX processing mill on June 1, 1955.[6]

In contrast to Durango, however, the AEC's announcement of the multi-million dollar processing plant found Moab wholly unprepared for the ensuing rush. Since the proposed Uranium Reduction Company was to be the largest uranium mill in the West, Chamber of Commerce officials predicted the present population of 1,800 could triple in one year. "Buildings are cropping up everywhere," declared Mayor Jack Corbin in his address before the Utah Municipal League in Salt Lake City. In early 1956 some skeptics viewed the situation as critical, while the local newspaper referred to Moab as "a city in distress." The onslaught of newcomers severely strained municipal water and sewage systems. The single schoolhouse, designed for only 450 students, bulged with double that number. The worst fears of city officials were realized scarcely one year after the AEC announcement when Moab's population jumped an amazing 267 percent to 4,600 people.

As an emergency measure, Moab hired a trained city planner from Provo, Utah, who appointed a seven-man commission to address the problems confronting the tiny desert community. Because of the city's importance to national defense, the federal government assisted Moab with municipal grants and low-interest loans. By mid-1956, the city had spent $200,000 to expand its water and sewer network to accommodate 7,000 inhabitants. San Juan County officials, meanwhile, approved a $600,000 bond issue to build a new elementary school. City building permits during that year soared from $100,000 to an astounding $2 million dollars. "The end is not yet in sight," clamored Dale Despain, chairman of the new planning commission. "Given its rate of growth, Moab should reach a population of 12,000 people."

Thus, the advocacy of the federal government both in sponsoring the construction of the Uranium Reduction Company and in providing much needed assistance for municipal improvements, created a new urban image for Moab. One approving journalist heralded the transformation, noting that Moab, once a sleepy village surrounded by magnificent scenery but virtually undiscovered, became "a breathless boom town," the target of hundreds of wealth-seekers.[7]

The determination of Durango and Moab to project an image of self-confidence and individual importance within the subregion greatly enhanced community development. Some historians describe such behavior as the "urban ethos"—the tendency among small municipalities to evaluate themselves in the context of regional and national surroundings.[8]

With good reason, Durango and Moab regarded themselves as significant contributors to national defense. Their phenomenal growth during these years, moreover, attested to their role in the federal government's commitment to uranium procurement. Boosterism, the outward manifestation of the urban ethos, and interurban competition provided the impetus for economic expansion as Durango and Moab each sought recognition as the premier "atomic city" of the Four Corners.

Durango residents had every reason to exude confidence that their future in uranium production was secure. To begin, the AEC had extended its contract with the VCA to purchase uranium concentrate through March 31, 1962. Secondly, the VCA had closed one processing plant near Naturita, Colorado, in an effort to consolidate all of its efforts into one facility. Four months later, the Durango plant had announced that it planned to increase milling capacity by 74 percent. Higher production quotas translated to greater employment as work schedules expanded to three shifts. During its peak years of operation (1950–1963), the Durango mill produced a total output of 7,851,425 pounds of uranium concentrate, which sold for an average price of $9.77 per pound. Durango's touting of the VCA's achievements and acknowledgement of the corporation's part in the city's remarkable growth was indeed justified.

Just as Durango celebrated the presence of the VCA, the city of Moab applauded the success of the Uranium Reduction Company. Not surprisingly, the mill provided the largest single payroll in the city. The Raw Materials Division in Grand Junction agreed to buy all nuclear material from the Moab plant through December 31, 1966. In addition, the plant's announcement in 1959 of a 30-percent increase in productivity promised "years of increasing stability" for all uranium facilities in southeast Utah.

On August 1, 1962, Charlie Steen sold out his interest in the Uranium Reduction Company to the Atlas Corporation, a fuel-producing giant headquartered in New York. When the sale was final, David Stretch, the firm's new president, reassured Moab residents of their future in the uranium industry: "We have every intention of remaining in the uranium and milling business after 1966. This company will be a major contributor to the atomic fuel industry." Moab residents had no cause to believe otherwise. The average annual output of 2.75 million pounds of uranium concentrate from the Moab plant more than quadrupled the output of the rival Durango mill.[9] These figures distinguished Moab as the uncontested leader in the production of radioactive material within the Four Corners.

On October 28, 1957, the AEC unexpectedly announced modifications to its domestic procurement program that forecast long-term consequences for uranium production in the Southwest. The regional office in Grand Junction published a recension of the 1956 circular that guaranteed the purchase of all uranium concentrates produced and delivered over the next ten years. "It is no longer in the interest of the government to expand the production of uranium concentrate," the circular read. The announcement meant that the federal government would no longer encourage new discoveries of nuclear material. Under the revised program, the AEC honored only current milling contracts, while providing extensions to only those companies already engaged in production. Assuring the public that this action in no way reflected a reduction in future atomic power needs, the AEC justified the measure as a "guard against serious overproduction which might occur under an unlimited purchase program."

The AEC's reversal of policy was in part a response to President Dwight D. Eisenhower's commitment of the United States to the peacetime industrial application of atomic power. In his "Atoms-for-Peace" speech before the United Nations General Assembly on December 8, 1953, President Eisenhower laid the foundation for a new domestic nuclear energy program. At that time, the president proposed the establishment of an International Atomic Energy Agency (IAEA). According to the Eisenhower plan, eighty nations were pledged to encourage research on peaceful as well as strategic uses of atomic energy. To supporters of nuclear arms control, the president's proposal was a call for eventual disarmament. To those favoring containment of the Soviets, however, the atoms-for-peace incentive was one way to neutralize the growing Russian military threat. Whatever its political motives, the president's proposal offered a workable alternative to the use of atomic power for exclusive military purposes. Accordingly, the government's urgency to stockpile uranium concentrate from the Four Corners in the interest of military defense subsided.[10]

This startling reversal of policy spelled disaster for the small, independent producers who had converged upon the Four Corners by the thousands in the early 1950s. According to one complainant, the AEC pronouncement "killed all prospecting, exploration, and development work in a single blow." Colorado Governor Steve McNichols, former attorney for the Uranium Ore Producers Association, lashed out at the new federal policy during a meeting with other western governors. First, he stressed the importance of the independents in the development of the "greatest uranium field in the world—the Colorado Plateau." Next, he criticized the AEC for intentionally freezing out the small operator while giving control of the industry to a handful of corporate giants. Asserting that the federal government had denied a market to the independents, McNichols predicted a bleak future for the domestic uranium industry.[11]

Independent mine owners speculated on the consequences of the new energy policy with regard to the future of uranium exploration in the Four Corners. One group met in Durango to discuss the increased complacency of the federal government in aiding small producers. A spokesman for the group concluded, "The government will have to treat uranium miners at least as good as the oil companies if the miners are to survive." In a letter addressed to Governor McNichols one mine owner lamented that his company held appreciable uranium deposits in reserve but had no market for them as long as the government favored the larger mining conglomerates. The Uranium Institute of America (UIA), an organization founded in Grand Junction, Colorado, for the regionwide promotion of uranium exploration and development, summarized the impact of the AEC announcement in a special report to the governor of Colorado. Revised federal policy, the institute advised, had removed all incentive for future exploration. The inevitable result would be a serious shortage of uranium concentrate.[12]

Meanwhile, on Capitol Hill the Joint Committee on Atomic Energy (JCAE), in an effort to comply with the new IAEA agreement, adopted measures to fund research for the peacetime application of nuclear power. "The program will bridge the gap between military uses of uranium concentrates and the development of a stable domestic market," committee chairman Clinton P. Anderson of New Mexico promised. In June 1957 the AEC appointed the Lawrence Radiation Laboratory of California technical directors for the so-called Project Plowshare program. Initially, the AEC limited experimentation to the use of nuclear detonations in harbor excavation and the recovery of petroleum products. In time, however, the AEC encouraged the scientific facility to broaden its research to investigate the potential for commercialized use of atomic power through the development of price-competitive nuclear reactors.[13]

The federal government's proposal to promote widespread industrial applications of atomic power had apparently taken precedence over military use by the 1950s. From the moment of the first nuclear explosion in 1945, scientists had hoped to convert the destructive power of the atomic bomb into a constructive, peacetime force. With the Soviet detonation of its first nuclear device in 1949, however, Washington placed maximum priority on military weapons development. In the beginning, the AEC committed more than 80 percent of its budget to military-related projects. Despite the climate of the Cold War, the JCAE also charged the commission with investigating peaceful applications of nuclear power. In response, the AEC established the Division of Reactor Development in 1949, which made slow but steady advances in the nonmilitary uses of atomic power.

In the early 1950s, industrial interest in electricity produced from nuclear reactors was negligible because of the abundance of petroleum and fossil fuels. As the decade advanced, government and private industry grew more concerned over the rapid depletion of traditional energy resources. The revised Atomic Energy Act of 1954 became the embodiment of President Eisenhower's plan to link industry with government in the production of fissionable material. Correspondingly, the AEC enticed major mining companies into nuclear energy production through the modification of its domestic procurement program. Thus, with the announcement of its revised policy in October 1957, the government made a conscious decision to lessen restrictions on uranium production in order to encourage its commercial use.

The United States also took global events into consideration in formulating a new atomic energy policy. It was no coincidence that the modification of America's uranium procurement program coincided with nuclear weapons test ban negotiations between American and Soviet diplomats in Geneva, Switzerland. In light of these diplomatic milestones, the AEC incentives offered to the fuel-producing corporations—at the expense of the independent prospectors in the Four Corners—were in keeping with the president's atoms-for-peace concepts. Consequently, AEC policy changes in 1957 shaped a new economic picture in the Four Corners as the area's great uranium rush drew to an uneventful close.[14]

In a speech before the Colorado Mining Association in March 1962, Jesse Johnson, director of the Division of Raw Materials in Grand Junction, outlined future prospects for the uranium industry. "Nuclear power requirements for uranium in relation to production capability will remain relatively small until the 1970s," Johnson predicted. Based on these trends, the federal government took steps to reduce the threat of overproduction. With future markets for uranium nearly a decade away, the financial requirements for deeper, more sophisticated explorations excluded the independent prospector in favor of multinational corporations. The AEC initiated what was called the "stretch-out" phase, meaning the agency would not enter into any new contracts to purchase uranium. According to Johnson, these measures were taken to help the uranium industry "survive in a limited market" until a substitute for nuclear weapons production could be fully developed.

The new AEC policy had an immediate impact on the Four Corners. In March 1959 the Raw Materials Division announced the closure of its plant at Monticello (the last federally owned uranium mill in the Four Corners). The government offset the shutdown, however, by extending its contract with the Atlas Corporation in Moab through December 31, 1970. Durango residents, on the other hand, were uneasy about the prospects of the AEC policy. In an editorial lamenting the clouded future of the industry, *Durango Herald* editorialist, Morley Ballantine, wrote, "There can be no enthusiasm at the possibility the demand for uranium is on the decline." Ending on a positive note, she added, "Durango can consider itself lucky that the Vanadium Corporation of America has a continuing interest in uranium production." The ink from her commentary had scarcely dried when in late 1962 the VCA stunned the city in announcing transfer of its entire operation to a newer, modernized processing mill near Shiprock, New Mexico. Undaunted, Ballantine published a follow-up editorial underscoring Durango's unfaltering self-confidence. "Durango has three natural resources that will always be in demand," she declared, "oil, natural gas, and scenery."[15]

Durango's hope to compete with Moab as the region's principal supplier of nuclear material faded with the VCA's departure in 1962. The city's prospects for an oil and gas boom, meanwhile, never fully materialized—despite the newspaper's profound optimism. After five years of explorations, geologists offered no more than a glimmer of hope for a major oil strike. A spokesman for the oil companies summarized their frustration, saying, "There is nothing wrong with our oil picture that a major discovery won't cure." Despite glowing predictions, Durango never met the expectation as a significant oil producer.

Durango's geographic remoteness further plagued oil executives with transportation problems. With the exception of a narrow gauge railroad, built in the 1880s for local mineral transport, the city had no viable means to transship petroleum products. Because of exorbitant trucking costs, Shell Oil Company and Standard Oil of California discussed the possibility of a transmission pipeline direct to Los Angeles. While this ambitious undertaking would have circumvented a serious obstacle to full-scale oil production in the Durango area, oil recoveries never reached levels sufficient enough to warrant implementation. If oil discoveries near Durango proved largely unsuccessful, the production of natural gas was a welcome reality. As noted earlier, southwest Colorado had placed its hopes for the future on the Pacific Northwest pipeline first proposed in 1952. While the FPC approval of that project two years later promised to make Durango competitive in the Four Corners petroleum industry, the anticipated bonanza faltered. In the first place, the Northwest Pipeline Corporation decided not to locate its headquarters in Durango as promised. Instead, the Houston-based firm selected Albuquerque as the site from which to oversee the completion of the $160 million transmission system.

Second, although gas fields discovered in southwestern Colorado in earlier years proved fruitful, petroleum engineers determined they were peripheral to major gas pools located in northwestern New Mexico. Thus, by the end of the decade, Durango appeared destined to experience only marginal success in the oil and gas industry. In October 1956 Gulf Oil Corporation declared a 50 percent reduction of its exploration forces in the Durango area. By the spring of 1959, petroleum employees had begun a mass exodus from southwest Colorado to newly developed fields in Wyoming and Nebraska. "It was kind of a blow when they started leaving," recalled one local realtor, "Lucky they didn't all leave at once, they left gradually." In 1961 Shell Oil Company, the last of the so-called majors to leave, packed up seismographic charts and core samples and moved its operation to Farmington, closer to the center of oil and gas activity.[16]

Although Durango's dream of an energy empire ended with the departure of Shell Oil, the short-lived petroleum boom had a lasting effect on community growth. According to historian Duane A. Smith, "The influx of the oil people altered the social, economic, and political description of Durango rather rapidly." Some oilmen served on the city council, while others held similar positions of influence in county government and local civic organizations. In this capacity, oilmen pressed for comprehensive urban improvements such as paved streets, a city recreation program, new housing developments, and expansion of the elementary and secondary school systems to accommodate a growing, middle-class population.

Their wives, meanwhile, sponsored community auxiliary programs and vigorously campaigned for a modern public library. In their quest to promote "a quality of life" that would attract other professionals to Durango, oilmen joined native residents in promoting the transfer of Fort Lewis A & M College from Hesperus, 30 miles west of town, to its present location on a high mesa overlooking the city. Shortly after classes convened on the new campus in the fall of 1957, civic leaders and academic administrators combined forces to petition the Colorado Board of Higher Education to convert the former military outpost, Indian boarding school, and A & M college into a four-year, degree-granting liberal arts institution; their request was approved in 1962. According to Smith, "The college transfused fresh blood into the local economy and enriched the cultural life." "The greatest thing that happened to Durango was the growth of Fort Lewis College," remarked local physician Leo Lloyd. "Its coming introduced an element of prosperity in the town." In April 1964 the local newspaper published the list of the first baccalaureate class.[17]

While Durango suffered some bitter disappointments in the energy resource industry, these setbacks did not inhibit measurable progress. In August 1956 Durango created its first city planning commission with the aid of a $50,000 federal grant. Later that year, the commission placed into effect the city's first land utilization master plan. The implementation of planned urban development was timely, as census records for 1960 showed Durango's population had surpassed 10,000 people. The figure represented a 41 percent increase in just ten years. One economic study predicted an additional 38 percent rise in population in the following decade, based upon the city's current growth rate. The same study also noted that retail trade figures had risen more than 25 percent in 1950 to an unprecedented $22.5 million. These findings forecasted a continuing upward economic trend in Durango.

Several factors accounted for Durango's unexpected growth in the wake of a collapsing petroleum industry. In the late 1950s the city enjoyed a diversified economy—agriculture, mining, timber, and nascent tourism—which offset the unfulfilled promises of oil and gas. Cattle ranching and mining, the economic mainstays of the frontier era, flourished in the decades immediately after World War II. Too, a significant rise in postwar housing construction fostered a healthy lumber and timber industry in southwest Colorado. More encouraging was the presence of a burgeoning tourist trade.[18]

The decision to promote tourism as a viable industry was in large measure Durango's response to a declining energy resource economy. Decreasing markets for uranium, coupled with only marginal success in the production of oil and gas, forced civic leaders to consider the area's geographic amenities as their economic salvation. Seeking to capitalize on the flavor of the "Wild West" as the main appeal to potential visitors, Durangoans placed their hopes on three available resources. First, they converted one of the nation's few remaining narrow gauge railroads into a popular tourist attraction. Second, they took advantage of the city's proximity to Mesa Verde National Park, widely recognized as some of the best-preserved cliff dwellings of the prehistoric period. Finally, civic leaders promoted the attractiveness of the surrounding San Juan Mountains as a year-round recreational area. Thus, as Durango's ambitions for recognition as an energy resource capital waned in the shadow of neighboring developments, municipal leaders purposefully shifted emphasis to tourism as that city's foremost economic endeavor.[19]

While Durango's economic progress in the 1950s was in part attributable the oil and gas industry, Farmington's reaction to the petroleum energy boom was nothing short of spectacular. According to census figures, the city experienced a phenomenal 554 percent population increase from 1950 to 1960! This mercurial growth rate transformed Farmington from an agrarian community, dotted with peach orchards and dairy farms, into a sprawling, industrialized oil town. Statistics published in 1965 show Farmington with a population in excess of 25,000 people. In a visit to the city in March of that year, celebrated radio commentator Paul Harvey proclaimed Farmington the "energy capital of the West." "In the most gigantic do-it-yourself project the mind of man can achieve," Harvey described in his own inimitable style, "they [Farmington] found gas, coal, and oil and made the most of it."[20]

Pipeline activities initiated during these years testified further that Farmington reigned supreme in the Four Corners subregion as a paramount producer of oil and gas in the West. Completion of the San Juan Basin pipeline to California in the summer of 1951 made the El Paso Natural Gas Company the sole supplier of the heat-producing element to the West Coast. In June 1953 the Federal Power Commission (FPC) granted the El Paso Company permission to double its deliveries via the pipeline from 400 million cubic feet (MCF) per day to 800 MCF. In its proposal, the petroleum firm planned to construct an auxiliary pipeline from gas fields located in the Permian Basin of West Texas to link with the West Coast transmission system located in Farmington. In this manner, El Paso Gas could draw upon its reserves from West Texas should San Juan Basin supplies prove inadequate to meet increased California and Arizona demands for natural gas. Farmington residents, meanwhile, anticipated that El Paso's plan to step up production and delivery of natural gas from the San Juan Basin meant increased explorations.

Concurrent with the El Paso Gas Company's expansion of operations in New Mexico, the Pacific Northwest Pipeline Corporation made its bid to become a serious competitor. The latter's proposal to build a transmission system from the San Juan Basin to Pacific slope states of Idaho, Oregon, and Washington in June 1952 touched off a heated court battle between the two energy giants. The El Paso Company protested the action on the grounds that a second major pipeline would infringe upon gas reserves already designated for use in California. In support of the El Paso argument, the New Mexico Oil and Gas Conservation Commission opposed

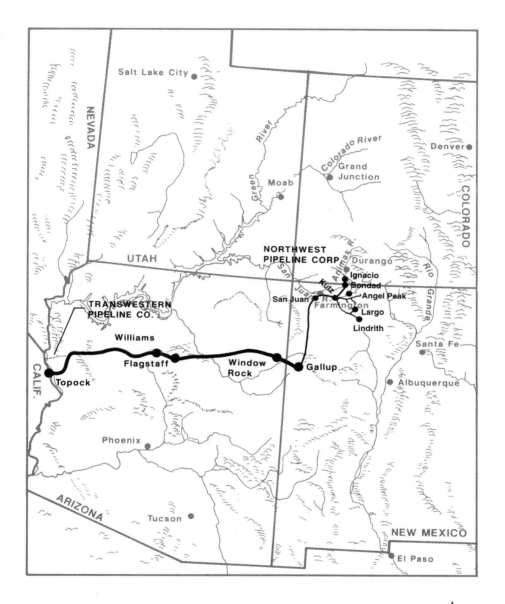

FOUR CORNERS PETROLEUM TRANSMISSION PIPELINES, 1950–1970.
(Map by Ernesto Martinez.)

an additional pipeline saying that it would cause a serious drain on the state's own supply.[21] Farmington entrepreneur Tom Bolack represented the faction in support of a second pipeline. Bolack insisted that the San Juan Basin held "plenty of gas for everybody." A second pipeline would only assure local producers of a ready market, he argued, thus increasing future explorations in the Four Corners to meet the demand. Bolack's motives were not entirely altruistic. In his determination to secure the Pacific Northwest Corporation project for the San Juan Basin, he sold thousands of acres of his own gas leases to guarantee that company an increase in natural gas reserves.

In a hearing before the FPC in November 1953, Robert R. Spurrier, director of the New Mexico Oil and Gas Conservation Commission, reversed the agency's earlier position in order to support the proposed Pacific Northwest pipeline. Citing the benefits that the project promised for future petroleum sales within the state, Spurrier predicted "reserves will eventually reach 20 trillion cubic feet." Spurrier added that new markets in the Pacific Northwest states meant 500–800 new wells would be brought into production in the Farmington area alone. Convinced that the San Juan Basin held sufficient reserves for both projects, the FPC authorized construction of the 1,400-mile pipeline in April 1955.[22]

Farmington's eagerness to support two major pipelines to meet natural gas requirements on the Pacific Coast was, in many respects, illustrative of the intraregional colonial tie that bonded the hinterlands to the metropolitan West. Not all southwesterners were eager to share energy resources with neighboring urban localities. Regional economic development at the expense of unlimited exploitation of local resources was a hotly contested issue, particularly among leading western politicians. New Mexico's senators, for example, were divided on the question of interstate exportation of state oil and gas reserves. Since the inception of the state's first pipeline proposal in 1949, Senator Dennis Chavez, the most outspoken opponent of interstate transport of natural gas, referred to all pipeline transmissions as a "robbery" of state gas resources.

Conversely, Senator Clinton P. Anderson, a member of the powerful Senate Committee on Interior and Insular Affairs, viewed pipeline construction not only as beneficial to the state economy, but also as vital to the national security of the United States. Anderson cited the importance of California as a central shipping point for war material in the event of another conflict in the Pacific. "There is a shortage of petroleum in California," he advised. "An abundance of oil and gas is available in West Texas and New Mexico." Privately, Anderson expressed his interests in securing a "firmer market" for New Mexico oil and gas products as the chief factor in motivating his support for the pipeline.

State officials relied less upon the "national defense" argument and more upon the economic needs of New Mexico as justification for unlimited exportation of petroleum to the West Coast. In November 1959 Governor John Burroughs, speaking in support of a proposed merger between El Paso Natural Gas and the Pacific Northwest Pipeline Corporation, applauded the measure because it promised to enhance purchases of San Juan Basin petroleum reserves. Two years later, Governor Edwin L. Mechem complained to the FPC that gas exportation levels were not keeping pace with production. "For the gas industry in New Mexico to remain active and healthy," Mechem warned, "new markets for gas produced in this state must be provided."

Not surprisingly, most New Mexicans agreed with Director Spurrier's conclusion that the San Juan Basin held enough natural gas in reserve to supply all of the Pacific coastal states plus Arizona for the next thirty years, while also meeting its own state obligations. In his decision to support the proposal for the Pacific Northwest Pipeline, Spurrier wryly commented, "I think that Pacific Northwest certainly ought to have that permit so it can take some of that gas before it becomes an obsolete fuel."[23]

The position of Farmington residents regarding the exportation of the subregion's energy resources mirrored the ambitions of the other Four Corners communities. Mayor Tom Bolack, spokesman for the city of Farmington, urged Senator Anderson's support for pipeline construction. Bolack argued that not only Farmington's economy but the livelihood of the entire Four Corners subregion was at stake. He feared it would take "a miniature WPA or Marshall Plan" to revitalize the San Juan Basin if the proposed pipelines were not constructed. Years later, Bolack restated the significance of the San Juan Basin and Pacific Northwest pipelines in fostering Farmington's remarkable growth. "History will reflect that it [pipeline construction] was the turning point, or the point beyond the embryonic stage," the former mayor recalled.

Thus Farmington, not unlike Durango and the other communities of the Four Corners, valued its economic link to the larger West. Expanding energy markets promised to help these remote, interior cities keep pace with twentieth-century developments. Despite occasional opposition, Four Corners residents appeared in favor of accommodating the metropolitan capitals of the West in the exploitation of the area's vital energy reserves.[24]

No other single event influenced Farmington's metamorphosis from agricultural community to industrial boom town as much as the discovery of oil and gas in the Four Corners. According to one county report in 1950, receipts from fruit sales represented the largest source of income. With the arrival of crews to begin construction of the San Juan Basin pipeline in the summer of 1951, the tiny city of 3,000 teemed with oil rigs, drilling equipment, and roughnecks. "Things were good," remarked one wildcatter. "We had one strip of pavement to represent Main Street." Early arrivals described Farmington as a big orchard with dirt roads emanating outward to Albuquerque, Gallup, Durango, and other outlying communities. Under the guiding hand of Mayor Tom Bolack, Farmington's population soon soared to 15,000 and boasted more than fourteen miles of paved streets. The completion of a modern, up-to-date airport during Bolack's tenure further signified Farmington's importance to out-of-state petroleum corporations as an energy-producing center.

Records indicate that 1959 was a peak year for the San Juan Basin oil and gas industry. A mammoth oil discovery in the Bisti Badlands near Farmington brought 400 new wells into production. Other recoveries, such as the San Juan–Blanco gas field, made Farmington a world competitor as a producer of natural gas. By 1960 petroleum deliveries from the San Juan Basin to the West Coast totaled 70,000 barrels of oil and 2.75 million cubic feet of natural gas daily. Additional pipeline construction during this period enabled the intermountain states of Colorado, Utah, and Wyoming to enjoy ample supplies of Four Corners oil and gas as well. That Farmington supported a population of nearly 25,000 in 1965 suggests that the city benefitted directly from its role as a chief supplier of critical energy commodities to the metropolitan West. Chamber of Commerce publications left no doubt that Farmington intended to perpetuate its colonial ties to the larger West in an effort to retain its title as the "energy capital" of the Four Corners.[25]

Despite predictions of a healthy economic future for Farmington, the petroleum boom lost momentum in the mid-1960s. Just as Moab and Durango absorbed the strain of a deteriorating uranium market, Farmington endured similar setbacks as the oil-and-gas boom subsided. Several reasons accounted for the decline of the Four Corners petroleum industry at this time. Most influential were the changes in federal policy regarding oil and gas regulation. In 1959 quotas imposed on foreign oil during the Eisenhower administration restricted imports to 10 percent of the total market. Protected from foreign competition under the terms of the Trades Agreement Act of 1958, domestic producers like those in the San Juan Basin, profited from unrestricted oil sales at $1.25 per barrel over the world market price. Increased dependency on imported oil, coupled with a push for the development of synthetic fuels during the Kennedy–Johnson years, forced an economic downturn in the domestic petroleum market. In addition, reductions in tax relief incentives such as oil depletion allowances during these years brought exploration to a near standstill. New Mexico, for example, recorded a 33 percent reduction in new wells drilled in 1963.[26]

Regarding natural gas, producers viewed the problem of federal price regulation as the main hindrance to unlimited development. The terms of the Natural Gas Act of 1938 authorized the FPC—not the producers—to regulate the cost of natural gas in all interstate transactions. A Supreme Court decision in 1954, known as the Phillips Case, not only upheld the FPC's authority to regulate the sale of natural gas but also expanded the agency's power to control the price of gas at the well head. In ensuing years, congressional leaders in favor of price deregulation tried in vain to reverse the findings of the Supreme Court. By the 1960s, intrastate prices for gas—not subject to federal control—exceeded the interstate market value, resulting in fewer gas reserves being committed to transmission pipelines. Thus, while the amount of gas held in reserve had not diminished, the number of new gas wells brought into production during these years decreased more than 25 percent. In effect, producers decided to keep their reserves in the ground until FPC prices were in line with drilling costs. One observer, recalling the effects of the gas crunch on Farmington, remarked, "With the price of gas at thirteen cents per MCF from 1960 to 1973 forty per cent of the wells did not return the cost of drilling. No wonder everyone was going broke!"[27]

A second related problem affecting the natural gas industry during these years was the increasing difficulty of recovery. Unexploited gas reservoirs, plentiful during the early days of the boom, required shallow drilling for relatively easy recovery. In later years, however, the low permeability of deeper gas-bearing formations made large quantities of reserves unrecoverable. In 1965 El Paso Natural Gas Company released a joint study suggesting that one solution to this problem was to "fracture" these formations with the use of an underground nuclear device. The proposed detonation would release an estimated seven times the amount of gas presently attainable. In theory, the nuclear explosion was expected to create extensive fracture systems that would permit gas to flow more freely into nonproductive wells. In the opinion of El Paso Natural Gas Company, the geologic formations prevalent in the San Juan Basin of New Mexico were an ideal setting for the test.

The plan to employ nuclear energy for the purpose of releasing petroleum reserves had been the topic of discussion among leading oil companies since 1959. At that time, twenty-four of the nation's major producers
expressed an interest in cooperating with the AEC and the U.S. Bureau of
Mines on such projects. Incorporated as a feature of the Plowshare Program initiated under President Eisenhower in 1953, "Project Gasbuggy,"
the code name for the experiment, would be the first cooperative effort
between private industry and the AEC to utilize atomic power for peaceful
purposes.

While President Kennedy authorized a pilot underground nuclear test
in October 1960, "Project Gasbuggy" was the first application of nuclear
stimulation for the expressed purpose of oil and gas recovery. On June 14,
1965, Assistant Secretary of the Interior John Kelly addressed a letter
to New Mexico Congressman Joseph M. Montoya and Governor Jack
Campbell informing them of the AEC's decision to detonate a 10-kiloton
nuclear device in gas fields located east of Farmington. In anticipation,
residents speculated that the experiment would undoubtedly revive the
sagging oil and gas economy.[28]

The discovery of seemingly unlimited reserves of oil and gas, coupled
with a favorable political climate for their exploitation and distribution,
made the years 1959–1961 the golden age of the petroleum industry in the
state of New Mexico. In November 1959, Governor Burroughs hailed
New Mexico as seventh among the nation's oil-producing states and third
in natural gas recovery before an Oil and Gas Association meeting in Santa
Fe. Statistics prove that the San Juan Basin contributed markedly to the
state's annual petroleum output during this period. Farmington's community development, meanwhile, corresponded to fluctuations in the petroleum industry. While the city enjoyed a population increase of more than
550 percent during the first decade of the oil and gas boom, census figures
recorded only a 15 percent gain from 1960 to 1970. Still, a population of
27,300 in 1960 made Farmington the largest of the Four Corners communities.

Despite indications of an economic downturn, civic leaders remained
enthusiastic about the future of oil and gas production in the San Juan
Basin. Their unshakable optimism suggested that Farmington residents
regarded the impact of the petroleum industry on their city as more than
simply a "boom-and-bust" phenomenon. Compared with Durango and
Moab, Farmington experienced a more comprehensive change in response
to the intraregional consumption of its energy resources. To be sure, the
arrival of the first drilling equipment in 1950 imposed a new social and

economic order in Farmington, in which the city gradually displaced all semblance of an earlier, agrarian society. As apple and peach orchards succumbed to shopping malls and instant subdivisions in 1960, little physical evidence remained of the frontier agricultural community from which Farmington had derived its name. Instead, a modernized, northern New Mexico municipality endeavored to assert a new profile as the leading industrial center in the Four Corners.[29]

Farmington's bid for recognition as the subregion's premiere industrial city did not go unchallenged. Growth patterns indicated that Flagstaff, too, was a major contender for the distinction. As already discussed, the forest and timber industry accounted in large measure for Flagstaff's early success. *Fortune Magazine* noted that other economic factors contributed to the city's meteoric rise. First, its proximity to surrounding national parks and recreational facilities—most notably the Grand Canyon—distinguished Flagstaff as an attractive tourist haven. Second, Flagstaff's location on U.S. Highway 66 and its traditional designation as a terminus for the Santa Fe Railroad stimulated growth. In summary, a balanced economy based largely upon a stable forest products industry coupled with a favorable geographic setting, gave Flagstaff greater economic flexibility than its counterpart cities.

Contrasted to the northern energy boom towns of Durango, Farmington, and Moab, Flagstaff relied more upon a traditional but highly diversified economy to account for its rampant community growth. In 1959 the Arizona Bureau of Business Research applauded Flagstaff as a planned community heavily dependent upon a stable industrial economy. City boundaries grew from 3 square miles to more than 60 square miles in just two years. The frequency with which new residential subdivisions were constructed during these years attested to the city's accelerated growth since World War II. Local boosters credited Arizona State College at Flagstaff as an important contributor to the community's livelihood. Since its establishment in 1895, the college had ranked second only to the lumber industry in employment of local residents. More promising to future development, however, was the Arizona Highway Commission's plan to build an east–west thoroughfare through northern Arizona. The proposed conversion of U.S. 66 to an interstate highway at this time assured Flagstaff—already widely publicized as the gateway to Grand Canyon National Park—recognition as a prominent tourist attraction in the West.

Census reports show that Flagstaff registered a 138 percent population gain from 1950 to 1960. This increase from 7,663 residents to an impressive 18,214 inhabitants in one decade was second only to Farmington's at the height of its petroleum boom. Local newspapers heralded the construction of a $3.5 million shopping center based on projected population estimates of 50,000 by 1965. Flagstaff's attraction of an electronics manufacturing firm from Los Angeles further evidenced a versatile economy.

Local newspapers applauded President Eisenhower's endorsement to build Glen Canyon Dam on the Colorado River as "a blessing due to reap bountiful harvests for Flagstaff." Although the Bureau of Reclamation selected Page, Arizona, as the primary construction site for the project, the agency designated Flagstaff as the central railhead for all incoming materials and supplies. Anticipating the arrival to Flagstaff of laborers, engineers, and federal employees associated with the Glen Canyon project, municipal officials authorized construction of 400 new homes. In addition, the Chamber of Commerce launched an all-out campaign in January 1957 to attract new manufacturing firms to the area. Finally, the adoption of a plan to build a new industrial park left little doubt of Flagstaff's intention to continue its dependency upon industry as the main determinant for future growth.[30]

Despite efforts of municipal leaders to attract high-tech businesses to Flagstaff during these years, the forest products industry remained the economic mainstay. The Flagstaff Federal Sustained-Yield Unit, sanctioned in 1949, provided that 85 percent of all saw timber cut in Coconino National Forest be processed in Flagstaff. In response, Southwest Lumber Mills merged with Saginaw and Manistee Lumber Company to give Flagstaff its first nationally recognized corporation. The following year, Southwest Lumber Mills announced expansion plans that promised to make the company "one of the few modernized sawmills in the West." Company vice president Freeman Schultz anticipated annual production at 44.5 million board feet (MMBF) from the updated facility.

Federally induced opportunities attracted other lumber and timber operations to Flagstaff. In the spring of 1956, Jay Whiting and Lee Kutch, two prominent Arizona lumbermen from Holbrook, announced their purchase of the Oak Creek Lumber Company, a Midwest firm with sawmills in northern Arizona. Once integrated with their Holbrook operations, Whiting and Kutch predicted their Flagstaff mill would manufacture an additional 35 MMBF of lumber annually. During the next five years, several lumber-related businesses established factories in Flagstaff, making lumber and timber production a multimillion dollar industry in northern Arizona.[31]

Compared with lumber production figures among sawmills in California and the Pacific Northwest (normally in excess of 100 MMBF), the projections for the two Flagstaff mills seem unimpressive. When contrasted to the amount of lumber produced statewide, however, Flagstaff clearly dominated the industry. Flagstaff-produced lumber, in fact, represented approximately one-third of Arizona's total output from 1954 to 1960. Significantly, Flagstaff manufacturers shipped 90 percent of their lumber to markets in California, Texas, Arizona, and Oklahoma. Regarding its importance to community growth, the lumber and timber industry employed 54 percent of Flagstaff's residents. Newspapers heralded the consolidation of the city's two largest producers as the main reason for a healthy employment future. An estimated payroll expenditure in excess of $2 million underscored the importance of Southwest Lumber Mills and the forest products industry to Flagstaff.[32]

Statistics showed Flagstaff not only as the leading lumber producer in northern Arizona, but confirmed that no other city in the Four Corners could compete. Among the other municipalities, only Durango produced lumber and timber. John Stanley Weidman, a veteran lumberman from Michigan, establish his Durango sawmill in 1946 and quickly gained recognition as the leading manufacturer of Englemann spruce in southwest Colorado. "Mister Weidman took his chances in pioneering a market for spruce among the western states in order to be competitive with the Arizona mills, who had access to all that ponderosa pine," recollected Grace Shoeber and Charlie Graves, two former employees of the Weidman enterprise. U.S. Forest Service records published in 1959 acknowledged the Weidman mill as the principal contractor for timber harvested in the San Juan National Forest during the decade of the 1950s. While the Durango mill absorbed most of the annual allowable cut for spruce that year, the Forest Service recorded a total harvest of only 54.5 MMBF of commercial timber.

During his twenty-three years of operation, Weidman depended upon the narrow gauge train to transport his product from Durango to the nearest main railroad terminus at Alamosa, Colorado. The lumber was then distributed to consumer markets in Texas, California, Missouri, Kansas, and Michigan. When the Denver & Rio Grande Western announced in 1967 the abandonment of the obsolete narrow gauge line, Weidman protested that his mill could no longer remain competitive with other southwestern producers. Two years later, he sold out his interest in the sawmill. Thus, by the 1960s, Flagstaff, with nearly twice the production capability as Durango and a reliable transportation outlet to interstate markets, emerged unchallenged as the region's foremost lumber producer.[33]

Flagstaff's domination of the lumber products industry in Arizona was destined to be short-lived, however. In November 1959 Southwest Lumber Mills officially changed its name to Southwest Forest Industries. The announcement had long-range implications for Flagstaff. The following year, the new corporation divulged plans to build a $32 million paper mill near Snowflake, Arizona, approximately 100 miles southeast of Flagstaff near the White Mountain Apache Indian Reservation. In response to the announcement, the U.S. Forest Service signed an agreement with Southwest Forest Industries to supply them with pulpwood. The Colorado Plateau Agreement called for 6,000,000 cords of pulpwood to be cut within the timber management units of the Kaibab, Apache-Sitgreaves, Coconino, Tonto, and Cibola National Forests in northern Arizona. The Forest Service viewed the agreement as an opportunity to make possible commercial thinning on a profitable basis. Southwest Forest Industries, in return, was guaranteed a continuous, thirty-year supply of pulpwood for the new paper-making enterprise.

While the agreement was beneficial to the Forest Service and Southwest Forest Industries, it did not prove agreeable to all concerned. For example, the Arizona Pulp and Paper Company, a small local firm recently located in Flagstaff, protested the contract on the grounds that a single large corporation could monopolize the paper industry at the expense of smaller competitors. James Potter, president of Arizona Pulp and Paper, charged that the sale was "a complete reversal of the long standing federal policy which viewed forest lands around Flagstaff as an integral part of the permanent economy of the town." The Flagstaff Chamber of Commerce argued that the agreement undermined its attempts to attract a Canadian paper mill. In agreeing to the contract with Southwest Forest Industries, the Forest Service had committed two-thirds of the area's pulp-sized timber to one company. Such large-scale sales of pulpwood to a single producer, lumbermen agreed, eliminated others from competing in the Arizona paper products business.[34]

Despite vehement protests from local interests, the Forest Service kept its contract with Southwest Forest Industries. The Phoenix-based corporation completed its new paper mill at Snowflake in December 1962 and commenced operations to satisfy the requirements of a growing newsprint market. Two years later, a corporate report informed stockholders that several publishing companies throughout the American Southwest were using Arizona-produced paper to publish newspapers. More importantly, the report speculated on the future of the paper products industry. Because of technological improvements, corrugated cardboard boxes were rapidly replacing wooden crates as material for shipping and transportation. In effect, increased uses of durable paper products for packaging literally eliminated the market for box shook, the mainstay of the World War II lumber economy. More revealing about future trends in the Arizona lumber industry was the prediction that sales in Southwest Forest Industries' paper products division were expected to surpass earnings from the manufacture of building materials.

The prospect that paper products might assume greater importance than lumber in future years foreshadowed an economic trend that was to have a long-term impact on community growth in Flagstaff. While the effects of these changes in the lumber industry were slow to evolve, sawmill activity in that city was on the wane by the mid-1960s. In August 1965 Kaibab Lumber Company, formerly the Whiting and Kutch operation, sold out to Southwest Industries, which proceeded to close down the sawmill. The company cited a reduction in the annual allowable cut of timber in the Coconino National Forest as the reason for the closure.

Concurrently, Southwest Forest Industries expanded its sawmill activities at McNary, Arizona, on the White Mountain Apache Reservation. In doing so, the company no longer depended exclusively upon Flagstaff facilities to supply its rough lumber needs. Located in the heart of northern Arizona's prime timberland, the McNary mill combined with the original mill in Flagstaff to form the nucleus of Southwest's forest products empire. By the end of the 1960s, a housing construction slowdown throughout the United States reduced national and regional demands for Arizona lumber even further. In response to a depressed market, civic leaders reevaluated Flagstaff's long-standing dependency upon the lumber industry as the city's principal economic endeavor.[35]

Continued intraregional dependency upon natural and energy resources produced in the hinterland West during the mid-1950s to mid-1960s accounted in large measure for the rapid economic development of at least four small cities in the Four Corners. As the energy needs of a postwar industrial society increased, the communities of the remote southwestern subregion were subjected to the dictates of overpopulated, metropolitan centers. Moab, Farmington, Durango, and Flagstaff, were, in effect, economic satrapies of an energy-consumptive West.

Not unlike the mineral rushes of the early frontier, the energy resource booms of the mid-twentieth century inevitably dissipated. In their wake, the scramble to exploit uranium, petroleum, timber, and other resources made an enduring contribution to the nascent urbanization of the Four Corners. All of the hinterland "boom towns" felt the stimulation of economic prosperity as they rebounded from the aftermath of virulent growth; permanent social and economic change was the irreversible result. Each municipality responded in its own way to the dynamics of change. These four cities, in particular, asserted their newfound individual identities in anticipation of regional and national recognition.

As the energy resource booms declined in the mid-1960s, each community reevaluated its broad-based economic relationships. The future of Moab and Farmington, for example, remained dependent almost exclusively upon energy resource exploitation. Neither city willingly accepted the fact that the energy boom era was over. Cooperative efforts between the federal government and private industry, as manifested in "Project Gasbuggy," gave Moab and Farmington a false sense of hope for the revival of the uranium and the petroleum industries.

In contrast, Durango early accepted its limitations as an energy producer. In response, that city pledged an unfaltering commitment to tourism as the leading profit-making industry of the future. Flagstaff, meanwhile, reaped the blessings of a fickle yet diversified economy, although impending changes in the lumber industry forced city fathers to also consider alternative economic measures.

Even at the nadir of the energy boom years, Durango, Moab, Farmington, and Flagstaff reaffirmed a willingness to engage in intraregional colonialism. In doing so, the Four Corners remained inextricably fused to the greater metropolitan West. The economic benefits and cultural enrichment gained from years of resource exploitation served to strengthened their resolve. Still, if the hinterland communities were to continue their economic association with the urban West, transportation and communication links between subregion, region, and nation were no longer a mere convenience, but an inescapable imperative.

VANADIUM CORPORATION OF AMERICA

The leeching plant located in Durango was in full operation when this photo was taken in 1942. (Photograph, Courtesy, Duane Smith Collection, Durango, Colorado.)

AEC, RAW MATERIALS DIVISION

Aerial view of the compound established as a uranium ore collection station at Grand Junction, Colorado, in 1947. (Photograph, Courtesy, Museum of Western Colorado, Grand Junction, Colorado, Image No. 1983.63, #44.)

MAIN STREET, MOAB, UTAH

On the eve of the great uranium rush ca.1950. (Photograph, Courtesy, Denver Public Library, Western Collection, Denver Colorado.)

URANIUM PROSPECTOR

Thousands like this unidentified uranium hunter with geiger counter canvassed the desert plateaus of the Four Corners in anticipation of a major strike. (Photograph, Courtesy, Museum of Western Colorado, Grand Junction, Colorado, Image No. 1983.63, #1.)

CHARLIE STEEN'S MI VIDA MINE
Site of southern Utah's earliest discovery of uraninite, which made the Four Corners competitive with international uranium producers. (Photograph, Courtesy, Western Mining and Railroad Museum, Helper, Utah.)

BARKER DOME FIELD

This rig near the Colorado–New Mexico border represented Southern Union Gas Company's earliest petroleum endeavor in the Four Corners in 1948. (Photograph, Courtesy, Museum of New Mexico, Santa Fe, Neg. No. 51–D–150.)

JAMES McNARY
Northern Arizona's lumbering pioneer and president of Southwest Lumber Mills.
(Photograph, Courtesy, Martha Chilcote Collection, Pinetop, Arizona.)

OAK CREEK LUMBER COMPANY

Later sold to Whiting and Kutch, was just one of Flagstaff's many lumber products producers in 1951. (Photograph, Courtesy, Arizona Historical Society, Pioneer Museum, Flagstaff, Arizona.)

SAN JUAN BASIN PIPELINE

The project to tranport natural gas from the Four Corners to California's sprawling cities was well underway when this photo was taken in 1953. (Photograph, Courtesy, El Paso Natural Gas Company, El Paso, Texas.)

"OIL PROGRESS WEEK" PARADE
Durango, 1956, underscored the city's hope of becoming a leading petroleum producer in the Four Corners. (Photograph, Courtesy, Fort Lewis College, Center for Southwest Studies, Durango, Colorado.)

CHARLIE STEEN (WITH GLASSES) AND ROSE SHUMAKER
Shown here with son Mark and an unidentified miner at the height of Moab's uranium activity ca. 1958. (Photograph, Courtesy, Western Mining and Railroad Museum, Helper, Utah.)

DURANGO, COLORADO

As the oil boom waned by 1960, local civic leaders placed their economic hopes upon the conversion of south Main Street (looking toward the train depot) into a replica of the "Old West." (Photograph, Courtesy, Fort Lewis College, Center for Southwest Studies, Durango, Colorado).

SAN JUAN RIVER PLANT
Construction of huge gasoline refineries such as the one pictured here, made Farmington the undisputed petroleum capitol of the Four Corners by the 1960s. (Photograph, Courtesy, Museum of New Mexico, Santa Fe, Neg. No. 57122.)

ARIZONA SNOWBOWL

A photo of the lodge (ca.1950) taken about the time the City of Flagstaff made its bid for the 1960 Winter Olympic Games. (Photograph, Courtesy, Arizona Historical Society, Pioneer Museum, Flagstaff, Arizona.)

NAVAJO–HOPI RESERVATION

El Paso Gas Company's effort to lay a transmission pipeline across northern Arizona resulted in the employment of hundreds of American Indian lineman. (Photograph, Courtesy, Museum of New Mexico, Santa Fe, Neg. No. 132488.)

INTERIOR THREE-BAND SAWMILL

This fully automated operation typified Southwest Lumber Mills operations throughout northern Arizona during the mid-1960s. (Photograph, Courtesy, Martha Chilcote Collection, Pinetop, Arizona.)

SIGNING OF "OPERATION GASBUGGY" AGREEMENT

Officials from the public and private sector sign an agreement in 1967 to apply nuclear energy for peacetime purposes. From left to right, Howard Boyd, President, El Paso Natural Gas Company; Stewart Udall, Secretary of the Interior; Dr. Glen Seaborg, Chairman of the Atomic Energy Commission; William Peacora; Charles F. Luce; Thomas Morris; Johnny Walker; John Kelly; Walter R. Hibbard. (Photograph, Courtesy, El Paso Natural Gas Company, El Paso, Texas.)

GOBERNADOR, NEW MEXICO

Lowering the 10-kiloton nuclear device in a gas field near Gobernador in the fall of 1967. Operation "Gasbuggy" was a cooperative effort between the private and public sector to enhance the production of natural gas. (Photograph, Courtesy, El Paso Natural Gas Company, El Paso, Texas.)

CONSTRUCTION OF COLORADO STATE HIGHWAY 160

Just east of Durango as it passed the newly established J. Stanley Weidman sawmill ca.1948. (Photograph, Courtesy, Colorado Department of Transportation, Durango, Colorado.)

HIGHWAY 550, NORTH OF DURANGO

Early visitors to the San Juan Basin must have found it tough going along precarious mountain highways such as these seen here under construction in the mid-1950s. (Photograph, Courtesy, Colorado Department of Transportation, Durango, Colorado.)

DRUID ARCH NEAR MOAB, UTAH

Secretary of the Interior Stewart Udall and Lee, his wife, visited Druid Arch with Bates Wilson (left) in 1961. Secretary Udall considered Canyonlands the capstone of his "Golden Circle" concept. (Photograph, Courtesy, National Park Service.)

CANYONLANDS PARK STUDY GROUP

Evaluated Canyonlands, Utah, for consideration as a national park in 1959 and 1960. Front Row (left to right): Darwin Snell, W. Robert Moore. Second Row (left to right): Paul Mayberry, Art Ekker, Bates Wilson, Paul Wykert. Third Row: Abijah Cook, Dean Guyman, Evan Rasmussen, Kent Frost, Lloyd Pierson. (Photograph, Courtesy, National Park Service.)

GOVERNOR JOHN LOVE

Business-minded Colorado executive addressing Durango civic leaders in 1964. L to R: Hal Tanner, Mrs. Arthur Wyatt, H. Jackson Clark, (?), Representative Arthur Wyatt, Leroy Goodwin, Governor John Love, Ann Love, Bill Watts. (Photograph, Courtesy, Fort Lewis College, Center for Southwest Studies, Durango, Colorado.)

PURGATORY SKI DEVELOPMENT CORPORATION

Seen here (ca. 1980), evolved into one of the premier ski facilities in the Southwest since it opened in December 1965. (Photograph, Courtesy, Fort Lewis College, Center for Southwest Studies, Durango, Colorado.)

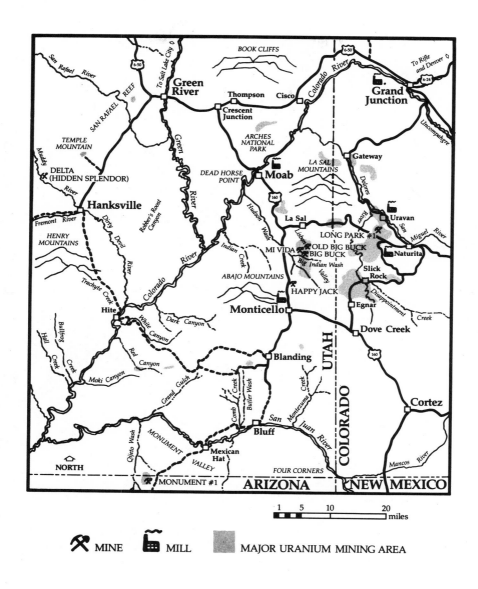

MAP OF THE URANIUM MINING INDUSTRY IN THE FOUR CORNERS REGION
(Map, Courtesy, W. W. Norton & Company, New York.)

95

MAP DETAIL OF PROJECTED NATIONAL SYSTEM OF INTERSTATE
HIGHWAYS IN THE AMERICAN WEST, 1947

The federal government planned no interstate highway construction through the Four Corners. (Map, Courtesy, Federal Highway Administration, U. S. Department of Transportation.)

FOUR

That Ribbon of Highways

"If you ever plan to motor west, just take my way the highway that's the best; get your kicks on Route 66."[1] Singer-songwriter Robert William Troup, Jr., former member of the celebrated Tommy Dorsey Band, penned these words scarcely one year after the conclusion of the Second World War. Entitled "Route 66," Troup's lyrical road map was a lively tribute to one of America's most popular overland thoroughfares. One of only a few interstate highways traversing the United States during the early postwar years, this well-traveled road wound its way more than 2,400 miles from Chicago to Santa Monica, California. In many respects, Bobby Troup merely echoed the enthusiasm that most Americans expressed about the United States national highway system in the mid-1940s. Over the next two decades, in fact, no fewer than a dozen recording artists popularized the now-famous composition.

Westerners, in particular, were grateful that U.S. 66, along with a handful of other transcontinental highways, linked the desert and mountain communities of the trans-Mississippi West to the remainder of the nation. Not unlike the transcontinental railroads that stretched outward into the pristine wilderness of the American frontier, the nation's bituminous highways etched a similar, arterial-like pattern across the United States in the twentieth century. Prior to 1945, however, America's single-lane, poorly maintained, ribbon of highways attracted only the hardiest travelers who dared challenge the astringent landscape of the desert Southwest en route to temperate climates and a "bohemian" lifestyle on the Pacific Coast.

Author John Steinbeck proclaimed Route 66 the "Mother Road" in his famous 1939 novel about the Great Depression. Indeed, the Joad family and thousands of itinerant escapees from the calamitous "dust bowl" region viewed the highway as an avenue of promised opportunity. After the war, that same highway became the vehicle by which a hitherto inaccessible West was opened to a hoard of pleasure-seekers expecting to recapture even a brief reminder of an untamed frontier.[2]

Despite its reputation as the most popular route to the West, U.S. 66 was one small segment of a comprehensive network of highways in the United States. The legislative offspring of the Woodrow Wilson era, the Federal Aid Highway Act of 1916 created the earliest concept of a federal system of highways. The act authorized an expenditure of $75 million for road construction through 1921. More importantly, this legislation introduced the idea of federal-state cooperative financing, the basis for the future implementation of a modern interstate highway system.

In its initial phase, the federal highways program evolved at a snail's pace. With Wilson's departure from the White House, only 11.5 percent of the nation's 2.5 million miles of farm-to-market roads were hard surfaced. World War I, however, demonstrated that the United States needed a coherent network of interstate highways, linking not only its farming communities, but also all of its major cities. In 1921 Congress responded with a new Federal Aid Highway Act that promised to provide the nation with a road system aimed at satisfying municipal as well as rural needs. Appropriately, the 1920s, regarded by many historians as the "age of the automobile," witnessed the greatest expansion of surfaced highway construction to date. According to one historian, "During the 1920s, more than seventeen million cars, trucks, and buses were added to the nation's motor fleet, the number of miles of surfaced highways reached 407,000." Everyone—politicians and motorists alike—demanded bigger and better highways.[3]

Thus, under the comprehensive umbrella of the Federal Aid Highway Act of 1921, U.S. 66 became a primary east-to-west thoroughfare. Originating in Chicago, the route made a sweeping arc southwest to St. Louis, then pierced the Great Plains to Oklahoma City. From there the road forged a westerly path to Albuquerque, where it paralleled the course of the Santa Fe Railroad across the Arizona-California desert until reaching Santa Monica. For years an unimpressive, rut-filled highway, U.S. 66 nevertheless promised economic survival to countless remote communities along its path. For this reason, local politicians were quick to adopt federal-state funding measures in an effort to surface their state's portion of the highway.[4]

During the depression years, the principal aims of Herbert Hoover and

Franklin Roosevelt with regard to road construction were employment and economic recovery. While Congress allocated a significant amount of federal dollars for the construction of new roads during these years, it earmarked most of the budget for the improvement and maintenance of the existing system. On July 21, 1932, President Hoover placed $300 million dollars into the hands of the Reconstruction Finance Corporation (RFC) for redistribution to construct, maintain, and improve America's system of public roads. In subsequent years, relief workers employed under the Civil Works Administration (CWA) constructed or repaired more than 500,000 miles of roads. When Franklin D. Roosevelt assumed the presidency in 1933, he continued the Hoover tradition of exploiting the public roads program as a means to national economic recovery. In early 1938 Roosevelt authorized an annual appropriation of $225 million for highway projects.

Because of the urgency for work relief during the early stages of the Great Depression, conscientious highway planning appeared for the most part as an afterthought. President Roosevelt's creation of the National Resources Planning Board (NRPB) in June 1934, however, stands out as the noteworthy exception. The chief purpose of this board was to discuss long-range economic planning based upon the development of existing national resources. Included in these plans were the ideas of economist Wilfred Owen on the development of a national system of interstate highways. New Deal road programs, he argued, were aimed mostly at providing jobs at the expense of sound planning and quality construction. More imperative was a wholesale revision of the public roads program that considered the future needs of American motorists. "Transportation planning," Owen asserted in his final report, "was second only to a basic land use pattern as a guide in developing the future city."[5]

The advent of the Second World War forced Roosevelt to consider long-term planning of highways, not only as an emergency war measure but also as an economic contingency for American postwar development. Partly in response to the NRPB's call for conscientious transportation development, Roosevelt appointed a seven-man panel designated the Interregional Highway Commission. The president charged the delegation with designing a network of planned interstate highways. Members of the commission included Bureau of Public Roads Director Thomas H. MacDonald, who submitted a proposal that called for a transcontinental expressway system not to exceed 40,000 miles. It was to be a highway system designed to connect all of the major urban centers in the United States. On September 8, 1941, the remaining members of the Interregional

Highway Committee voted to adopt the so-called MacDonald Plan with some modifications. In their recommendations to the president, the committee suggested an annual expenditure of $500 million for three years to implement the proposed national system of interstate highways.

As United States involvement in global war became more imminent, national defense requirements took precedence over domestic planning. The MacDonald Plan was temporarily shelved. A more pressing concern in late 1941 was the condition of the nation's highways in the face of all-out war. For this reason, President Roosevelt directed the War Department to conduct a survey of all highway systems as they related to national defense. In its report, the Army recommended upgrading 78,000 miles of highways that were determined to be vital to national defense. With America's entry into the war, Congress responded to War Department recommendations for more defense highways by passing the Defense Highway Act of 1941. Section 6 of the act authorized funds for the construction, maintenance, and improvement of access or replacement roads determined to be either essential to the war effort or necessary for defense in the event of an enemy attack. One feature that distinguished this bill from previous highway legislation was the provision that the federal government assume 75 percent of the all-defense-related costs.[6]

Passage of the Defense Highway Act of 1941 had a lasting effect on postwar development in the Four Corners. First, the act authorized the federal government to spend millions of dollars to subsidize new road construction throughout the subregion, making even the most desolate stretches of the interior West accessible to vehicular traffic. In accordance with defense priorities, all sections of the country determined to have strategic value were to have improved access to existing national highways via newly constructed trunk roads. As it applied to California, Nevada, Texas, and portions of southern Arizona, the Defense Highway Act provided that all military installations used for testing or other defense-related activities, be linked to the nation's primary roads network. Regarding the Four Corners, the act stipulated that those areas rich in strategic minerals—vanadium, and later, uranium—should also become part of the interstate system through a system of secondary roads.

With the conclusion of World War II, President Roosevelt signed the Federal Aid Highway Act of 1944, which incorporated both military and civilian highway requirements into a single piece of legislation. In essence, the act became the legal embodiment of the MacDonald Plan. In anticipation that Americans would become increasingly mobile, the new legislation pledged to connect "principal metropolitan areas, cities, and industrial centers, [and] to serve the national defense" through the establishment of a 40,000-mile "expressway" system. Upon final passage of the bill, Senator Carl Hayden of Arizona, concerned about the future of western regional development and a personal advocate of improved national highways, expressed his approval, saying, "The American people cannot enjoy prosperity without an adequate highway transportation system." Significantly, the act recognized the importance of postwar national security as it provided for the continued construction of defense roads.[7]

Despite good intentions, national highway development bogged down during the early years of the Truman administration. Cognizant of material shortages and rampant economic inflation after the war, President Truman subordinated highway projects to more pressing reconversion demands. Initially, Truman delayed highway construction in an effort to hold down consumption of scarce building materials such as steel and concrete. On August 6, 1946, Truman ordered the suspension of federal highway aid altogether. When in early 1938 the Senate Committee on Public Works reevaluated the 1944 Highway Act, they recommended that the federal government spend no more money beyond the $500 million authorized in the legislation. Because of these restrictions, the government funded only 18,000 miles of surfaced highways from 1944 to 1947. Expressing his disappointment, Public Roads Director MacDonald predicted that 42 percent of the original primary system of national highways would be completely worn out by the next decade.[8]

As the national highway program slowly took effect with the new decade, American response to the Korean Conflict, the Cold War, and the AEC Domestic Uranium Procurement Program prompted unparalleled highway improvements on the regional level. In December 1950 the AEC approached MacDonald to discuss the inadequacy of access roads in Colorado, Arizona, Utah, and New Mexico. "Uranium is one of the most critical and urgently needed metals in our defense program," an AEC spokesman noted. "The Colorado Plateau area is the only large domestic source of this metal." A dependable system of access roads leading to and from active mining operations was critical to maintain "a continuous flow of uranium in the event of a national emergency."

The unusually rugged canyon country of the Four Corners, AEC officials argued, required massive federal subsidization to ensure the success of the access roads program. "This desolate but spectacular scenic land contains the most isolated regions of the United States," noted Charles A. Rasor, chief of the AEC's ore procurement branch in Grand Junction, and later supervisor for the agency's roads program. "The largest section of the country in which there are no improved roads, now furnishes a large part of the domestic supply of uranium ore."

Under the guiding hand of Senator Dennis Chavez, senior legislator from New Mexico and chairman of the Senate Committee on Public Works, Congress passed the Federal-Aid Highway Act of 1950. "Motor transportation is the lifeblood of America's economy," Chavez declared in a dramatic appearance before Congress. "The highways are its arteries—we cannot let them harden." A mirror image of earlier legislation, the latest version of federal highway policy again appropriated $500 million for interstate road construction. More important to the Four Corners, the act funded the AEC's access roads program proposal. "There is a need at the present time to provide for emergency highway funding to essential defense installations in the event of a national emergency," the bill read. Section 12 of the act allocated $10 million for road improvements in sections of the country deemed strategically important. Notably, the same bill earmarked money for road building on federally owned lands such as Indian reservations and national parks—a provision that also would have an impact on the future economy of the Four Corners.[9]

From 1951 to 1955, the four years during which the access roads program was in effect, the Department of Defense built more than 800 miles of arterial roads in the Four Corners at a cost of $5.9 million. Among the four contiguous states, Utah benefited most from the federally sponsored roads programs. Recognizing Utah as the principal contributor of uranium-bearing ore to a growing national stockpile, the AEC underwrote the construction of 508 miles of roads at the phenomenal cost of $5,135 per mile. Notably, the state incurred only 5 percent of the initial cost, while the Defense Department absorbed the remaining 95 percent. Colorado, which housed most of the uranium processing mills, was second. It saw 223 miles of highways built at an even more astounding cost of $11,216 per mile! Arizona followed with 97 miles, most of which traversed the Navajo Reservation, where several uranium mines were in operation. Curiously, New Mexico, Senator Chavez' home state, reported only 32 AEC-built miles of new road during this period.[10]

The AEC's commitment to implement an access roads program further underscored the importance of the federal government in the postwar economic development of the hinterland West. Up to this time, Four Corners residents labored under the ever-present burden of inadequate transportation. For years, only an obsolete narrow gauge railroad serviced the area. Before the AEC there was no link to the national highway system; only remnants of weather-worn cattle and sheep trails rendered vague impressions of a serviceable road network. "The few trails kept open by local cattlemen," remarked one resident, "were determined by the topography." While prewar federal projects, such as the Civilian Conservation Corps (CCC), made notable improvements, it was the AEC's access roads program that finally breached the bonds of isolation to revolutionize the local economies. In subsequent decades, the infrastructure of roads sponsored by the AEC were incorporated into the primary highways network of the various Four Corners states.

Before 1950 San Juan County, Utah, was among those reporting the lowest road use of any section located in the southeastern part of the state. In their investigation into the problem, county officials cited poor highway conditions as the chief cause for limited traffic usage. Although the National Park Service since 1929 endeavored to lure visitors to Arches National Monument, poorly serviced roads precluded significant traffic visitations. Other factors, too, contributed to the area's isolation. Located nearly 30 miles south of U.S. Highway 50 (today's I-70), Moab maintained at best a tenuous link to the state's most important interstate thoroughfare. To the dismay of the Defense Department, Moab—the nation's leading supplier of uranium concentrate—remained far removed from the mainstream of traffic moving east-to-west across America.

The arrival in the early 1950s of the AEC, on whose heels trailed thousands of get-rich-quick prospectors, substantially altered conditions in southeastern Utah. First, the agency funded the construction of a paved highway (present U.S. 191) south from the Lisbon Valley Mining District near Moab to Monticello, site of the government's uranium processing mill. Next, the AEC extended the road to Blanding and other neighboring communities, linking uranium-bearing lands of that area to mining operations in Monument Valley, Arizona, the heartland of the Navajo Reservation. In addition, the AEC built a network of dirt and gravel roads connecting all the major mining facilities in the area. Finally, the federal agency, in cooperation with the Utah State Highway Commission, bulldozed a new highway from Moab north to U.S. 50. With these achievements the AEC provided the much-desired hookup between Utah's uranium mining districts and the national interstate system.[11]

Southwest Colorado residents also hoped to reap benefits from the AEC's access roads project. With the arrival of the VCA mill to Durango in 1949, company president Dennis Viles lobbied for the improvement of local roads leading to and from Durango. More importantly, he campaigned for a modern interstate highway to cut through the heart of the Four Corners, linking Denver to Phoenix. Viles argued that a route across the Navajo Reservation would "make easily accessible a giant section of known uranium-bearing ore deposits." Employing the time-honored national defense argument before a joint commission of Colorado and Arizona state highway officials, Viles predicted that a modern paved highway through the Navajo Reservation would "contribute vitally to United States self-sufficiency in uranium production." Responding to the plea for improved roads, the AEC combined forces with the Colorado Highway Department to upgrade present U.S. Highway 160 from the mineral-rich counties of southeast Utah and northeast Arizona to the VCA processing plant in Durango.[12]

New Mexico benefited least from the AEC's road building activity. Instead, the petroleum industry's requirement for highway improvements superseded all other resource development needs in that state. Oil companies located in the San Juan Basin clamored for good roads from Farmington—considered the "largest oil and gas industry service between Denver and Phoenix." Oilmen desired a route to either Albuquerque or Gallup, where petroleum products could be transshipped by rail to market. Similarly, pipeline contractors pleaded for a reliable access road into the Four Corners. While U.S. 66 facilitated transport from major distributors in Oklahoma and West Texas to Albuquerque, only a primitive, rut-filled passage extended to the San Juan Basin oil fields. When in 1950 the FPC authorized construction of an interstate transmission pipeline from Four Corners to southern California, the New Mexico Highway Commission funded a surfaced, two-lane bituminous highway (present State Highway 44) between Farmington and Albuquerque. Within months of its completion, state officials ordered that a 90-mile stretch of graveled road be built between Gallup and Shiprock (present U.S. 666). This latter highway, commissioners hoped, might one day extend to the Arizona–New Mexico state line to connect with the much-discussed "Navajo Trail" across northern Arizona.[13]

The notion to build an interstate highway across the vast Navajo Reservation had for years been a topic of discussion. In 1946 various municipal chambers of commerce in the Four Corners met to deliberate the possibility. One year later, a newly formed Navajo Trail Association submitted a formal proposal to the Bureau of Indian Affairs (BIA). The resolution proposed that the BIA construct a 200-mile-long, blacktop road from Tuba City, Arizona, to Shiprock, New Mexico. The committee hoped that state agencies would eventually link the Navajo Trail, once built, to U.S. highway 66. In this manner, travelers bound for the West Coast could easily divert into the Four Corners via the Reservation highway. The result of such a plan would be increased exposure of the Four Corners to tourist traffic.[14]

Despite great expectations, the BIA was hard-pressed to comply with the request. Until the Highway Act of 1950, there were no provisions for highways on federally owned lands. Even with the 1950 legislation, agency construction on reservations was restricted to secondary-class roads. The proposal for a surfaced highway across Navajo lands, therefore, did not fall within the BIA's jurisdiction. BIA Commissioner John R. Nichols discussed the matter with New Mexico's freshman senator Clinton P. Anderson, advising him that while the Bureau recognized the need for such a route, the agency did not intend to build a road to "high speed highway standards."

Despite some obvious limitations, the 1950 Act transformed the dream of a Navajo Trail into reality. Because of its proven uranium reserves, the importance of northern Arizona to national security increased comparably to that of Utah. Thus, under the provisions of the Federal Aid Highway Act of 1950, the Navajo Reservation was linked to the AEC's access roads program. The establishment of the Rare Metals Corporation uranium reduction mill near Tuba City, moreover, shifted responsibility for highway improvements from the BIA to the AEC.

From 1950 to 1954, the AEC funded the lion's share of road construction along the originally proposed Navajo Route No. 1. The Ore Procurement Branch constructed 61 miles of road from Monument Valley, where many of the VCA uranium mines were located, west to Teec Nos Pos near the Arizona–New Mexico border (present U.S. 160). In addition, the AEC improved the BIA-constructed secondary roads running east from Monument Valley to Tuba City. These roads were not built for public access; rather, they were used for heavy ore truck traffic. For the most part, the AEC-sponsored roads were graveled and subject to closure during poor weather conditions. Nevertheless, even these limited improvements increased haulage of Arizona-produced uranium ore to Durango and Tuba City for processing.[15]

If the AEC roads program was significant, the Navajo Indian Relief Bill, sponsored during the last months of the Truman administration, was equally important to future highway building in the Four Corners. Part of a bipartisan plan to reduce federal responsibility for reservation Indians, the bill promoted Indian economic self-determination, calling for "better utilization of resources on the Navajo and Hopi reservations." Among the bill's many important provisions was the allocation of $20 million dollars for road improvements on the Navajo and Hopi reservations. Proponents of the bill contended that the roads program not only would provide employment and training for hundreds of Indians, but also would increase the overall economic potential of their tribal lands. President Truman signed the rehabilitation bill into law on April 19, 1950.

The ten-year road-improvement package outlined in the new legislation promised to fulfill the hope of the Navajo Trail Association. One plan called for construction of an all-weather, two-lane highway starting in southwestern Colorado, continuing along the AEC ore road in northern Arizona, and ending at the junction of U.S. 89, approximately 50 miles north of Flagstaff. Local boosters believed the proposed highway would become a popular alternative to Route 66 for travelers heading west. Supporters estimated a 500 percent increase in motorist visitations to the scenic Four Corners with the completion of the new road.

Furthermore, the proposed route would reduce the distance between Durango and Flagstaff by 135 miles, and travel from Denver to Phoenix by approximately 260 miles. The Navajo Trail thus had the potential to replace the more circuitous Route 66 as the principal means of travel between these important western cities. State officials in Colorado were so enthusiastic at the prospect, they pledged to appropriate $1.5 million dollars for a new bridge across the San Juan River near the Arizona–Colorado border to expedite completion of the Navajo Trail. Thus, the goals of American Indian policy-makers in Washington combined with the defense imperatives of the AEC to improve accessibility to the isolated communities of the Four Corners.[16]

While boosterism ran high on the local level, politicians in Washington were remiss in appropriating the $20 million earmarked for the Navajo–Hopi roads program. In an appearance before the Senate Committee on Public Works in February 1952, BIA Roads Chief J. Maughs Brown reported less than $1 million a year had been appropriated since the rehabilitation act had gone into effect. Most of these expenditures, Brown added, went toward maintenance of existing roads rather than new construction. "In order to bring the Navajo–Hopi program into balance," the BIA official advised, "four million dollars annually will be required during the fiscal years 1954 and 1955." Because of fiscal delays, the federal government made little progress on the Reservation highways beyond what the AEC had achieved. The BIA, Brown admitted, improved only 73.6 percent of the proposed 170-mile-long highway.

Interurban rivalry among the Four Corners municipalities also impeded progress. In anticipation that the proposed highway would serve as a natural link between Mesa Verde National Park near Durango and Grand

Canyon National Park north of Flagstaff, the Durango and Cortez Chambers of Commerce petitioned the BIA to divert the Navajo Trail into Colorado once it crossed Arizona. The request infuriated the city of Farmington because of the recommendation that the Navajo Trail bypass New Mexico altogether. "A larger number of Navajo Indians would be aided if the new road started in the vicinity of Shiprock rather than Cortez where there are no Navajos," rebuffed George Roberts, Farmington Chamber of Commerce Manager. Advocates noted further that New Mexico had already made a significant commitment to the Navajos in paving the 90-mile stretch of road between Shiprock and Gallup (present U.S. Highway 666). In the view of most northern New Mexicans, connecting the Shiprock–Gallup road to the proposed Navajo Trail provided cross-country motorists even greater access to the interstate system.[17]

Utah and Arizona residents were equally disturbed about the Navajo Highway proposal. Former San Juan County Commissioner Calvin Black recalled that Moab officials rejected a BIA plan to divert the Navajo Trail through Monument Valley and Moab before passing into southwest Colorado. The San Juan County Commission petitioned Utah Governor George Clyde to make a public statement that there would be no cooperation with Arizona or Colorado to facilitate the highway through his state. This early yet consequential decision to prevent the Navajo Trail from entering Utah in part accounted for Moab's inability to sustain a high-level tourism economy after the uranium rush years. "We really goofed, we were so tunnel-visioned," Black later lamented.

Similarly, Flagstaff officials feared a northern route across Arizona would distract traffic from U.S. 66, which up to that time had served as an economic lifeline to communities along its path. According to an Arizona Highway Commission survey, Route 66 was the most popular year-round thoroughfare in Arizona. Traffic passed through Winslow, Holbrook, and Flagstaff at the rate of 2,728 vehicles daily. A more northerly route, municipal leaders feared, would no doubt have an adverse effect.

State Congressman Edward Ellsworth stressed the importance of U.S. Highway 66 to national defense. "In case of an attack on the West Coast," the Flagstaff representative advised, "Highway 66 would carry a major share of traffic loads of people leaving the area." Ellsworth argued that if the road was expected to meet its civil defense capabilities, funding for maintenance of the existing interstate system was preferable to costly expenditures on the underpopulated Navajo–Hopi Reservation.[18] Thus, congressional inefficiency in appropriating federal funds to complete the Navajo Highway, plus the failure of the project to generate unanimous approval among rivaling Four Corners cities, postponed construction of the Navajo Trail for nearly a decade.

Federal funding for interstate highways markedly increased when Dwight D. Eisenhower entered the White House in January 1953. Ike's fascination with highway improvement dated back to July 1919, when as a young officer he accepted the army's challenge to organize a "coast-to-coast" convoy to dramatize the strategic importance of good highways. The convoy, which included forty-two trucks, mobile field kitchens, ambulances, and a complement of motorcycles, usually managed only four to five miles an hour on good roads. Most of the time, Captain Eisenhower's command either bogged down in muddy, rain-soaked fields or, in some cases, "the heavy trucks broke through the surface of the road and we had to tow them out one by one with the caterpillar tractor." On September 6, after months of arduous travel, the convoy arrived in San Francisco. Eisenhower later recollected that the journey "started me thinking about good, two lane highways."

After World War II, Eisenhower, like other top-level officials, returned home much impressed by the strategic value of the German *Autobahnen*. Eisenhower remarked, "During World War II, I saw the superlative system of German national highways crossing that country and offering the possibility, often lacking in the United States: to drive with speed and safety at the same time." It was no surprise, then, that President Eisenhower, three and a half decades after his miserable, cross-country ordeal, championed a vast system of interstate highways for America.

In support of the president's views on the military need for good, public highways, New Mexico Senator Dennis Chavez rendered an emotional appeal to Congress for long-term improvements. "Hitler's General Staff laid out across Germany a system of magnificent four-lane highways capable of moving military men and equipment to any front without delay," Chavez noted. Expressing alarm about the state of America's preparedness for war, however, Chavez warned that in defense planning the nation was dangerously negligent. "America is slogging along in 1952 on roads that are scarcely adequate for even 1935's traffic."¹⁹

Increased global tension during Eisenhower's tenure made him more determined to improve the defense capabilities of the nation's highways. In a special White House meeting in April 1954, the president charged personal aide Sherman Adams, and Arthur Burns, chairman of the Council of Economic Advisors, to coordinate their efforts in proposing a funding package to accelerate the federal highways building program. Eisenhower's objective was to place "50 billion dollars worth of highways under immediate construction." In the interest of national defense, the president gave the interstate system top priority. Eisenhower enlisted the services of an old military colleague, General Lucius D. Clay, to design the so-called "Grand Plan."

The president selected the Governor's Conference of 1954, held at Lake George, New York, to unveil his plans for national highway improvement. Vice President Richard M. Nixon informed state executives that Eisenhower hoped to inaugurate a public highway program "to challenge the imagination as did the road building era in the days of ancient Rome." Ike's plan called for a ten-year program costing $5 billion annually. "The proposed $50 billion dollar price tag," Nixon advised, "shall have made only a good start on the highways that the country will need for a population of two hundred million people." While the vice president acknowledged congressional authorization of an unprecedented $875 million for federal roads, he contended that America's politicians "lacked imagination" with respect to the real needs of the American public highways system.[20]

In early January 1955 the Clay Committee submitted its report to Eisenhower. Essentially, the recommendations mirrored the MacDonald Plan of pre–World War II years. Accordingly, the Clay Plan outlined a thorough modernization of 40,000 miles of interstate highways. The federal government would, through a Federal Highway Corporation, finance 90 percent of the project. In contrast to the MacDonald proposal, however, the Clay program would be self-liquidating, since the funds to be capitalized would be equivalent to revenues anticipated from the imposition of federal taxes on gasoline and other petroleum products. In a ten-point objective summary of the recommendation, the committee stressed military and civil defense along with improved highway safety and efficiency. The final report read, "There can be no serious question as to the need for a more adequate highway system. Only the cost and how it is to be met poses a problem."

Six weeks after receiving the Clay report, Eisenhower sent a special message to Congress advocating its adoption. "The National System of Interstate Highways, although it embraces only 1.2 percent of total road milage, joins 42 state capital cities and 90 percent of the urban and 45 percent of the rural population." He argued for the interstate system to receive top priority in all future highway legislation. "At the current rate of development," Eisenhower declared, "the Interstate network would not reach even a reasonable level of extent and efficiency in half a century. State highway departments cannot effectively meet the need." Following his opening statement, Eisenhower outlined the recommendations of the Clay Committee.[21]

Despite almost universal agreement on the need for modern highways, devising a sound fiscal approach to finance the "Grand Plan" divided Washington lawmakers. Advocates of the Clay proposal, among them Senators Milliken of Colorado, Chavez and Anderson of New Mexico, and Hayden of Arizona, viewed the measure not only as critical to the growth of the West but also as beneficial to the national economy. Most supporters concurred with the president that a major road-building program would end recent downturns in the post-Korean War economy. The federal government's intent to assume 90 percent of the overall costs, moreover, assured state and municipal officials that local and regional expenditures would be marginal. According to the Clay Plan, truckers and other motorists would share the primary costs of construction and maintenance through increased gasoline taxes.

Dissenters of the Clay Plan, principally congressional representatives from the more populous eastern states, determined that a gasoline tax increase was unfair as well as unwarranted. Led by Senator Harry F. Byrd of Virginia, the chairman of the powerful Senate Finance Committee and a self-declared fiscal conservative, detractors argued that the heavier-traffic states located in the East would bear most of the financial burden for the national highway program. Opponents agreed that toll roads, a popular method of financing road and bridge construction in the East, was more equitable.

Spokesmen for the western states, which lacked the traffic to support toll highway reimbursements, adamantly rejected this approach. Though not a westerner, General Clay also spoke out against the toll road measure, saying, "If tolls were charged on previously free roads, there would be a revolution in several western states." Thus, the arguments presented for and against the Clay proposal were, in large measure, in line with regional differences. Although the Clay Plan conformed to President Eisenhower's thinking on interstate highway construction, political factionalism struck down the bill during its initial appearance before Congress.

In an effort to end the political impasse, House Roads Subcommittee Chairman, George H. Fallon of Maryland co-sponsored a new bill with Congressman Hale Boggs of Louisiana in July 1955. The key to the success of the Fallon–Boggs bill was that it provided something for everybody. First, it satisfied Ike's mandate to give interstate highways top priority within the nation's internal improvements. Second, while the new bill acknowledged the urgency of reducing the problems of congested urban areas, interstate highways would not be at the expense of road building in the nation's rural sectors. Finally, the bill recognized the needs of the military as well as those of various federal agencies.

Financing for all of this construction would come not only from a graduated tax increase on petroleum products but also from automobile registration revenues collected in each state. While the Fallon–Boggs proposal also required the federal government to pay for 90 percent of interstate construction, all other local and state improvements would be completed on the traditional 50–50 matching fund basis. In an appeal to western interests, there would be no toll assessments on newly built highways. To appease easterners, the federal government pledged to compensate the states for all toll roads absorbed into the national system. Finally, the new bill established a Highway Trust Fund from which all revenues from taxes on fuels, tires, and new vehicles would be redistributed for future maintenance and construction needs. The reaction was an overwhelming adoption of the compromise bill in Congress. Indeed, the Federal Aid Highway Act of 1956 passed with only one dissenting vote.[22]

The new legislation provided a comprehensive financial umbrella for transportation needs in the West. First, the act created the National Interstate and Defense Highway System, which by its own definition was designed to link the more isolated states of the nation to the more populous ones. Secondly, it continued the policy of special funds for road improvements determined essential to national defense. No less important, the act set aside special allocations for the construction and maintenance of roads located on federally owned properties such as Indian reservations, National Parks and Monuments, and U.S. Forest Service lands. The latter provisions were to have special meaning in the economic future of the interior West.

In accordance with the Federal Highway Act of 1956, the Four Corners states received their share of the apportionment in early 1957. New Mexico got more than $14 million to start construction on its portion of three interstate routes. U.S. 66, redesignated Interstate 40, ran west from the Texas Panhandle through New Mexico to northern Arizona. A second highway, U.S. 85, which joined New Mexico with Texas on the south and Colorado on the north, was rechristened Interstate 25. Finally, a third route from Texas to Arizona was designated Interstate 10. In all, the New Mexico State Highway Department anticipated the completion of more than 1,000 miles of four-lane superhighways by 1970.

The new legislation allotted Arizona $20 million to complete its portion of Interstates 40 and 10 west to the California state line. Arizona agreed to link the two parallel thoroughfares with the construction of Interstate 17 (Black Canyon Highway) running north-south between Flagstaff and Phoenix. Colorado and Utah, meanwhile, also received a share of federal funds to extend I-25 north from New Mexico through Colorado to Wyoming, and to join Colorado and Utah via construction of Interstate 70. Upon receipt of his state's share of the total allocation, Governor Ed Johnson of Colorado remarked, "This is the dawn of a new era in road and street construction in Colorado." Not unlike the days when the railroads linked the mineral resource West to the industrial East, the Interstate and Defense Highway System symbolized a new transportation revolution that promised economic paybacks to the interior West.[23]

The Four Corners well understood the importance of the federal highways program as it related to subregional growth. The Four Corners states not only reaped the benefits of accelerated interstate construction; they also expanded primary and secondary roads because of increased federal funding. Local commissioners in San Juan County, Utah, authorized improvements to U.S Highway 191 leading south from Moab toward the Navajo Reservation. Arizona officials responded by extending U.S. 89 north beyond Tuba City to the Utah state line, where the Eisenhower-sanctioned Glen Canyon Dam project was in its early stages of construction. Utah countered with a 57-mile stretch of paved highway from the dam site to Kanab, Utah.

Like their neighbors, Colorado and New Mexico utilized their portion of the 1956 Federal Highway Act funds to improve roads adjoining the two states. Anticipating that the federal highway program might stimulate completion of the Navajo Trail, the New Mexico Highway Department ordered the road between Shiprock and the Arizona state line surfaced. Colorado, in turn, authorized substantial improvements along U.S. 160 from the Arizona border through Durango toward the San Juan range. In addition, Colorado highway workers made remarkable progress along U.S. 550, which linked southwest Colorado to northwest New Mexico.

In a Durango Chamber of Commerce annual report, Manager Robert L. Beers summarized the importance of the new federal and state highway programs to the local economy. "It can be said that the future of Durango will be molded in 1957," he declared. "Both highways U.S. 160 and 550 respectively are vital to Durango." Elaborating on the economic benefits of future projects, Beers noted, "When the road through the Navajo Indian Reservation is completed and the Four Corners cut-off is built, a tremendous flow of traffic that previously traveled U.S. 66 will be funneled into our city."[24]

Beers's acknowledgement of the highways and their importance to the future of Durango's economy anticipated a change in the making since the mid-1950s. As earlier discussed, the phenomenal postwar growth of the Four Corners' communities was attributable in large measure to mineral and natural resource development. Recent highway improvements, therefore, assured national and regional exploitation of valued Four Corners resources. For a decade, the AEC, in the interest of civil and military defense, had laid the foundation for improved highways throughout this remote subregion. In 1955, the year the AEC terminated its access roads program, Congress failed to appropriate additional funding for that specific purpose. In his evaluation of the AEC contribution to early road building, Raw Materials Division Chief Jesse Johnson prophesied, "These roads which are opening up new areas in the West may possibly have—undoubtedly will have—a future value even after the uranium ores have been mined out."[25]

Johnson's prediction could not have been more accurate. By 1957 the energy resource boom in the Four Corners began to show signs of recession. Durango civic leaders—Robert Beers and others—saw tourism as the logical economic determinant for the future. Representatives from other Four Corners communities concurred with Durango. In effect, the modernization of state highways—many of which were built originally with AEC defense funds—became the necessary measure for tourism to flourish on a major scale. With the enactment of the Federal Highway Act of 1956, the Four Corners states paved most of the AEC-constructed dirt roads and incorporated them into the state highway system. In the minds of most residents, however, any roads network in the Four Corners remained incomplete without the construction of a bituminous, multilane, Navajo Highway.

There was no stronger advocate for the proposed reservation thoroughfare than the Navajo tribe. In the summer of 1957 Navajo Tribal Chairman Paul Jones forwarded a resolution to Senator Clinton P. Anderson of New Mexico containing the names of several residents of the various Reservation Chapters located in each of the Four Corners states. The petition urged the completion of Navajo Reservation "Highway Route #1," the numerical designation that referred to the portion of the road from Shiprock via Tuba City to U.S. Highway 89. Jones stressed the importance of the highway for continued exploitation of uranium and petroleum reserves. He also emphasized its tourism potential noting that the road, once completed, would reduce the distance between Denver and Phoenix by some 260 miles. The Navajo leader argued that the number of east-west travelers across the Reservation would undoubtedly increase, because "Route #1 traverses an area known for spectacular, but at present almost inaccessible, scenery."[26]

Despite the expectations of tribal officials and municipal leaders, bureaucratic gridlock in Washington delayed the long-awaited Navajo Trail Project. As the AEC domestic uranium program lost impetus in the late 1950s, the Defense Department's responsibility for road improvements on the Colorado Plateau lessened. The issue between the energy commission and the BIA, the two agencies most responsible for road improvements on the Navajo Reservation, was clearly one of jurisdiction. In a letter to General Manager K. E. Fields in early 1957, Senator Anderson probed the extent of the AEC's commitment to finish its work on the Navajo Highway. Stressing the importance of the roadway to Southwest Indians, Anderson inquired if the AEC intended to cooperate with the BIA in upgrading the existing dirt road to primary highway status. In response, Acting General Manager R. W. Cook advised that such an undertaking would cost approximately $8.5 million, the equivalent of $50,000 per mile. "While the improvement of the route to bituminous standard would be desirable in the general development of the Navajo Reservation," Cook agreed, "we do not believe that the project can be justified under an AEC program."

Clinton Anderson made similar inquiries of the BIA in his letter to Commissioner Glenn L. Emmons dated January 30, 1957. Apparently unaware that the AEC had responded unfavorably to his request, Anderson assured the BIA director that "assistance from the Defense Department was forthcoming." "Since this would beneficially affect the Indians, and as the area comes under the control of the Bureau of Indian Affairs," Anderson remarked, "I believe that you have a major interest in coordinating any efforts in this regard."

To Anderson's displeasure, the BIA response to his letter was equally noncommittal. Emmons told the New Mexico senator that the agency had informed both the Navajo Trail Association and the Navajo tribe of the jurisdictional complications in upgrading the road to "transcontinental highway" status. If the road were surfaced and widened for public use, the improvements would force the project out of a county road class category. In effect, upgrading the Navajo Highway to superhighway specifications would take the responsibility out of BIA hands. The only recourse, Emmons advised, was to seek funding under "the special provisions for roads on federal reservations contained in the Federal Aid Highway Act."[27]

The type of funding Emmons referred to, as Anderson well knew, was provided for in the Navajo–Hopi Rehabilitation Act of 1950, which established the precedent for highway improvements on the Reservation. Senator Anderson was also aware that since the inception of the bill, Congress was slow to appropriate the funds needed for such critical internal improvements as the roads program. It was true that the federal government provided for projects on federal lands; nevertheless, Anderson considered the Navajo–Hopi Act useless in its present form.

The New Mexico senator was not the only critic of the legislation. Concerned with the economic well-being of his Indian constituency, Congressman Stewart L. Udall, Arizona's newest and extremely popular representative, lobbied to improve upon the 1950 version of the Navajo–Hopi Rehabilitation Act. In April 1958 Udall and Anderson joined forces to co-sponsor an amendment to the Navajo–Hopi Act allocating 20 million federal dollars toward the completion the Navajo Highway.

The Anderson–Udall alliance was just one of several examples in which western politicians combined efforts to win legislation favorable to the region. Over the years a powerful western lobby had emerged on Capitol Hill; Udall and Anderson were among its latest members. In many respects, Congressman Udall personified the western politician. A descendent of Mormon pioneer heritage, Stewart Lee Udall was a native of the Southwest. His father, Levi, was for many years a respected Superior Court judge in Apache County, Arizona. Udall's inherent passion for the West made him one of the leading advocates of conservation legislation in Congress. In the years to come, Udall's reputation would make him the logical choice for an appointment as secretary of the interior by John F. Kennedy.

New Mexico's Clinton Presba Anderson, on the other hand, had come to the Southwest, like many others before him, to recuperate from tuberculosis. Before his election to the United States Senate, the former South Dakota farm boy gained invaluable experience as a newspaper journalist, an insurance agent, a U.S. Representative, and secretary of agriculture in the Truman administration. An ardent conservationist, Anderson's carefully honed political skills eventually won him the chairmanship of two of the Senate's most prestigious committees, Interior and Insular Affairs and the Joint Committee on Atomic Energy. As junior members of Congress, Udall and Anderson relied upon the support of their more influential and senior colleagues to help push their amendment through Congress. Senator Carl Hayden of Arizona, the seemingly ageless and powerful chairman of the Senate Appropriations Committee, was by far their strongest ally. It was no coincidence that Senator Hayden, who hoped to see the completion of the Navajo Highway, pressed his committee to appropriate the necessary funding for the project.[28]

It appeared that the Udall–Anderson bill would provide the stimulus needed to bring the Navajo Trail to fruition. Still, even though Congress had agreed to allocate $20 million for the Reservation project, the House Appropriations Committee was slow in distributing the money to contract engineers. After several delays in construction, Congressman Udall, a Democrat, criticized his Republican colleagues—constituting a majority in the House but not in the Senate—for not meeting their obligation to the Navajo and Hopi tribes. "Eisenhower administration officials have been so preoccupied with the long-run goal of Termination that they have failed to lay emphasis on the only step-by-step programs that will logically lead to independent status for American Indian Tribes," Udall exclaimed in a speech before the National Congress of American Indians. If the Navajo and Hopi Indians of Arizona were ever going to achieve economic self-determination, Udall urged, internal improvements—such as completion of the Navajo Trail—were a vital first step toward that end.

While Udall's public recrimination may have shamed Republican members of Congress into action, more important to the ultimate success of the Navajo Highway was an administrative change in the White House. In his first days as president, John F. Kennedy nominated Stewart Udall to be secretary of the interior—an act that virtually assured the completion of the slow-moving project. As a result, in January 1962 Kennedy made a personal commitment to the Navajo Highway by setting aside a record $70 million dollars for reservation improvements in his first budget proposal. Nine months later, engineers announced that the last segment of road connecting northern Arizona to southwestern Colorado had been surfaced. Thus, in the fall of 1962, an increasingly strong coalition of western congressmen in cooperation with a sympathetic White House administration, terminated the twenty-five year struggle to build a modern highway across the windswept landscape of the Navajo nation.[29]

Appropriately, Secretary of the Interior Udall gave the dedication speech before hundreds of spectators gathered at the spot where the borders of four southwestern states converge. "The Navajo Indians whose lands occupy three corners of this unique point, and the Mountain Utes, who own the fourth, have remained isolated because of the lack of passable roads," Udall explained. "Too, this lack of roads has been one of the barriers between the four states." Enumerating the economic benefits of the heralded achievement, Udall hailed the Navajo Highway as a symbol of unification between subregion, region, and nation. Cognizant of the contribution that the new road would make to future growth of the Four Corners, Secretary Udall predicted, "We look forward to a generation of all American travelers discovering the unparalleled scenic beauties and colorful history of America's first settlers."

Western newspapers echoed the optimism expressed in Udall's stirring dedication. The *Denver Post* publicized the highway as "a vital east-west connecting link between Mesa Verde and the Grand Canyon." Editorials noted that tourist visitations to the San Juan Basin alone were expected to increase from 700,000 to 5 million people in one year because of the new highway. The *Arizona Republic*, meanwhile, speculated that the Four Corners states would, for the first time, become economically bonded because of the new, all-weather route. Noting the contribution of the Navajo Trail to modernized transportation in the West since World War II, the writer predicted, "The mystic and scenic attractions of the Navajo Indian Reservation will put many vacationers from the Midwest and the East on the reservation highway rather than on the crowded U.S. 66."[30]

In a comprehensive endeavor that spanned four presidential administrations, the federal government successfully united the remotest sections of the country via an interstate system of highways. During the Cold War years, American preoccupation with civil defense provided the impetus for this major undertaking. As nuclear disarmament became the focus of American diplomacy during the Kennedy years, military imperatives gave way to domestic internal improvements as a long-term goal of national planning. In 1963 Secretary of the Interior Stewart Udall cited "conservation of resources" as the key to national and regional growth. The preservation of the nation's resources for future use, he believed, would bring western economic success in the years to come. Secretary Udall's pledge to conservationism promised a new era of prosperity in the Four Corners.[31]

Locally, the citizens of Durango, Farmington, Moab, and Flagstaff awaited the revitalization of the Four Corners economy that was to be based, ironically, upon the preservation rather than the exploitation of the subregion's resources. Municipal leadership viewed the projections of increased western tourism as crucial to the future economy, and improved highways the catalyst that would enable the tourist industry to flourish. By 1965 most of the interstate system was in full operation. Shortly after its completion, the Navajo Highway became nationally recognized as the shortest and most scenic all-weather route between Los Angeles and Kansas City. Route 66 no longer held the distinction as the most-traveled highway to the Pacific Coast. The Navajo Trail linked the Southwest to mainstream America and, in the process, improved interstate communication throughout the Four Corners. While thousands of American tourists journeyed west to revel in the scenic wonders of the Four Corners, a geographic and economic kinship brought the municipal communities of this vast and arid subregion ever closer.

FIVE

The Golden Circle

Beneath a mild, Utah summer sky in July 1961, Secretary of the Interior Stewart L. Udall peered into a campfire that illuminated the faces of the weary campers gathered around it. Udall had personally recruited the entourage of Washington dignitaries, including Senator Frank E. Moss (D-Utah), Congressman David S. King (D-Utah), Secretary of Agriculture Orville L. Freeman, and Assistant Director of the National Park Service George B. Hartzog, Jr. The purpose of the gathering was a hands-on, river raft investigation of the canyon country of southeastern Utah. At the outset, Udall challenged the group to determine if the area warranted nomination as America's newest national park. That evening, camped at Anderson Bottom near the confluence of the Green and the Colorado Rivers, Udall recounted the day's events. "Surely," he exclaimed, "the boundary of this remarkable region is a golden circle, encompassing the greatest concentration of scenic wonders to be found in the country, if not the world."

The golden circle to which the secretary referred was an imaginary line drawn around the Four Corners linking a chain of national parks and monuments into a single, comprehensive scenic area. The outer perimeter of the circle, as Udall perceived it, passed through southeastern Utah, southwestern Colorado, northwestern New Mexico, and northeastern Arizona. Enclosed within were a number of units of the national parks system unmatched anywhere in the country in ruggedness and natural beauty.

Within the circle were Zion and Bryce National Parks as well as Arches National Monument, all in the state of Utah. The Colorado segment contained Mesa Verde National Park. Arizona contributed Canyon de

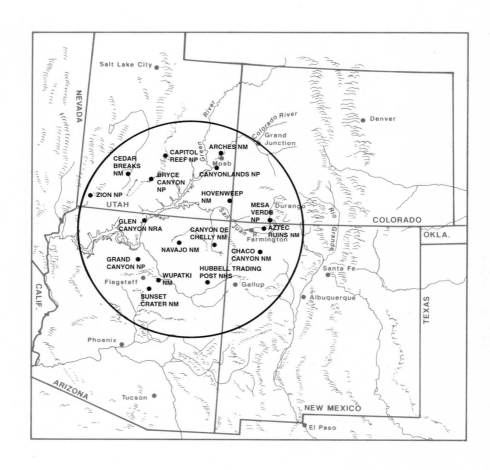

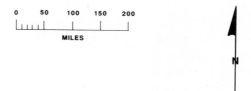

THE "GOLDEN CIRCLE" OF NATIONAL PARKS
(Map by Ernesto Martinez.)

Chelly, Sunset Crater, and Wupatki National Monuments, in addition to the world-renowned Grand Canyon National Park. New Mexico claimed the archeological units of Aztec Ruins and Chaco Canyon National Monuments near Farmington. That summer's night in 1961, Udall announced that the canyonlands of Utah, which he intended to propose as a national park, coupled with the recently established Glen Canyon National Recreational Area in northern Arizona, would make a fitting nucleus for the so-called "Golden Circle." As he envisioned it, a carefully planned network of paved highways would unify all of the parks and monuments in this remote subregion of the West into a wondrous Four Corners vacationland.[1]

The probability that a circle of scenic wonders concentrated in the American Southwest could be linked one to the other via a system of access parkways portended significant social and economic changes in the Four Corners. Prior to World War II, tourism, notable in the Southwest since the turn of the century, had ranked well below mining, agriculture, ranching, timber production, and other extractive industries as an economic determinant. As earlier discussed, the growth of the interior communities depended in large measure upon their colonial link to expanding metropolitan regions of the West. Intraregional exploitation of energy and natural resources became the standard means by which hinterland subregions maintained continuity with regional and national economic trends.

Improvements to the national system of highways after World War II, however, precipitated the expansion of the tourist industry to these once-isolated subregions of the American Southwest. Rising urban congestion, technological advances in travel and transportation, and increased leisure time among America's working class, were factors that contributed markedly to increased tourist visitations to the Four Corners. By the mid-1960s tourism not only replaced energy resource development as the area's leading industry, it also facilitated the reversal of the intraregional colonialism pattern that had characterized the relationship between the hinterlands and the metropolitan West since the end of the war. City dwellers, seeking their escape from the hectic pace of urban and suburban living, became increasingly dependent upon the scenic amenities located in the remote interior subregions.

During the 1950s and 1960s, thousands of pleasure-seekers, many of whom resided in the sprawling, populous cities of California, Texas, Arizona, and other so-called "sunbelt" states converged on the Four Corners in search of the Golden Circle. While not immediately realized, the visions of Secretary Udall, as well as other proponents of western conservationism, came to fruition in the mid-1960s. During this decade, the number of visits to the national parks and monuments of the Four Corners soared to unprecedented levels. In the process, millions of tourists spent an equivalent amount of dollars that trickled down to local economies. No longer were the Four Corners communities restricted to a continuous outward flow of money and resources, a tendency that in the past confirmed their colonial bondage to the whims of the metropolitan West. As the tourist industry fostered an influx of money and human resources, traditional colonialism gave way to a new codependency between the metropolitan capitals and their hinterland counterparts.

The notion that the American Southwest would some day emerge as a popular tourist attraction had surfaced well in advance Stewart Udall's excursion through the scenic canyons of Utah. The Antiquities Act of 1906, which provided for the establishment of federally protected lands, caused westerners to view national parks and monuments not only in terms of their contribution to scenic preservation, but in the context of their economic potential. During the First World War, Washington officials expressed alarm over the estimated $500 million that American tourists reportedly spent each year in Europe. Notably, western congressmen were among the first to promote the scenic amenities of the United States as an alternative to overseas travel. "The American people have never yet capitalized [on] our scenery and climate as we should," remarked Colorado Congressman Edward T. Taylor in 1915, "It [scenery] is one of our most valuable assets, and these great assets should be realized upon to the fullest extent." In effect, Taylor proposed an environmental and cultural nationalism that would, in time, attach monetary as well as aesthetic importance to the nation's scenic attractions.

Those dedicated to the ideals of preservationism embodied in the Antiquities Act found their needs satisfied with the creation of the National Park Service (NPS) in 1916. While the move to create federal preserves and national parks was evident as early as the 1870s, a relatively obscure professor of history from the University of Wisconsin provided impetus to the movement in 1893. In his speech entitled, "The Significance of the Frontier in American History," Frederick Jackson Turner boldly proclaimed that the United States had reached the limits of settlement, and as of that year no longer maintained a discernable frontier.

In response to the idea of an evaporating American wilderness in the wake of urban development, John Muir, Stephen T. Mather, Horace B. Albright, and other conservationists, pressed for federal legislation to protect the few remaining vestiges of our national heritage. The result was the Antiquities Act of 1906, which in effect served as the legal instrument for scenic preservation. Ten years later, Woodrow Wilson affixed his signature to the National Park Service Act, enabling the creation of an agency to establish as well as administer America's parks and monuments for "future generations."[2]

With the creation of the earliest national preserves, the question of natural resource conservation versus the ideals of scenic preservation surfaced as an issue for contention. John Muir, strident preservationist and popular founder of the Sierra Club in California, argued for total restriction of the nation's scenic resources. Conversely, Gifford Pinchot, Theodore Roosevelt's outspoken director of the United States Forest Service, advocated proper and efficient management of natural resources for utilitarian purposes.

Nowhere was the threat of "locking up" the bounty of the public domain more vigorously debated than in the West. Cattlemen, lumbermen, and miners especially demanded assurances that the creation of national parks would not conflict with long standing policies of resource exploitation and free enterprise. According to one historian, the federal government could not possibly have made such concessions. "By its very nature," wrote Alfred Runte, "scenic protection hinged on the exclusion of logging, mining, and grazing." Thus, one overriding criterion for the uncontested establishment of a national park or monument during these early years was to prove that the territory set aside had no other intrinsic value except scenic preservation. This issue remained a barrier to the creation of national parks in the West well into the twentieth century.

One approach that federal preserve advocates employed to gain regional support for their ideas was to demonstrate how increased tourism might generate even greater revenues than resource exploitation. With the establishment of the first national parks in the West, local boosters joined forces with transcontinental railroad promoters to initiate the "See America First" campaign. The Santa Fe Railroad, for example, announced its support of the scenic protection movement not out of altruism, but in hope that the attraction of more tourists to the West would translate to greater profits to the company. Railroad officials hoped to lure wealthy American travelers away from popular European resorts in favor a an adventurous outdoor experience midst the unspoiled grandeur of the American West.

The "See America First" campaign had the personal endorsement of powerful western politicians like Senator Reed Smoot of Utah, the former Mormon banker and mercantilist who introduced the National Park Ser-

vice bill to Congress. A second supporter, Oklahoma Congressman Scott
Farris, summarized the importance of the nationalistic movement in an
address before the first National Parks Conference in 1917. "The best
estimate available is that more than $500,000,000 is expended by our
American people every year abroad vainly hunting for wonders and beauties only half as grand as nature has generously provided for them at
home."[3]

If the success in attracting more tourists to the remote Southwest was
contingent upon the prevalence of federal preserves, the Four Corners
stood to reap early rewards from the "See America First" campaign. Mesa
Verde, established near Durango in 1906, was one of America's earliest
national parks. Since his cowboy days out West, Theodore Roosevelt had
expressed a keen interest in the now famous archeological site. Just months
after his authorization of the Antiquities Act, Roosevelt endorsed Mesa
Verde for national park status. Mesa Verde National Park was unique
among the other early federal parks in that archeological significance
rather than scenic landscape determined its cultural value to the nation.
The congressional act of June 29, 1906 that provided for the establishment
of the park stated: "Regulations shall provide specifically for the preservation from injury or spoliation of the ruins and other works and relics of
prehistoric or primitive man within said park."[4] Federal protection of
archeological ruins such as those found at Mesa Verde added a new and
important dimension to the original concept of national park planning.

Other parks and monuments in the Four Corners were established
along more traditional lines. In 1908 Congress enacted legislation to establish the scenic Grand Canyon of northern Arizona as a national monument; then, in 1919, it became a national park. A stellar attraction for
railway travelers in the nineteenth century, Grand Canyon National Park
enjoyed greater attention with increased automobile travel in the twentieth century. "The automobile represented a new democratization of vacation travel," wrote historian Earl Pomeroy. With the invention of the
automobile, tourism was no longer restricted to the affluent; more people
could now afford cross-country travel. The popularity of the Grand Canyon by the mid-1920s inspired Arizona Congressman Carl Hayden to
introduce a bill to provide money for road and bridge improvements
throughout the park. Attributing the latest surge of tourism in Arizona to
increased automobile use, Hayden declared, "The park is a great economic asset to the county and to the state. . . . Many tourists are potential
settlers and investors, and we want more of them in Arizona."[5]

Utah offered similar natural amenities to early travelers. Although secondary in importance to Zion (1919) and Bryce Canyon (1924) National Parks, Arches National Monument near Moab was an extension of the spectacular rock formations that lured tourists to sparsely populated Mormon communities in other parts of the state. Since the exploits of John Wesley Powell, the one-armed Civil War officer who led a party of scientists down the Colorado River in 1871, Americans had been infatuated with the canyon country between the La Sal and Henry Mountains. In 1929 President Herbert Hoover authorized Arches National Monument, said to contain "more natural stone arches, windows, spires, and pinnacles than any known section of the nation." Compared with the Grand Canyon, however, this latest federal preserve attracted only a limited number of visitors in the early years because of its inaccessibility to vehicular traffic.[6]

Somewhat slower to evolve as a tourist attraction, the archeological ruins located on opposite extremes near the town of Farmington were nonetheless important to the federal government. Chaco Canyon National Monument, established in 1907, ranked with Mesa Verde National Park as one of the oldest federal preserves in the Four Corners area. A veritable showcase of early Pueblo architecture, these ruins, though well preserved, remain to the present day remote and difficult to reach. Located fifty miles in any direction from a natural water source, these ancient Anasazi dwellings held little appeal to visitors other than to scholars interested in their scientific and cultural value.

While more accessible, Aztec Ruins National Monument, located just off U.S. Highway 550 approximately 15 miles north of Farmington, was also slow to pique the curiosity of tourists. On January 24, 1923, just six months before suffering a fatal heart attack, President Warren G. Harding signed the legislation that established Aztec Ruins National Monument. Notable Southwest archeologist Earl Morris, a New Mexico native who had spent his childhood in Farmington before achieving national renown for his work in Central America, spent the next decade excavating and restoring the ruins for public view. Like most other parks and monuments in the Four Corners, Aztec Ruins had minimal visitation during the Depression and the war years. In the postwar period, however, both sites enjoyed modest increases in tourist visits.[7]

While the presence of these parks and monuments in the Four Corners region aroused the interest of early travelers, difficulty in reaching them—either by train or automobile—precluded significant visitations until after the Second World War. Grand Canyon National Park was by far the most popular as well as the most accessible scenic attraction in the subregion.

The Santa Fe Railroad wasted no time in building a trunk line from Williams, Arizona, to the canyon's famous south rim. With the arrival of the Santa Fe Railroad, Fred Harvey, famous resort entrepreneur and promoter of the American Southwest, built El Tovar, one in a chain of luxury hotels strategically positioned along the route from Albuquerque to San Diego. Some found the palatial resort "too beguiling," insisting that luxurious accommodations prevented guests from venturing too far out into the canyon beyond well-placed benches along the rim.

The importance of the national park to the economy of northern Arizona inspired the city of Flagstaff to promote itself as the "gateway to the Grand Canyon." By comparison, other national scenic areas in the Four Corners suffered harsh criticism. One early arrival to Mesa Verde National Park, finding the site barren and parched, described it as "one of the very worst portions of the United States." To make matters worse, park administrators blamed hazardous road conditions, especially those ascending precariously from the main entrance, as another inhibition to frequent visitations. After his trip to assume the position as manager of Mesa Verde National Park, Superintendent Jesse Nusbaum cursed the nearly impassable roads from the Colorado state line to the park as "one hour of grief, ruts, chuck holes, and bouncing all over the road."

In 1930 Mesa Verde officials counted a paltry cumulative total of 114,022 visitors for the first quarter-century of operation. These figures were unimpressive when compared with other western parks. Rocky Mountain National Park near Denver, for instance, boasted regular annual visitations in excess of 50,000. Still, Superintendent Nusbuam remained hopeful that the facility would "come into its own as an educational park." Arches, Aztec Ruins, and Chaco Canyon National Monuments were even less approachable than Mesa Verde. "Until 1936," noted one local historian, "Arches National Monument had been seen only by those sturdy outdoor people who could ride horseback or a jolting wagon through its primitive trails."[8]

National parks in the West endured meager visitations during the height of the Depression. Still, the 1930s proved to be a benchmark period for internal improvements throughout the federal preserve system. President Franklin D. Roosevelt and Secretary of the Interior Harold L. Ickes targeted national parks and recreation areas as ideal settings for New Deal work relief programs. The Civilian Conservation Corps (CCC), conceived to link work relief to the conservation of natural resources, was the cornerstone of the New Deal. Between 1933 and 1942, federal relief agencies accounted for nearly 80 percent of all expenditures toward national and state park improvements. The CCC boys reconditioned roads, trails, and camping facilities; they constructed bridges, drainage systems, and reservoirs; and they installed communications networks in many of America's parks. The nearly $500 million in government subsidies expended during these years left the national park system in the best physical condition ever.

While the coming of the Second World War found the national parks in excellent repair, it also found them without visitors. In the first place, wartime demands forced Congress to reduce park appropriations more than 50 percent, resulting in Roosevelt's termination of the CCC program in 1942. More devastating was the government's imposition of gasoline rationing and the use of the national railroads for wartime needs over commercial transport, reducing tourist travel to negligible proportions. Annual tourist visitations to Mesa Verde during the war years, for example, averaged less than 5,000. "Those were very discouraging and very trying times," recalled former National Park Service Director Conrad L. Wirth. "Many of our best people were the first to leave for military service, our organization had been greatly reduced, and not all who had left came back." In the view of the Four Corners communities that had placed their hopes upon the national parks as the key to ensuring economic security in an expanding West, it appeared as though the war had all but shattered their dreams.[9]

Since the decision in 1906 to set aside federally protected land for America's national parks and monuments, western promoters had recognized the economic advantages of the nation's preoccupation with monumentalism and scenic preservation. The "See America First" campaign was perhaps the first comprehensive attempt to capitalize on the scenic amenities of the West in an effort to develop tourism as a viable region-wide industry. Not all westerners, however, welcomed the tourist industry nor the concepts of preservation as the best way to economic enrichment. Cattlemen, miners, and timber producers asserted their right to pursue the exploitation of mineral and natural resources. They vigorously opposed federal infringement upon individual states rights through the reduction of the public domain.

While the presence of federal preserves in the Four Corners promised to augment the local economy, isolation and primitive facilities reduced them to marginal significance. Consequently, tourism had very little effect on the local economy of this area before World War II. Government restrictions upon travel and leisure time imposed during the war delayed the full impact of the tourist industry even longer. As a result, the Four

Corners remained a colonial subregion, continuing to rely principally upon mining, ranching, agriculture, and forest production for its economic livelihood.

The termination of World War II in the fall of 1945 unleashed a mass migration of tourists to the West in unprecedented numbers. Visitations to the nation's parks and recreation areas jumped to an all-time high of more than 21 million people scarcely one year after the surrender of Germany and Japan. As the end of the war triggered an increase in tourism, National Park Service Director Newton B. Drury informed Americans in 1949 that the national park system was ill-prepared to meet their recreational needs. In a public report entitled "The Dilemma of Our Parks," the disgruntled administrator declared that congressional funding for improvements within the national parks and monuments had not grown proportionately with the rise in visitations.

In effect, Drury declared the national parks system in a state of drastic deterioration. The $14 million appropriated for that year could hardly meet the demands placed upon the NPS by the recent deluge of postwar travelers. Drury estimated a more realistic financial needs figure for park rehabilitation at $140 million for physical improvements and $175 million for roads and trails. These estimates were in addition to $181 million required to modernize access highways to carry visitors to and from the facilities. The pleas of the NPS Director found no sympathy among congressional leaders concerned more with designing policy for postwar economic reconversion than developing a national recreation program.

Problems of inadequacy and overcrowding in the national park system continued unabated in the ensuing years. The number of tourist visits reached unwieldy proportions in the mid-1950s, as nearly 55 million people invaded the nation's recreational areas armed to the teeth with cameras and camp gear. In 1953 Bernard DeVoto, prophetic journalist-historian and champion for the conservation of national scenic areas, clamored for the closure of the nation's parks. He argued that inadequate staffing and poor facilities within the parks placed America's scenic treasures in jeopardy. "So much of the priceless heritage which the Service must safeguard for the United States is beginning to go to hell," DeVoto lamented. He singled out parks experiencing particular difficulty. "The ranger force at Mesa Verde National Park is the same as it was in 1932," DeVoto noted, "but seven times as many people visited there in 1952. All facilities are strained to the utmost."

Others felt compelled to reveal the "shocking truth" about the condition of the national parks. Magazine correspondent, Charles Stevenson, charged that Congress had lost sight of the goals of the preservation movement. In effect, Washington had sold out to the pressures of increased tourism at the expense of scenic preservation. Preoccupation with "recreational projects" and "fancy highway programs" perverted the original intent of the parks and monuments system. In Stevenson's opinion, too much of the money allocated for national parks from 1945 to 1955 had been spent on road improvements and not enough on operations, maintenance, and protection programs. "New roads should be built only when there is a need for traffic to reach an essential destination," he argued. "Even then, the realization that every road is an encroachment upon the wilderness must be kept clearly in mind." Assuming a hard-line preservationist stand, Stevenson cautioned that overmodernization of highways would reduce the parks to "the equivalent of drive-in movies."[10]

After a brief interim period in which Arthur B. Demaray was head of the National Park Service, the administrative yoke passed to Conrad L. Wirth in December 1951. Wirth, the son of a professional park planner, grew up in the East and the Midwest enjoying the great outdoors with his parents and two brothers. With his second-hand Studebaker "ragtop" filled to capacity in the summer of 1925, Wirth and two other college graduates toured the great national parks of the West. Early impressions of Yellowstone, Yosemite, Mount Rainier, and Glacier National Parks influenced Wirth to seek a career in Washington as a landscape architect with the National Capital Park and Planning Commission. In 1931 he transferred to the National Park Service and shortly thereafter was assigned to help administer the agency's CCC program. After twenty years of field experience, Conrad Wirth became director of the National Park Service. Cognizant of the public's criticism toward the national park system, Wirth took the helm determined to fix the problem.[11]

The accession of Conrad Wirth to the directorship coincided with a grandiose scheme for park improvements that the agency designated "Mission 66." Mission 66 was a long-term rehabilitation program projected to reach its zenith in 1966, the golden anniversary of the establishment of the Park Service. During the proposed ten-year period, agency officials as well as park supervisors were asked to identify major problems and deficiencies affecting the various national parks and monuments. Once he defined his objectives, Director Wirth appealed to congressional leaders for appropriations needed for the systemwide rehabilitation. The general idea, according to one writer, was to upgrade the national parks so that they could properly accommodate soaring visitations.

In October 1955 the bureau presented the Mission 66 plan to President

Eisenhower, who endorsed the proposal in his message to Congress on January 5, 1956: "During the past year the areas of our national parks have been expanded; visits of our people to the parks have increased much more rapidly than have the facilities to care for them." He added, "The administration will submit recommendations to provide more adequate facilities to keep abreast of the increasing interest of our people in the great outdoors."[12]

When Wirth appeared before the Senate Appropriations Committee on March 6, 1956, he estimated that tourist visitations to the national parks would exceed 80 million people during the next decade. Wirth's appeal to the Senate committee was simple and direct. "The 120 percent increase in visitor use of the areas since World War II has placed an excessive burden on existing buildings, utilities, and other facilities." Wirth estimated that the total cost of the proposed ten-year rehabilitation program would be $786 million. Perhaps fearful that the request may have appeared excessive, the director emphasized that a 25 percent increase in revenues during 1955 alone guaranteed at least some return on the government's investment.

Throughout the presentation, the NPS chief was careful to link interstate highway development policy to the improvements plan for the national parks. First, he applauded Congress for authorizing funds under the Federal Highway Acts of 1954 and 1956 for the improvement of roads leading to and from America's most treasured scenic and historic sites. Bearing in mind earlier criticisms of hard-line preservationists, Wirth stressed that his appeal for increased appropriations was principally for the construction, operation, and maintenance of new facilities needed to accommodate the anticipated arrival of millions of tourists in response to the federal highways program.

The overwhelming support from the president and the Congress for the Mission 66 concept spawned an era of unequalled postwar expansion of the national park system. The federal government responded generously, providing appropriations of more than a quarter of a billion dollars during the first five years. Coupled with congressional approval of a federal interstate system of highways, Mission 66 contributed immeasurably to making national parks and monuments more attractive and more accessible than ever before. Inasmuch as some of the oldest and most scenic federal preserves were located in the West, California, Texas, Arizona, Colorado, Utah, Wyoming, and New Mexico reaped impressive benefits from the federally sanctioned program.

Among the Four Corners states, Congress granted parks in Utah and

Colorado apportionments amounting to about $18 million each for fiscal 1957. Arizona, meanwhile, received approximately $20 million, while New Mexico was awarded only $10 million.[13] Not since the "See America First" campaign of the 1920s had the West generated such wide-range attention toward its scenic amenities. Surrounded by some of the most spectacular natural beauty in the United States, the communities of the Four Corners stood poised to capitalize upon the postwar invasion of a new and seemingly inexhaustible economic resource—the American tourist.

According to an Outdoor Recreation Resources Review Commission (ORRRC) report entitled "Outdoor Recreation for America," several factors accounted for the dramatic rise in tourist travel to the West in the postwar decades. The survey, undertaken in the late 1950s but not released in its published form until 1962, noted first the steady increase in the general population of the United States. Based on the current national rate of growth, authors of the report forecast a 30 percent population increase to 230 million people by 1976. Of that figure, they estimated 73 percent would be city dwellers. In the commission's opinion, these factors of steady population growth and rapid urbanization significantly influenced the growing demand for outdoor recreation. In summarizing its findings, the commission remarked, "The demand for outdoor recreation including tourism is surging; it is clear that Americans are seeking the outdoors as never before. Not only will there be many more people, they will want to do more, and they will have more money and time to do it with." The commission further predicted: "By the year 2,000 the population should double; the demand for recreation will triple." Rising personal and family income, plus increased leisure time among American working classes, also contributed to postwar tourism activity. The ORRRC report verified that America had become an "affluent society" since the end of the war. Average consumer incomes above $10,000 were expected to increase by a total of 40 percent over current levels by 1976. "With this new affluence, more Americans will be able to afford a variety of activities," the report stated. Reduced work weeks, paid vacations, and comfortable retirement plans—more common among laborers by the late-1950s—enabled Americans greater enjoyment of leisure time. As hours on the job diminished, American participation in sightseeing, camping, picnicking, fishing, hunting, and other recreational activities correspondingly increased.

Equally important to postwar tourist travel in the West were highway improvements and technological advances in transportation. As already discussed, the federal government's commitment to the construction of an interstate highway system afforded the American public unprecedented mobility. Interstate turnpikes, like the transcontinental railroads before them, opened the West to tourists. With regard to the interior communities, the completion of the Navajo Trail across northern Arizona in 1962 made the once-unapproachable subregion of the Four Corners accessible to anyone who could drive an automobile. As air travel reduced distances in the West to a matter of a few hours flight time, technological amenities such as air conditioning, mobile homes, camper bodies, and recreational vehicles made highway travel enjoyable. The development of roadside motels, auto courts, and public campgrounds, offered motorists a comfortable respite from long-distance travel. National Park Service statistics indicate that 85–90 percent of the visitors to the recreational facilities of Arizona, Utah, Colorado, and New Mexico from 1955 to 1962 arrived in a car or a truck. Meanwhile, the luxury tour bus replaced railroad travel for those unable or unwilling to withstand sustained drives across the arid landscape. In short, Americans became more urbanized, more mobile, and more affluent. Thousands converged upon the Four Corners in anticipation of experiencing the mysterious wonders of this alien but scenic land.[14]

Northern Arizona assumed an early lead in the race to lure its share of pleasure-seekers. Figures released from Grand Canyon National Park in 1954 revealed that travelers who visited there spent more than $20 million dollars annually. In December 1956 visitations to the Grand Canyon exceeded the 1,000,000 mark for the first time since its establishment as a national park. Chamber of Commerce officials anticipated that the expansion of the federal highways program as well as the NPS commitment to Mission 66 objectives promised greater recreational dollars in the near future. Indeed, Flagstaff newspapers predicted 1956 as a record tourist year for northern Arizona. Municipal leaders anticipated more than 400,000 tourists would traverse Route 66 en route to nearby parks and monuments. Chamber of Commerce Manager Hal Jackson cited the completion of the Black Canyon Highway from Phoenix to Flagstaff (present I-17) as a second factor for the increase.

That Flagstaff—and the other Four Corners communities—counted heavily upon tourists from neighboring metropolitan areas to augment their economies is evidenced in early tourism reports. An economic study released in 1966 revealed that 66.0 to 78.5 percent of the visitors to northern Arizona from 1954 to 1962 lived in the West. With California at the forefront, Texas, New Mexico, and Colorado provided most of the out-of-state tourist trade to Arizona. These figures were an early indication that westerners, mostly urbanites living in metropolitan localities like

Los Angeles, San Francisco, Denver, Dallas–Fort Worth, Houston, El Paso, and Albuquerque, looked to interior subregions as a means of recreational escape. This tendency for western city dwellers to become more dependent upon the scenic amenities of the interior West reversed somewhat the colonial economic tradition prevalent in earlier decades. At the very least, tourism helped to establish a codependency in which residents of western suburban communities contributed millions of dollars annually to the Four Corners economy in an effort to escape the pressures of city life and "get away from it all."

Northern Arizona did not limit its appeal to tourists simply through the promotion of its national parks. As outdoor activities increased in popularity, Arizona communities advertised year-round recreational enjoyment. In 1956 Flagstaff launched an ambitious campaign to attract tourists to the Arizona Snow Bowl, a small ski development established for local use before the war but expanded to attract out-of-state enthusiasts in the later years. Considered an activity restricted to the wealthy leisure class, skiing developed slowly as a tourist attraction in North America. Most of the major ski resorts were located in Europe, while a few operated in the New England region of the United States. Only a handful of ski recreation facilities existed in the West before 1960. For this reason, Flagstaff city officials expressed considerable pride in their unique but semideveloped facility.

In the winter of 1956 the Flagstaff Olympics Committee addressed a letter to U.S. Olympic Association Chairman Avery Brundage. The letter was an appeal to the chairman to consider the Arizona Snow Bowl as the site for the 1960 Winter Olympic Games in lieu of Cortina, Italy, which reportedly had suffered from unusually poor snow conditions. The Flagstaff committee assured Brundage that a municipal airport "capable of accommodating the largest planes," and two cross-country bus lines could provide adequate transportation for those interested in viewing the events. The letter committed the entirety of Flagstaff's "35 motels and a dozen or so hotels" to house both athletes and spectators. At the top of Spruce Cabin Run, "served by the world's longest rope tow," committee members boasted, "one may look into the depths of the world-famed Grand Canyon." While it is not known whether Brundage seriously entertained Flagstaff's offer, history records that the 1960 Winter Olympics were held in Grenoble, France, not in northern Arizona.[15]

The Navajo Reservation was another unique curiosity for visitors to the Four Corners states. While the severity of the desert instilled anxiety among its travelers, it also wielded an alluring appeal. Motorists from New

York or Chicago bound for the Pacific Coast via the Southwest found the Navajo Reservation virtually inescapable. Completion of the Navajo Trail made the cross-country trek less demanding because it reduced the distance by approximately 150 miles. Encompassing nearly 25,000 square miles of federally protected lands, Navajo country included portions of northern Arizona, northwestern New Mexico, and southeastern Utah. To most motorists, Navajo land appeared austere on the one hand while mystical on the other. Since the 1930s, Hollywood westerns had captured the compelling beauty of Monument Valley and other familiar landmarks on film. To those bold enough to attempt the crossing, the Navajo Reservation represented one of the few remaining vestiges of the wild and rugged West.

Washington legislators, cognizant of the increasing popularity of the Navajo and Hopi Reservations, seized the opportunity to promote their rugged appeal. The BIA, for instance, capitalized on the Navajo–Hopi Rehabilitation Act of 1950 to channel millions of federal dollars into the Four Corners. These funds enabled Navajos to develop a lucrative tourist trade centered essentially upon the creation of national parks and monuments. By 1965 Congress had authorized no fewer than six archeological and historical monuments in northern Arizona. Thus, in an attempt to develop their scenic amenities for the purpose of promoting western tourism, Navajo and Hopi Indians, with financial aid from the federal government, converted a once intimidating desert wasteland into a vacation wonderland.[16]

Southwest Coloradans, meanwhile, were equally enthusiastic about perpetuating the myth of the Old West. Shortly after World War II, local civic leaders clearly perceived that the image of the western frontier was a salable commodity. According to historian Duane Smith, "Durango attempted to live off a legend, a legend that never actually existed." Smith continued, "The gunfights, the glamorous red-light district, the heroic cowboys, and the days of simple rights and wrongs lived only in imagination, a glory that never was." Still, the popularity of the western motif provided a wonderful setting for Hollywood films and popular comic strips. The very name *The Durango Kid* conjured up images of adventure, the true spirit of the American West. By the end of the war, thousands of would-be cowboys, constrained by the concrete boundaries of the nation's outstretched cities, scrambled to the Four Corners in hopes of recapturing one fleeting glimpse of a vanishing frontier. Dude ranches were the San Juan Basin's earliest contribution to the "rugged" West legacy. While the heyday of the industry was actually the 1920s, dude ranching enjoyed a brief renaissance across the region in the early 1950s. Indeed, the *Durango Herald News* listed dude ranching in 1953 as one of the fastest growing industries in the San Juan Basin. There were no fewer than seventeen facilities accommodating 500 guests. "There is a guest ranch to suit every taste," the paper boasted. Outdoor enthusiasts from all over the nation traveled via plane, bus, or private automobile to relax in the mountainous trappings of southwest Colorado. Frontier Airline, Durango's main commercial carrier, proudly portrayed itself as the "Dude Ranch Airline."

To the urbanite, the dude ranch offered an escape—though admittedly artificial—from the frenzied, day-to-day routine of city life. "Often the guests outnumbered the cattle and the cowboys," observed one writer about the atmosphere dude ranch owners hoped to recreate. In later decades, as the need to perpetuate the image of the rugged West gave way to rising demands for state-of-the-art recreational facilities in a pristine setting, the addition of golf courses, tennis courts, and swimming pools transformed dude ranches into the luxury resorts of the 1960s. A new genre of businessmen from Denver, Dallas, Tucson, and Scottsdale replaced local ranch hands as managers of fully modernized facilities. In the process, the new owners maintained the facade of western authenticity while offering a variety of recreational services to their guests.[17]

More enduring than the dude ranch to the Durango tourist economy was William Jackson Palmer's 1880-vintage narrow gauge railroad. Although a true symbol of the western frontier, the Denver & Rio Grande Western (D&RGW) line, which serviced Farmington, New Mexico, as well as Alamosa and Silverton, Colorado, struggled to survive in the early 1950s. D&RGW officials determined that the train had become a financial liability to the company and announced plans to suspend all passenger and freight service beginning in the new year. While some local residents merely protested the impending suspension, others discussed alternative uses for the antiquated line. Advertise the train in all major cities of the nation as "the most scenic route in America," local businessmen proposed. Steam railroad buffs in Chicago, St. Louis, Los Angeles, San Francisco, Salt Lake City, Memphis, Oklahoma City, and other traditional rail centers would no doubt pay for the privilege of riding the last fully operational narrow gauge train in existence.

After a decade of court litigation, coupled with trial-and-error experimentation, the Interstate Commerce Commission (ICC) ruled that the D&RGW could operate the narrow gauge railroad strictly as a tourist attraction. What began in 1950 as a local curiosity in which a total of 4,500 passengers booked passage to the mining town of Silverton, had evolved

into a formidable tourist enterprise by the mid-1960s. In 1963 the
D&RGW added a second train to accommodate the overwhelming national response to the Four Corners attraction. Six hundred passengers
daily reveled in their "trip into yesterday," bringing the total number of
tourists serviced between 1960 and 1965 to nearly 300,000. These figures
were especially impressive in view of the fact that the train operated only
during the summer months.

The long established reputation of Mesa Verde National Park as a
center of Southwest Indian culture combined with the popularity of the
narrow gauge train to make tourism Durango's leading industry by 1965.
If D&RGW passenger figures delighted the local Chamber of Commerce,
the number of tourist visitations to Mesa Verde's famous prehistoric ruins
rendered them euphoric. In 1956, on the eve of the park's golden anniversary, Mesa Verde admitted its one millionth visitor. A decade later,
tourists, hoping to view the well-preserved Anasazi site, arrived by the
hundreds of thousands each year.

National Park Service records for 1966 indicated that slightly less than
four million people passed through the park entrance during Mesa Verde's
first sixty years of operation. Superintendent reports for this period credited a nationwide infatuation with the Southwest—not the Mission 66
program—for the phenomenal interest. Superintendent Chester Thomas
complained that internal improvements "were slow to develop at Mesa
Verde although they were noticeable elsewhere." Conversely, the NPS
official cited the completion of the Navajo Trail, which local reporters
referred to as the Park to Park (Grand Canyon to Mesa Verde) Highway,
a far greater contribution to widespread tourism increases in southwest
Colorado.

The most direct, snow-free route from southern California and Arizona,
the highway attracted a growing number of travelers from those states to
the Four Corners. Statistics for the years just prior to the completion of
the Reservation highway confirm Mesa Verde's popularity among westerners. Figures indicate that the West furnished more than 60 percent of
the out-of-state visitors to Mesa Verde; California led the way, followed by
Texas, Arizona, New Mexico, and Utah. After the completion of the
all-weather route from Kansas City to Los Angeles in 1962, NPS records
show the Great Plains region and the Midwest just behind the western
states in tourist visitations to Mesa Verde.[18]

In early 1960 Durango's enthusiasm over expanding tourism in the
Southwest inspired a movement among business and municipal leaders to
commit the town to year-round recreation. Development of a regional ski

industry was judged the immediate solution. While the sport was more than a novelty to many residents, local facilities were generally small and marginally developed. Durango skiers benefitted from municipal facilities like Calico Hill (present Chapman Hill), though it was serviced only by a rope tow. "They had lights up there, and we'd have chili suppers," one resident recalled fondly. Others weathered blinding storms and icy roads to take advantage of more sophisticated—yet still restrictive—poma-lift operations at either Colbank Hill in the San Juan Mountains north of Durango, or Hesperus Hill near the La Plata Range to the west.

For the most part, Durango's winter sports advocates appreciated skiing more as a local recreational activity. Still, a handful of bankers, merchants, restaurant, and motel owners recognized the potential for the ski industry to provide the stimulus for a healthy, year-round economy. Up to this time, Durango's vacation appeal was largely limited to the summer season. "We made all of our income in three and a half months," remarked banker, Nick Turner, "Most of the motel and restaurant people went south for the winter." With the exception of a few weeks of big game hunting in October and November, the community seemed hard-pressed to develop a suitable attraction to fill the economic void endured during blustery, prolonged winters. Duane Smith notes that the absence of a year-round tourist economy "made Durango a federally designated depressed area with many unskilled and semiskilled workers unemployed half of the year."

Thus Durango's desire to promote the ski industry as a winter recreational attraction grew as much out of economic necessity as it did out of local appreciation for an increasingly popular winter sport. One of the earliest proposals for a the development of a modern ski area near Durango was the so-called Sultan Mountain Winter Sports Area. The plan called for construction of a ski complex that was to be located in San Juan County between Durango and Silverton about 51 miles north of town. Despite local support for the proposed development, U.S. Forest Service limitations on multiple use of the national forests at this time precluded the Sultan Mountain project from materializing.

Understandably discouraged at their failure to win approval for a ski facility in southwest Colorado, Durangoans perhaps took heart in the ambitious predictions of John Love, the state's newly elected Republican governor. "We must recognize that the best utilization of a resource is not necessarily the same in this generation as it was in the past," explained the new chief executive in his initial address before the Colorado State Assembly. Alluding to the future economic direction of the state, the governor continued, "I propose to encourage the most intensive development in those areas that meet the modern demands of the people." Doubtless the governor of one of the most mountainous states in the nation early recognized the potential for initiating an active ski industry promotional campaign, one that would have immediate and long-term impact upon the Four Corners subregion.[19]

The combination of federal preserves, scenic topography, and an incurable nostalgia for the Old West made the Four Corners enormously popular as a tourist attraction in the first two decades after World War II. While Flagstaff used tourism principally to augment a vacillating industrial economy, Durango made an unfaltering commitment to tourism as its principal economic undertaking. The growing popularity of the "little train," Mesa Verde, and a burgeoning ski industry by 1965 coincided with declines in uranium processing and oil production. Durangoans emphatically promoted their community as the "vacation capital of the West." Flagstaff, meanwhile, while appreciative of the economic value of the Grand Canyon and other scenic enhancements in northern Arizona, placed implacable faith in an erratic but nonetheless enduring lumber industry.

Unquestionably, the completion of the Navajo Trail elevated the importance of tourism within the consciousness of municipal leaders in both communities. In the summer of 1962, the year of the road's completion, Durangoans celebrated the First Annual "Navajo Trail" Fiesta. A marching band from Huntington Park, California, the all-Navajo contingent from Window Rock, Arizona, and Durango's very own nationally recognized "Goldenaires" high-stepped in militarylike unison to a lively cadence to mark the momentous occasion. On that sweltering July afternoon, the faces of jubilant onlookers could not contain their excitement over the impending economic renaissance that the asphalt highway promised the Four Corners.

In contrast to Flagstaff and Durango, Farmington officials remained skeptical that tourism could ever overshadow energy resource development. After all, it was widely accepted that oil and gas, not spectacular desert scenery, accounted for the city's meteoric growth since 1945. In many respects, Farmington's attitude toward tourism mirrored the general feeling of New Mexico's leadership at that time. In an address to his constituents in the fall of 1959, New Mexico Governor John Burroughs emphasized his state's continued reliance upon energy resource development as imperative to future economic growth. "It is almost impossible to imagine the effect on New Mexico if the petroleum industry should suddenly cease to exist," Burroughs declared, "If that ever happens, that's the time when I don't want to be governor."

Burroughs's dramatic proclamation, while it underscored the importance of the energy resource industry to New Mexico, ran counter to the emerging views of other executives of the Four Corners states. In a Western Governor's Report published in late 1958 entitled "The State of the West," Governor Ernest W. MacFarland of Arizona and Governor Steven McNichols of Colorado, though proud of their state's industrial achievements, singled out scenic beauty and the enormous appeal of the American Southwest to the nation's vacationers as the keys to regional economic stability in the coming years.

Despite Governor Burroughs's unfailing commitment to the resource industry, to suggest that neither he nor the state showed interest in tourism would be a gross overstatement. On the contrary, it was Burroughs who created the Department of Economic Development in April 1959 to investigate the long-term potential for tourism in New Mexico. "Every tourist we persuade to stay a day longer is a step in the right direction," the governor asserted.

Nevertheless, a statewide economic survey published in early 1960 showed New Mexico, in particular the counties in the northwestern portion of the state, still heavily dependent upon oil and gas as the mainstay of their economy. Although the report noted that most residents believed their state capable of attracting more visitors, officials admitted that New Mexico "lagged behind" Colorado and Arizona in competition for tourists. As for Farmington's potential as a major tourist attraction, a more obvious deterrent was the fact that it harbored neither rugged snow-capped mountains nor breathtaking canyons to lure vacationers away from neighboring states.[20]

By the mid-1960s a series of events occurred in New Mexico to enable tourism to assert a stronger influence in the Farmington area than in previous years. First, in 1962 the gubernatorial election placed Jack M. Campbell, a business-minded, tourism-oriented Democrat, in Santa Fe. From the moment he became governor, Campbell committed himself to tourism, as evidenced in his inaugural address before the State Assembly. Distinguishing northern New Mexico as "one of the most scenic but largest contiguous areas of economic underdevelopment in any part of the country," Campbell pledged to improve the recreational as well as the industrial resources of the region. "It must be obvious," the governor asserted, "that perhaps New Mexico's greatest long-range economic potential is its tourist industry." Criticizing the absence of adequate transportation routes into the remote northern counties as the main cause for the state's unimpressive tourist record, Campbell also blamed state agencies for failing to initiate a more assertive publicity campaign. Compared with neighboring states, Campbell lamented, New Mexico was too slow in promoting skiing, hunting, fishing, and boating as popular outdoor attractions within the state.[21]

Ending his speech on a positive note, Campbell expressed confidence that Navajo Dam, completed in 1962 to retain New Mexico's share of water from the Upper Colorado River Storage Project, added a tourism dimension to San Juan County. "The new Navajo Lake is expected to develop into one of the major water and land recreational sites in the Southwest," he boasted. Early visits to the man-made reservoir bore out the governor's predictions. In its first year, Navajo Lake attracted 135,000 visitors to fish, sail, and water ski, most of whom approached the facility through Farmington. Although Navajo Reservoir greatly enhanced Farmington's image as a tourist attraction, most residents understated its value in the shadow of more time-tested traditions like the petroleum industry.[22]

Unlike northwestern New Mexico, southeastern Utah was blessed—or cursed, depending upon one's point of view—with abundant scenic amenities. Kennedy cabinet officials, especially Stewart Udall, who grew up in one of the neighboring Mormon townships of northern Arizona, championed the canyon country of Utah as a site for a new national park. It was in early summer of 1961 that Udall invited his Washington colleagues to join him on the rafting tour of the Green and Colorado Rivers. In Udall's opinion, the completion of Glen Canyon Dam and Lake Powell, Utah and Arizona's contribution to the Upper Colorado Storage Project, was certain to stimulate renewed tourist interest in this once-inaccessible backcountry of the Four Corners. The presence of the giant reclamation project on the Utah–Arizona border, coupled with the sheer magnificence of its canyonlands, made southeastern Utah a splendid choice for the proposed federal park.

While Democrats Frank E. Moss and David S. King responded enthusiastically to Udall's invitation and his proposal for a canyonlands unit, Republican legislators flatly opposed the idea. Senator Wallace F. Bennett was one of the most virulent detractors of the plan. In declining Udall's invitation to participate in the inspection tour, Bennett made his position clear, declaring, "I do not share your belief that it would be in the best interests of my state of Utah to set aside great areas as a national park and forever remove them from the possibility of future development." The senator further criticized the raft trip as a stunt designed to win public approval for the proposed Canyonlands National Park. Time could be better spent, Bennett argued, investigating the possibility of highway improvements leading to and from the uranium-rich mining regions of Moab. "My participation," he explained, "could not help but compromise my position as well as subject me to criticism for using public funds designed to influence potential legislation."[23]

Despite Bennett's acrimonious assault, Udall returned from the 250-mile land and aerial survey of the Colorado and the Green Rivers convinced that the unique landscape of southeastern Utah warranted federal protection. Expressing his personal beliefs to long-time friend and celebrated archeologist, Alfred V. Kidder, Udall vowed that Canyonlands would one day "take its rightful place beside such areas as Yosemite and Olympic National Parks." In conjunction with his desire for a new national park, Udall made public his philosophical construct of the "Golden Circle" in July 1961. Speaking before a curious ensemble of city officials, uranium hunters, and private citizens in Moab, he detailed a plan to consolidate the national parks and monuments of Utah, Arizona, Colorado, and New Mexico. In an attempt to convince listeners of the need to create a 1,000-square-mile recreational zone, Udall predicted the "Golden Circle" would make the Four Corners subregion unsurpassed as a tourist destination. Glen Canyon National Recreational Area and the proposed Canyonlands National Park would form a natural bullseye for the circle, he explained. The secretary concluded by asking his audience to consider the creation of a national park in southeast Utah an "investment in the future."

The proposal to establish a national park in Utah rekindled animosities among western politicians reminiscent of Washington's earliest attempts to establish federal preserves in the West. For one thing, the Canyonlands issue divided Utah's congressional leadership along partisan lines. Senator Bennett allied with Republican Governor George D. Clyde in opposition to Senator Moss and Congressman King. In a scathing critique of Bennett's unyielding position, Moss accused his opponent of placing partisan favoritism above the best interests of the state. "For the first time in many years we have a Secretary of Interior with the interest, drive and gumption to do something to develop and utilize Utah's matchless scenic beauties," Moss declared, "But he happens to be a Democrat, so you automatically oppose his suggestion for a park. Come, Wallace, do you want National Parks in Utah—or don't you?"[24]

Both Moss and Bennett were aware that problems arising from the Canyonlands proposal transcended simple partisan rivalry. At the heart of the matter was the recurring issue of multiple use versus total preservation.

Secretary Udall favored setting aside approximately one million acres of state property as a scenic preserve, federally protected against mining, grazing, and other commercial activity. In addition to its aesthetic value, park supporters argued that a tourist attraction of such magnitude would more than compensate Utah's economy for any losses in industrial utilization of the land. "Tourists are flocking to the West from everywhere giving Utah and other western states a new, big business," remarked one newspaper reporter. Perhaps hopeful that Canyonlands and other similar attractions would ensure that the trend continued, the author wrote, "Signs show the future tourist crops will be larger than ever." Meanwhile, local supporters noted that the combination of improved national and state highways, federally funded programs such as Mission 66, and Udall's plans to enhance tourism in the Four Corners on a grand scale, forecasted economic revitalization for Moab.

Governor Clyde, a conservative Republican and former economics professor who helped guide his state to industrial prominence, was the principal spokesperson for the multiple-use advocates. Careful to assure his constituency that he was neither against national parks in Utah nor adverse to the concepts of scenic preservation, the governor outlined his position on Canyonlands. First, he objected to the estimated size of the proposed federal preserve. "I am not against parks. We should have them, but it is a matter of degree. It is economically unsound and morally wrong to spread them all over the map." Clyde expounded, "No one, not even Secretary Udall, knows all that would be encompassed in 1,000,000 acres!"

More objectionable than the size of the proposed park was the federal government's commitment to limit the enclosure to single use. In the governor's view, such restrictions would kill San Juan County's livestock business while placing serious limitations on its mining industry. "We have in this area a great scenic wonderland, but we also have a great industrial potential," Clyde declared. "What I object to is locking up these areas before they have been surveyed, before they have been economically explored." In a compromise offer, Governor Clyde agreed to establish the park, but with a reduction in size from the original 1 million to slightly more than 250,000 acres—50,000 to be placed under federal jurisdiction and the remainder under state protection.[25]

It was painfully obvious to Udall that also at issue was the right of the federal government to impose its will over the individual states. The governor's position on Canyonlands challenged the federal government's power to restrict the use of the public domain. In his original proposal, Udall included a section of the canyon known as Dead Horse Point, located five miles southwest of Moab. A few years before, the state of Utah had set aside the public lands surrounding Dead Horse Point as a state park; now it appeared Udall wanted the land included in the federal preserve.

Even Frank Moss, Udall's staunchest ally and cosponsor of the Canyonlands bill in Congress, cautioned the secretary against asserting too much federal authority in Utah. In a confidential letter to Udall, the senator warned that the inclusion of the state facility in the Canyonlands package would be totally unacceptable. "Had the federal government taken action to create a park in this area before the state, I would have supported it heartily," Moss advised. "But now that the state has created the park, it cannot afford to relinquish to the federal government." Utah's position was clear; Udall realized that compromise was inevitable. He agreed to reduce the size of Canyonlands from 1 million acres, but the question remained: How much could he compromise before jeopardizing the scenic integrity of the park itself?

Secretary Udall ordered the size of the proposed national park reduced to 300,000 acres. Further, he requested that the Bureau of Land Management (BLM) and Humble Oil Company conduct surveys of the lands to be set aside in an effort to determine their commercial value. The BLM report stated that those areas with the greatest scenic interest had little commercial value since the terrain was considered too rugged and too remote for proper industrial development. The surveyed portion, however, did have value from the standpoint of grazing and wildlife use. The BLM advised that limited use in these areas be allowed within the park boundaries. While there appeared to have been mining activity in previous years, most claims were now abandoned. "The significance of the area for minerals is still somewhat speculative," the report concluded.

The Humble report supported the BLM findings. Although oil discoveries in the Aneth field south of the proposed park had proven profitable, the oil industry in Utah was, on the whole, slow to evolve. The company's seismographic surveys indicated that the bulk of unrecovered reserves lay outside the proposed boundaries. Based on these findings, Udall made a counterproposal to Governor Clyde, stressing that the majority of the 300,000 acres required for park use was essentially "inaccessible to other forms of development."[26]

Hard to convince, Governor Clyde countered that a state-commissioned economic survey revealed the Canyonlands area to be heavily mineralized. In response to Udall's compromise, Clyde insisted that 300,000 acres was too large an apportionment. The governor admitted the area was

presently underdeveloped, but with an adequate road system the probability of mineral and petroleum recovery increased dramatically. Clyde
reiterated that a 50,000-acre park would more than satisfy the needs of
outdoor lovers. In an emotional appeal to the interior secretary, Governor
Clyde asserted, "I, as Governor, have a special responsibility to the people
of this State and both of us have a larger responsibility to the people of our
nation. I feel that we can satisfy both, but not by locking-up 300,000
acres."

Casting support for Udall, Senator Moss, Congressman King, and Congressman Blaine Peterson (D-Utah) cosponsored legislation in February
1962 to establish Canyonlands National Park. Udall defended the bill in a
letter informing Governor Clyde that he could not in good conscience
further reduce the size of the facility. "I am confronted with the fact that
the best independent park experts have concluded that the area covered in
the bills of Senator Moss and Representatives King and Peterson includes
only the very minimum area necessary for a true national park," the secretary affirmed. Salt Lake City newspapers, while recognizing the economic value of the proposed park in terms of visitors to Utah, were split
on the issue. The *Deseret News* voiced support for Udall's "Golden Circle"
concept in a bold headline: "Let's Move on Canyonlands." Rival *Salt Lake
Tribune* called for less rigid protective measures to allow for both scenic
preservation and limited resource exploitation.[27]

Secretary Udall's proposal to enlarge the national park system in the
Four Corners also won the approval of the White House. In a special
message to Congress on February 21, 1962, President John F. Kennedy,
concerned with a growing imbalance in the national economy, appealed to
Americans to stay at home rather than travel abroad. The president noted
that service industries such as restaurants, hotels, resorts, and recreational
centers had become an important feature of the total national economy. "I
would urge that Americans enjoy the recreational opportunities which this
country offers," Kennedy said. For this reason, the president cast his
support in favor of the interior department's ambitious program to create
more national parks for an increasingly active population. Kennedy's endorsement underscored his administration's pledge to increase federal
sponsorship of recreational programs in the United States.

President Kennedy's commitment to outdoor recreation mirrored a
growing appreciation among Americans for the country's national parks
and monuments that came with the end of World War II. During the
Truman years, national parks legislation reached a nadir, in part because
recreational pursuits listed well below industrial needs in his postwar re-

conversion program. Eisenhower, on the other hand, endorsed the Mission 66 program for improvements within the existing parks system, but placed only 19,000 acres of land under federal protection during his two terms. Kennedy's plan to launch a "See the United States" campaign signified a commitment on the national, regional, and local level to promote tourism and outdoor recreation as vital to the American economy.[28]

In the end, residents of the Four Corners determined the outcome of the Canyonlands National Park debate. Stressing the uniqueness of his city's scenic environment, Moab's Mayor Norman G. Boyd supported the park before a Senate committee hearing. First, Boyd outlined the economic potential of Canyonlands to southeastern Utah. A good portion of the 16 billion vacation dollars spent in the U.S. in 1960 would affect Utah if the park were established. "In 25 of the 50 states, recreation travel is regarded as one of the three most important sources of income," Boyd noted. "Utah stands 11th largest in the United States."

Next, Boyd objected to Governor Clyde and Senator Bennetts's position that Canyonlands would become a national refuge without regard to the feelings of those who lived nearby. In support of President Kennedy's commitment to develop tourism as a national industry, the mayor concluded his testimony saying: "I believe it to be the obligation of the people of southeastern Utah to willingly preserve this national sanctuary for the benefit of the Nation." By that evening, Mayor Boyd had received affirmations from the neighboring communities of Monticello, Blanding, and Bluff, all of whose economies had collapsed with the decline of the uranium industry. Notably, representatives from adjoining Four Corners states testified that a national park in Utah would enhance their local economies as well.

That national parks and monuments contributed markedly to the Four Corners economy was well documented. A University of Utah report published in 1962 estimated federal preserves already established within the so-called "Golden Circle" had attracted 2.8 million visitors the year before, with estimated expenditures of $28.6 million dollars. More than 70 percent of the vacationers were from cities located in the West. The anticipated completion of Interstate 70—the shortest route between Denver and Los Angeles—in 1965 promised a growing number of tourists from outside the region as well. Bureau of Business Research economists projected 10,000 visitors to Canyonlands in the first year. Coupled with Arches National Monument, the outdoor attractions could conceivably bring more than a half million people to Moab during the following decade.

Economist Elroy Nelson, a member of Governor Clyde's investigative committee on the park issue, advised that the university study might lead to "false conclusions and unfortunate generalizations." While tourism no doubt would enhance the economic development of southeastern Utah, it should not be at the expense of mineral exploitation, Nelson insisted. Others less skeptical criticized the governor's attempts to reduce the size of the park. "The inclusion of the Canyonlands within the national park system is a great and big idea," some argued. "The territory should be in keeping with a grand idea." Tired of the political bickering, one exasperated critic suggested President Kennedy declare a national park by executive order.[29]

The debate over Canyonlands park raged on for nearly two more years, during which time Senator Frank Moss guided through passage of the bill that he and fellow House Democrats had introduced in 1962. In his effort to neutralize the opposition, Moss carefully aligned himself with powerful western legislators who viewed national parks as economically beneficial to state economies. Senator Clinton P. Anderson of New Mexico, chairman of the Senate Committee on Interior and Insular Affairs and the most formidable proponent of outdoor recreation and wilderness legislation, counted himself a supporter of both Senator Moss and the Canyonlands Park proposal. With the aid of a powerful western alliance, the bill won congressional approval, and on September 3, 1964, President Lyndon B. Johnson signed the legislation to establish Canyonlands National Park.

From Secretary Udall's point of view, a hard-fought political battle had been won, but not without concessions. The final boundaries of the park enclosed 257,000 acres, one-quarter of the original amount proposed in 1961. In addition, Senator Moss introduced an amendment to his own bill providing for multiple use within the park on a twenty-five-year "phase out" basis. This gesture mollified Governor Clyde and others who opposed the park on the grounds that it would endanger mineral resource development. The twenty-five-year period, Moss explained, allowed time to explore the area for mineral and petroleum reserves. After that time, Canyonlands would be restricted to scenic and recreational use only. While the issue of multiple use versus scenic preservation forced modifications to the original concept, the addition of Canyonlands and Glen Canyon Recreational Area brought Secretary Udall's vision of a "Golden Circle" of national parks and outdoor recreational facilities to fulfillment.[30]

The issues that surfaced in conjunction with the Canyonlands debate were illustrative of the economic concerns affecting not only the Four

Corners but the entire West. The 1950s saw a flurry of unequalled energy resource explorations. As a result, subregional community growth was tied proportionately to national and regional demands for oil, uranium, natural gas, and lumber products. By the next decade, the nation's intensive energy policies showed indications of decline. The AEC commitment to uranium procurement, for example, waned as the agency proclaimed its "stretch-out" phase. The outright termination of the uranium program, moreover, coincided with reductions in petroleum explorations within the private sector. In effect, energy resource exploitation reached its lowest point in the West since the termination of the Second World War.

In the view of a growing number of western politicians in Washington, as well as a handful of municipal leaders in the hinterland communities, the tourist industry offered not only a promising alternative to energy resource development, but a seemingly undepletable resource for future exploitation. Tourism enabled the Four Corners municipalities to develop an import economy for the first time, one in which American—and later European, Asian, and Latin American—vacationers became exploitable commodities willing to spend millions of dollars in exchange for relaxation, recreation, and outdoor pleasantries. By the mid-1960s the scenic amenities of Utah, Colorado, Arizona, and New Mexico acted like a magnetic force to attract thousands of urbanites seeking refuge from the rigors of city life.

The issues surrounding the creation of national parks in the Four Corners did not abate. Those who embraced the concept of the "Golden Circle" promoted tourism and outdoor recreation as their latest salvation. Multiple use advocates, meanwhile, remained implacable in their commitment to energy resource exploitation, seemingly unwilling to accept the notion that the energy boom in the Four Corners had, for all intents and purposes, played itself out.

An assassin's bullet in November 1963 prevented John Kennedy from implementing a nationwide tourism campaign. His ideas on national outdoor recreation, however, passed to Lyndon B. Johnson, who incorporated them into a comprehensive federal program known as "See America Now." Unlike its predecessor of the 1920s, the new campaign moved beyond national parks and summer outdoor recreation areas as a stimulus to the national economy. Johnson's program also encouraged a broad range of winter recreational activities. As it pertained to the Four Corners, municipalities already committed to a nascent ski industry stood to reap additional economic rewards.

With the "Golden Circle" of national parks and outdoor recreational areas in place, the Four Corners stood ready and eager to commit to tourism as their number one economic undertaking. In contrast to the resource economy of previous years, which had evolved more or less independently within each state, tourism generated a regionwide response. In succeeding years, political leaders in Utah, Arizona, Colorado, and New Mexico championed the Four Corners as a unique subregion poised to assert itself within the larger economic framework of the West. As state leaders worked collectively to maximize the appeal of their scenic amenities, the Four Corners—a distinct economic subregion of the West—assumed a more well-defined identity.

SIX

Tourism and the Regional Ethos

The room silenced as D. Howe Moffat, chairman of the Utah Industrial Promotion Commission approached the podium. He commenced his keynote presentation before the Second Annual Rocky Mountain Governors' Conference in Salt Lake City. The audience that morning of September 2, 1966, consisted mostly of state dignitaries from Utah, Arizona, New Mexico, Colorado, as well as representatives from the neighboring Rocky Mountain states. Moffat emphasized the importance of regional planning as it pertained to the economic development of the Four Corners. His message, a follow-up to a proposal initiated the previous year in Denver, championed the Four Corners as a distinct economic subregion rather than a composite of individual states. In doing so, Moffat presented an analytical framework for state and federal legislators to consider in their quest for a regional solution to economic issues within the western hinterlands.

The Utah bureaucrat first defined the economic and political boundaries of the Four Corners Economic Development Region. In all, ninety counties—nine in Arizona, forty in Colorado, twenty-one in New Mexico, and twenty in Utah—comprised the area. "The Four Corners," he noted, "has a land area of 288,460 square miles; while 8 percent of the nation's total landmass, it contains only 1 percent of its population."[1] On a more disturbing note, Moffat revealed to the governors of the four inclusive states that both congressional and executive officials in Washington had determined the Four Corners to be well below the national average in economic development. Recent studies indicated that high unemployment, population decreases, and limited industrial expansion were shared characteristics among the four states. Moffat tendered his solution to the economic dilemma, saying: "The four states must develop a plan that will consider geography, cultural uniqueness, federally owned lands, tourist potential, and greater utilization of scenic and recreational amenities."[2]

Moffat's advocacy in 1966 that southwestern governors adopt a policy of intraregional cooperation as a step toward economic revitalization would probably not have received strong endorsement among conservative leaders in earlier decades. The legislative records of Governors McNichols of Colorado, Clyde of Utah, Mechem of New Mexico, and McFarland of Arizona indicate a stronger commitment to enhancement of state revenues than to improvements in the regional economy. Using "national defense" as their watchword, western governors of the mid-1950s competed to satisfy a growing military-industrial complex with vital mineral resources.[3]

If the governors of the four southwestern states appeared unconcerned with the broader issues of subregional growth in the 1950s, the principal cities of the Four Corners were even less interested. Durango, Farmington, Flagstaff, and Moab scrambled to establish identities as economically self-sufficient cities in competition for subregional preeminence. As earlier noted, intense production of energy resources enabled the four southwestern municipalities to develop independently in the postwar decades. The 1960s brought the boom era to an end, and with it the beginning of a lingering economic recession. Thus, political leaders, especially those representing the hinterland communities of the West, showed growing interest for the idea of cooperative regional planning as the panacea for collective economic ills. This was especially true of the governors of the southwestern states in attendance at the Salt Lake City conference in the fall of 1966.

The chief executives of Colorado, New Mexico, Utah, and Arizona in the mid-1960s contrasted remarkably with their predecessors. All were business professionals who endorsed economic and regional expansion above partisan politics. Colorado's John A. Love, the hand-picked, Republican candidate for governor, had no established political record before winning the election in 1962. While admired for his legal talents, the only executive experience Love claimed was an uneventful term as president of the Colorado Springs Rotary Club. Marine Corps veteran Jack M. Campbell of New Mexico, decorated for service in the Pacific theater during World War II, similarly proved himself a capable businessman with the New Mexico Oil and Gas Association before rising to his state's highest political office on the Democratic ticket.

Calvin Rampton, a moderate Democrat from Bountiful, Utah, and son

of a Mormon salesman, allied with Republican, business-minded supporters to win his gubernatorial post. Before seeking office in 1964, Rampton
had established the Utah Industrial Promotion Council and the Utah
Travel Council. Popular radio talk show host Jack Williams was the personal favorite of Senator Barry Goldwater and other pro-business, right-
wing Republicans for governor of Arizona.[4] Based upon personal
experiences in the private sector, the executive leaders of the Four Corners
states in the mid-1960s naturally equated good government with healthy
economics. Accordingly, they interpreted Moffat's proposal for interstate
cooperation as not only effective politics but also sound business practice.

Besides compatible leadership, the Four Corners states shared other
similarities that encouraged subregional development in the mid-1960s.
First, its physical setting made the Four Corners unique among other
areas of the nation. Most geographers agree that the Rocky Mountains,
the Great Plains, the Colorado River, and the United States–Mexico border loosely delineate the parameters of the American Southwest. Within
this larger definition, however, are extraordinary natural features that dis-
tinguish Durango, Moab, Farmington, and Flagstaff as a distinct physiographic subregion nationally known as the Four Corners. Like other small
cities in the West, those of the Four Corners states share common characteristics: arid climate, geographic isolation, and abundant natural resources. Unlike anywhere else in the nation, however, the municipalities of
the Four Corners proximate a common point where the borders of four
individual states merge into one.

To be sure, the Indian, Hispanic, Mormon, and Anglo presence in the
Southwest influenced historical differences among these neighboring
states during their formative years. Nevertheless, a shared physical boundary provided Arizona, New Mexico, Colorado, and Utah with some measure of political cohesiveness. As previously discussed, the topography of
the Four Corners separated the hinterland cities from one another in
earlier years, causing each to evolve more or less independently. Still, a
shared boundary forced inhabitants of Durango, Moab, Flagstaff, and
Farmington to acknowledge at least some attributes of subregional com-
monality.[5]

Strong cultural affiliations among its inhabitants have also shaped a
Four Corners subregional identity. Referring to the American Southwest,
geographer Raymond Gastil wrote: "Nowhere in the country are so many
distinct cultures persisting side by side." Gastil identified the major sub-
groups living in the southwestern states as follows: (1) Hispanic American,
subdivided into those people of Mexican and Spanish descent; (2) Amer-

ican Indian, composed of both Pueblo and non-Pueblo tribes; and (3) Anglo American, further categorized as Mormon, Texan, Californian, and Midwesterner. Without question, the perseverance of traditional culture coupled with resistance to change, especially among its Native American and Hispanic residents, account for the cultural heterogeneity of the Four Corners. "Because of distance, low population density, and the character of the original peoples," Gastil argued, "the area [Four Corners] has added on new versions of life without destroying the old, and attempts to preserve the old alongside the new seem less strained here than they do elsewhere."[6]

Development of extractive resource economies is a third common trait shared among the Four Corners communities. As we saw in the early postwar years, Durango, Moab, Farmington, and Flagstaff established a classic colonial relationship with the metropolitan West. For more than two decades, Denver, Phoenix, Dallas–Fort Worth, Los Angeles, San Francisco, San Diego, Seattle, and other industrial cities were the chief beneficiaries of Four Corners-produced resources. By the 1960s traditional economic ties to the metropolitan consumers of the West had weakened because of declines in traditional industries such as mining, timber, and agriculture. In response, the hinterland cities shifted emphasis to tourism and service-related industries, the one aspect within their failing economies that promised a reversal of the time-honored colonial pattern.

It was no coincidence, then, that the focus of D. Howe Moffat's Salt Lake City presentation in the fall of 1966 also addressed the enhancement of tourism in the Southwest. According to the Utah spokesman, an underdeveloped tourist industry was one final—and perhaps most important—similarity that all cities in the Four Corners shared. In his speech Moffat stressed the importance of tourism as a major business. "Leisure has become a multi-billion dollar industry in the United States," he exclaimed. "Tourism provides jobs in the construction of roads and facilities to meet the needs of tourists all the way from service stations and garages to motels and camp grounds."

The Utah industrialist proposed to his audience that they make the scenic and recreational amenities found in abundance throughout the Four Corners more accessible to outside users, in particular to those living in the high-density population centers of the West. In effect, the governors of the various states should view leisure and relaxation as marketable commodities to be exchanged for tourist dollars. Increased development of tourism through interstate cooperation, Moffat insisted, would improve the economic stature of the entire subregion. Thus, the central purpose of the Second Annual Rocky Mountain Governors Conference was to challenge its participants to adopt a regional approach to economic recovery in the hinterland West; the tourist industry, according to the resolution endorsed by the participants, became the principal feature of that plan.[7]

As intriguing as his appeal for interstate cooperative planning sounded, D. Howe Moffat's ideas were not original. Nevertheless, Moffat revealed some disturbing statistics on the economic status of the interior West that warranted serious attention from all of the executive leaders present in Salt Lake City. The prototype for regional economic planning in the United States had been proposed more than three decades earlier. In May 1933 at the height of the Great Depression, President Franklin D. Roosevelt had endorsed legislation to create the Tennessee Valley Authority (TVA). Essentially, the TVA was designed to carry out a program of flood control while utilizing to the fullest extent the power of the Tennessee River system as an energy resource. Inasmuch as the flow of the Tennessee River affected seven southern states, political expediency demanded that the Tennessee River valley be considered a single, economically depressed region. In its effort to stimulate a revitalization of the region's economy, the TVA built dams and powerhouses, cleared rivers, replenished soil, replanted forests, and brought the miracle of electricity to residents along the Tennessee River.

The TVA's most enduring contribution to the Four Corners region, however, was in its role as a tool for understanding regional economic development. Columbia economist Rexford G. Tugwell, one of Roosevelt's key advisors in the New Deal recovery plan, revealed years later his belief that the TVA had to "approximate a government and supersede the states" in matters related to regional development. In this capacity, some post-Depression critics rate the TVA a tremendous success. "In its role as a regional planning agency," wrote one scholar, "the TVA undertook and carried out activities that were too great, or too broad in scope, to be accomplished by state or local agencies or by private enterprise." Despite Republican claims that the TVA weakened state and local initiative, the TVA did bring a sense of economic unity to an otherwise fragmented region. As a model for future organizations, "it [TVA] provides a means by which regions can be studied, described, and understood as an integrated whole," noted Gordon R. Clapp in *Regionalism in America*.[8]

In a more comprehensive approach to resource planning, Roosevelt authorized the creation of the National Resources Planning Board (NRPB) on June 20, 1934. The president's establishment of the NRPB, to

provide some measure of protection for the nation's land and water resources, stemmed in part from his childhood love affair with nature. According to historian Gerald D. Nash, Roosevelt, soon after assuming the
presidency, recognized the need for some type of systematic approach to
resources planning. "Unlike most of the leading nations of the world,"
Roosevelt declared in early 1934, "we have so far failed to create a national
policy for the development of our land and water resources." The NRPB,
the organizational embodiment of Roosevelt's desire to protect America's
natural resources, "did much to stimulate local resource planning and
encouraged development of regional plans," Nash wrote. While it did not
attempt to impinge upon the powers of existing government departments—interior, agriculture, or the Corps of Engineers—the NRPB acted
as an advisory bureau to direct national attention to regional planning
needs.

Regarding the NRPB's role in the development and management of
natural resources in the West, the federal agency served to coordinate
efforts between the executive departments and various regional, state, and
local planning boards. One scholar observed that the tremendous ordeal
suffered during the Depression years made most westerners susceptible to
the comprehensive planning efforts imposed on the region during the
New Deal. While Bernard De Voto and other avid conservationists debated who was ultimately responsible for the resource exploitation of the
West, New Dealers "avoided the question and made strenuous efforts,
through planning, to manage the arid environment so that people could
live utilizing nature's treasures without substantially depleting them from
one generation to the next."

Thus, the most notable contributions of the NRPB and the New Deal
to the West were in the area of planned management of the region's land
and water resources. While regional planning won strong support among
state and local New Deal advocates during the Roosevelt years, the movement lost impetus in the early postwar decades. The planning legacy, with
the notable exception of massive reclamation and irrigation projects completed in the 1940s and 1950s, became increasingly ignored by future
administrations.[9]

In the mid-1960s New Deal regional planning concepts resurfaced as a
solution to economic revitalization in the Four Corners. The Public
Works and Economic Development Act of 1965 established the legal
foundation for regional planning in the hinterland West. The legislative
offspring of several attempts to reestablish planned economic growth during the Kennedy–Johnson years, this legislation represented the first of-

ficial recognition of the Four Corners as a distinct geographic and economic entity in the United States. In May 1961 President Kennedy, disturbed by the impoverished conditions that he had observed first-hand on his presidential campaign through Appalachia, signed the Area Redevelopment Act (ARA), authorizing federal expenditures in support of local economic development. The thrust of this program was to stimulate industrial and commercial enterprise through the distribution of low-interest loans. Congress expanded the concept in 1962 with the passage of the Accelerated Public Works Act (APWA), which provided funds to finance the construction of public facilities within economically depressed regions.

In 1965 Congress focused attention on particularly hard hit areas like Appalachia when it created the Appalachian Development Act (ADA). President Lyndon B. Johnson, a staunch New Dealer since his early days in Congress, supported the legislation as a way to reintroduce New Deal approaches to contemporary regional economic issues. The ADA authorized a planning commission designed to initiate as well as direct commercial and industrial activity within a specified area. The Public Works and Economic Development Act was, in effect, the logical extension of the ADA. In early 1965 members of Congress from states outside Appalachia, but with similar economic problems, sought comparable federal benefits. Under Title V of the new law, Congress designated seven more regions— including the Four Corners—as economically disadvantaged and thus eligible for federal assistance.[10]

In effect, D. Howe Moffat's presentation to the Rocky Mountain Governors' Conference in Salt Lake mirrored the thinking of federal officials in Washington. Specifically, Moffat echoed the position of congressional spokesmen from the sparsely populated western states who believed that the consolidation of economic issues into a single, comprehensive plan was the most effective and least expensive way to foster regional growth. In January 1965 Senators Joseph M. Montoya [D–N.M.] and Frank E. Moss [D–Utah], two of the most vocal proponents of regional economic planning, introduced the Public Works and Economic Development bill. Their intent was to provide for the establishment of other regional planning commissions, including one in the Four Corners. While lobbying on behalf of the proposed legislation in Albuquerque, Montoya, chairman of the Senate Committee on Public Works, cited the bill as "the most sensible way to promote interstate cooperation and economic development in the Four Corners."

Equally supportive of the proposal for a Four Corners regional planning agency, the governors of the respective states welcomed the initiative in

Salt Lake City. Host governor Calvin Rampton summarized the commitment of his colleagues, declaring: "We feel there is room for cooperation
among the states and cooperation between the states and the federal government in solving regional problems." Calling for greater decentralization of government in favor of regional self-determination, Rampton
assured his listeners that the Four Corners could better resolve its economic problems on a local level rather than in Washington. Casting their
support for the Utah executive's call for interstate cooperation, the remaining governors voted to meet at some future date to discuss the creation of a Four Corners Regional Planning Commission, as recommended
in the Public Works and Comprehensive Employment Act of 1965. Meanwhile, President Johnson applauded the new legislation, which he signed
into law on December 19, 1966, as a vehicle for a kind of "creative federalism" that he hoped would address issues affecting national economic
development. "Appalachia teaches us many lessons," remarked the president. "Its recent progress tells us that the partnership of federal, state, and
local governments can work in Appalachia as well as in other regions."[11]

A declining traditional economy coupled with a steady increase in unemployment underscored the recession that engulfed the Four Corners in
early 1965. A study published by the Bureau of Business Research at the
University of New Mexico showed unemployment running about 4 percent throughout the four-state region, which conformed to the national
average during the first years of the Johnson administration. Within the
ninety-two counties encompassing the Four Corners, however, the unemployment figure averaged 6.3 percent. The study also showed that the rate
of population growth in the Four Corners had fallen well below the national level.

Economists attributed these statistics to sharp declines in agriculture
and mining—mainstays of the postwar economy. Except for northern
Arizona, manufacturing and transportation were virtually nonexistent,
while retail sales made no appreciable gains. The only detectable signs of
encouragement were in the area of tourism and service-related industries.
These categories, studies indicated, rose nearly 25 percent over 1960 levels, an increase of 5 percent above the national average.

Industrial decline in the Four Corners economy hit Moab the hardest.
A government investigation of San Juan County's economy in 1965 revealed that agricultural employment had dropped from 2,200 ranchers at
the beginning of World War II to a paltry 500 people engaged in the
industry. The U.S. Bureau of Reclamation study showed mining activity,
too, in a state of recession. Southeast Utah's uranium industry, which

produced 1.36 million tons of ore in 1959 during the peak years of the uranium rush, had dwindled to slightly over one-half million tons by 1965.

Anticipated demands for fissionable material for use in nuclear electric generating plants caused only a minor resurgence of the industry. Huge stockpiles of carnotite ore, deposited in government warehouses during the boom years, precluded serious reactivation of mining. As noted earlier, the Atomic Energy Commission's uranium procurement program had entered its "stretch-out" phase by the mid-1960s. As a result, the federal government no longer guaranteed purchases of newly recovered uranium.

Because of these fluctuations, San Juan County enjoyed only moderate growth. From 1950 to 1960, the decade registering the highest influx of people into southeast Utah, population figures had soared from 5,300 to 9,100 inhabitants. Four years later these numbers had slumped to 7,700 after the initial boom subsided. Curiously, the 1967 count rose to 9,000 people, 70 percent of whom lived in the three largest urban communities of Moab, Monticello, and Blanding. These slight increases were attributable in part to government construction of nuclear power generating stations. Many local residents anticipated renewed mining activity. More significant, however, were the Bureau of Reclamation findings linking population increases to scenic and recreational amenities in the Four Corners, attractions that were especially appealing to retired couples living on fixed incomes. According to the survey, the establishment of Canyonlands National Park—in its infancy at the time of the study—greatly enhanced Moab's potential as a tourist and recreation area.[12]

While Farmington projected outward signs of economic progress and municipal growth in 1965, the oil and gas industry in New Mexico showed signs that it too had reached a production plateau. In a personal letter to Frank Ikard, director of the American Petroleum Institute, Governor Jack Campbell expressed concern over the steady out-migration of oil industry personnel from his state. Arguing that New Mexico had always put forth its best effort to create a favorable climate for the oil and gas industry, Campbell lamented, "I suppose that is why the movement of personnel from our state has disturbed me so deeply and why I believe that this may be a serious business error on the part of the companies involved."

Oilmen apparently were not moving far. Campbell noted that some had returned to their point of origin in the Midland–Odessa area of Texas, while others moved to Denver, closer to new petroleum fields under development in Wyoming and Nebraska. In a closing statement to Ikard, Governor Campbell declared: "It is extremely difficult for me and for the members of the legislature to continue to maintain a favorable climate for industry when 90 percent of the oil produced and 75 percent of the gas produced is being exported, and at the same time the limited number of employees that we have are being removed from the state."[13]

The problem in New Mexico was not that petroleum reserves were being rapidly depleted; rather, they simply were not being exploited. Statistics indicate that the peak years for the oil industry in New Mexico were 1962–1965. During that time, production levels increased from 109 million barrels to 119 million barrels. In addition, "Operation Gasbuggy," the AEC and El Paso Natural Gas Company's joint project to expose new gas reserves through nuclear detonation, had been judged an overall success. The experiment to employ innovative fracturing techniques nearly doubled the estimated state reserves of natural gas after the first detonation in December 1967.

In later years, Tom Dugan, a former production manager for Phillips Petroleum, one of the early producers in the San Juan Basin, summarized the oil and gas situation in New Mexico in the mid-1960s. "We had all those reserves," Dugan recalled, "and no way to make a profit on them." According to the veteran oilman, the Federal Power Commission (FPC) maintained such a low price for oil and gas at the well-head during these years that "the cost of drilling exceeded the price companies were receiving for their products." In response, many of the companies that had established operations near Farmington and other oil-producing areas of New Mexico, brought their exploration and drilling activities to a near standstill. Others, as Campbell suggested, left the state entirely to explore untapped reserves elsewhere. "Prices in the gas and oil industry did not significantly change until the Arab oil crisis of 1973," Dugan remarked.[14]

Tom Dugan's reference to the Arab oil embargo in the early 1970s underscored the importance of national and international oil politics and their long-term affects on the New Mexico petroleum industry. In the first place, legislators from oil-producing states had tried unsuccessfully to deregulate the field price of natural gas shortly after the Korean War. In 1956 President Eisenhower had vetoed the Harris–Fulbright bill, in part because he feared that he might be accused of showing political favoritism toward the increasingly powerful oil and gas lobby in Washington. The FPC hold on field price regulation was strengthened during the Kennedy and Johnson years, resulting in drastic declines in the interstate transfer of natural gas in favor of intrastate markets that did not fall under FPC domination. In the meantime, consumption of natural gas more than doubled in the West as the number of new gas wells brought into production declined by more than 25 percent. By 1970 the debate over gas deregulation continued. In the end, the lion's share of New Mexico gas was distributed to intrastate markets. Thus, while New Mexico had actually doubled its gas reserves through technological experiments such as "Operation Gasbuggy," the amount of reserves committed to the interstate pipelines located in the San Juan Basin had decreased.

Other supply-and-demand problems clouded the future of oil production in the Four Corners. Actually, the issue was one of oversupply, as domestic producers increasingly surrendered their markets to exporters of foreign oil from the Middle East, Canada, and Latin America. In July 1969 Senator Joseph Montoya of New Mexico drafted a stern letter to Secretary of Labor George P. Shultz, chairman of President Johnson's task force on oil importation. In his letter, Montoya advised the secretary that he and twenty-eight of his congressional colleagues were sponsoring Senate Bill 2332, legislation designed to promote the "general welfare and national security of the United States" by imposing stringent quotas on importation of foreign oil. "Excessive imports threaten the existence of our domestic petroleum industry," challenged the self-proclaimed spokesman of western oil-producing states. "Simple economics explains the threat to our defense capability posed by excessive imports."

Montoya claimed that a glutted oil market made new exploration of domestic reserves unprofitable. If the trend toward underproduction of domestic petroleum continued, "A time of crisis would find us with inadequate supplies; our survival would then be dependent upon the willingness of foreign sources to provide us with oil." Speaking on behalf of his own constituency, Montoya cited oil and gas activities as vital to New Mexico's economy in the absence of a strong industrial base.[15]

Durango also felt the strain of a sagging petroleum economy, but local officials had already pledged their commitment to tourism as a way to offset depreciating revenues. As already discussed, oil production near Durango was at best marginal. By the summer of 1965 most of the major oil companies—Shell, Conoco, and Phillips—had moved their operational staffs to Denver and Cheyenne, Wyoming. The Pacific Northwest Pipeline Corporation, meanwhile, continued its transshipment of natural gas, but suffered from the same deprivation of reserves affecting neighboring pipeline facilities. Lumber production and coal mining still contributed to Durango's industrial base, but ranching and agriculture suffered a drastic downturn. Only tourism—and its related service industries—demonstrated the potential for reversing a downward trend in the economy.

Thus, by 1965, in the wake of a vanishing traditional industrial base, tourism had emerged as the capstone of the Durango economy. The expenditure of millions of federal dollars for improvements to Mesa Verde National Park contributed profoundly to the expansion of tourism in southwest Colorado. With the completion of the Mission 66 Project, the National Park Service internal improvements program that affected most federally owned parks and outdoor recreational facilities, Mesa Verde enjoyed a national reputation as an archeological attraction. One reason for its increased recognition was the completion of the multimillion dollar Wetherill Mesa Project in 1963. This massive excavation project had uncovered more than 800 new archeological sites and had stabilized three previously unexplored Anasazi cliff dwellings. Park Service officials determined that Wetherill Mesa doubled the number of cultural amenities accessible to the public.

Equally important was the rehabilitation of entrance roads and access highways, the construction of restaurants and general concessions, the expansion of camp facilities, and other improvements that made Mesa Verde National Park a year-round attraction to tourists. In July 1965 park registers indicated that Mesa Verde experienced monthly visitations in excess of 100,000 people for the first time in its history. By 1970 the same records documented average monthly figures of 130,000 visitors and revenues of $8.7 million dollars during the peak summer months. Significantly, planning documents for future expansion acknowledged the importance of Durango, located less than a half-hour's drive from Mesa Verde, as the principal accommodation center for a number of park visitors.[16]

In contrast to the other Four Corners cities, only Flagstaff enjoyed steady growth in the mid-1960s, based upon both a solid industrial foundation as well as a steady stream of tourists. Inasmuch as national forests represented 28 percent of the state's land surface, most of which were located in northern Arizona, lumber remained the principal consumer commodity produced in Flagstaff. One notable difference from earlier years, however, was a greater concentration of the industry among fewer producers. After World War II, more than sixty sawmills were reported in operation in northern Arizona. Two decades later, that number had been reduced to four major wood products corporations. More revealing, perhaps, was the fact that these four firms accounted for 96.3 percent of all lumber produced in the state between 1965 and 1975.

Several factors accounted for the domination of a handful of manufacturers in the lumber industry during these years. First, most of the merchantable timber accessible for logging operations during the postwar years had been harvested by the mid-1960s. As a result, only those companies able to meet the cost of advanced logging methods—cable skidding and helicopters—designed to harvest remote timber areas remained competitive in the industry. Second, intensive forest production during the first two decades after the war had resulted in a generally lower quality of timber available for commercial harvest in later years. Therefore, only the firms that could afford to diversify their operations to include the manufacture of paper and packaging materials, plywood, particle board, and other forest products derived from smaller, low-grade logs, achieved economic success. Finally, most small operators were unable to afford compliance with the federal government's air pollution standards imposed industrywide beginning in 1970. Conversion to federally approved, pollution-free equipment proved too costly for most individual sawmill operators. Eventually, these small sawmills sold out their logging interests to the larger corporations.[17]

Southwest Forest Industries, Flagstaff's only remaining lumber manufacturer, best represented the direction of the Arizona lumber industry in the late 1960s. "Once a small lumber firm with a limited number of products, we have emerged in recent years as a company with an ever increasing range of capabilities," summarized President Gene C. Brewer in the firm's *Annual Report* of 1969. Indeed, since the company's first major expansion ten years earlier, Southwest claimed ownership of three of the state's largest and most modernized sawmills, located at Flagstaff, McNary, and Eagar, Arizona. Combined, these operations produced more than 200 million board feet of timber annually. In 1961 the corporation diversified to include a pulp and paper mill at Snowflake, and a corrugated container plant at Glendale. In addition to its Arizona holdings, Southwest Industries had purchased plywood mills and pole treatment plants throughout New Mexico and Colorado.

One intriguing facet of Southwest's Flagstaff operation was the construction of a particle board plant in late 1969. Southwest's decision to manufacture particle board, the conversion of wood chips and other sawmill waste products into marketable building materials, was in part an effort to comply with federal environmental standards imposed during the Nixon administration. More importantly, particle board manufacturing was the lumber industry's response to a promising new market. Increased construction of mobile homes and recreational vehicles, designed to accommodate the demands of a growing leisure class in the United States, resulted in an important commercial outlet for this relatively new and inexpensive forest product.

Noting the importance of the American commitment to a more vacation-oriented lifestyle, President Brewer declared: "The new affluence, the new leisure time, and the desire for a fuller happier life have led to a new concept in home building." By 1970 Southwest Forest Industries had absorbed all of its former competitors in Flagstaff under the corporate umbrella of a giant, multistate organization. Equally impressive, their combined forest activities accounted for nearly 85 percent of all sawtimber produced within the Flagstaff Timber Unit of the Kaibab and Coconino National Forests.[18]

Despite the impressive accomplishments of Southwest Forest Industries, there were indications in the mid-1960s that the lumber industry would no longer enjoy a dominant position in the Flagstaff economy. Since 1949, the year that the Flagstaff Federal Sustained Yield Timber Unit was established, logging and primary wood manufacturing combined to become the number one industry in Flagstaff in employment and dollar value. The wood products industry accounted for 75 percent of all employment in Flagstaff from the 1940s through the 1950s. Indeed, the city's population, nearly tripled from 9,000 in 1950 to 25,500 in 1970, owed much to the forest products industry.

Still, one Arizona economist noted: "When the unit was reevaluated for the first time in 1970, the wood products industry had dropped to fourth place in economic importance." Southwest Forest Industries' annual reports for 1967 and 1968 bore out these findings. Gene Brewer announced the shocking news that the company's paper products division—not wood products manufacturing—accounted for the majority of all corporate sales for the first time in the firm's history. The announcement confirmed a nationwide slump in the building construction industry, which also had a negative impact on sawmill operations throughout the timber state.[19]

Meanwhile, surveys of the Flagstaff area from 1960 to 1970 showed an increasingly varied local economy, one clearly less dependent upon a single industry for employment. By 1970 Northern Arizona University, along with federal, state, and county offices, had become the largest employers in the city. Notable too was the growth of the service industry, a response to the completion of Interstate 40—formerly Route 66 from Chicago to Los Angeles—and the Black Canyon Highway (I-17) from Phoenix. The proliferation of restaurants, motels, gas stations, and campground facilities during these years furnished a promising job outlet to local residents. Thus, while the remainder of the Four Corners endured a general recession in the mid-1960s, Flagstaff sustained a fairly stable economy. For the moment, the city seemed immune to the economic worries that befell its neighboring municipalities.[20]

Such were the pervading economic conditions in the Four Corners when executive leaders from the four southwestern states gathered to formulate a comprehensive plan for the proposed Four Corners Regional Planning Commission (FCRPC) on September 19, 1967. Orren Beaty, Jr., a New Mexico-born bureaucrat well known in Washington circles, chaired the meeting held in Cortez, Colorado. Scarcely a month earlier, President Johnson had appointed Beaty, whom the president described as the "right arm of Secretary of the Interior Udall," as the first federal cochairman for the newly formed FCRPC. As he called the meeting to order, Beaty opened with a dramatic statement on the objectives of the nation's newest regional commission. "The FCRPC has the largest economic region geographically and the smallest population," he said. "There are vast areas with no railroads and virtually no highways." It was incumbent upon the new commission to rectify long-standing problems such as geographic isolation and economic underdevelopment through conscientious and cooperative planning. The purpose of the FCRPC, in Beaty's view, was to strengthen relations between the federal administration and state governments through greater decentralization. Washington was prepared to give the states a "bigger voice in the formulation and administration of federal-state programs."

Imbued with the spirit of President Johnson's "creative federalism," the governors devised an "Initial Action Plan." The principle aim of the plan, as stated in its preamble, was to create a "doctrine of regionalism." In the text, state executives targeted areas for improvement through interstate cooperative planning. Topics assigned the highest priority in order of importance were transportation, tourism and recreational development, health and education, and the high-tech industry. In a departure from earlier economic planning, the governors in attendance at the FCRPC meeting in 1967 ranked mining and natural resources second to last in the plan. The maximum utilization of the subregion's resources, members determined, should be enhanced, but only through the wider application of new technology such as the use of nuclear power as demonstrated in "Project Gasbuggy."

The plan made its most cogent statements in the area of transportation improvement and the development of a regionwide tourist industry. "National economic growth and development cannot be divorced from regional economic growth and development," began the introductory statement on transportation needs. "A region with chronic economic problems cannot contribute its full potential to the national output and wealth."

With the termination of the uranium procurement program and the departure of the AEC in the mid-1960s, the United States government no longer considered mineral resources in the Four Corners vital to national defense. Consequently, the subregion suffered from a general lack of investment capital available for road and highway construction. The Navajo Trail across northern Arizona best illustrated this point. Although the project began in the late 1950s with the AEC attempt to facilitate uranium processing, the desire to increase tourism on the Navajo Reservation—not the need to ensure national defense—became the driving force for the road's completion a decade later.

Some months after the organizational meeting in Cortez, Colorado, Governor John A. Love, elected state co-chairman for the FCRPC, argued for improved transportation in the Four Corners at the annual meeting of the Rocky Mountain States Federation. In Colorado, the governor argued, railroads served only one out of every thirty-nine miles of land, compared to the national average of one out of every eleven miles. According to Love, "Mountain States have become more dependent upon truck transportation than have other parts of the country because of the character of the region and its economy." The problem of isolation was even more acute in Durango, serviced only by inadequate air transportation and an antiquated narrow gauge railroad. Unless transportation needs in the Four Corners were improved through regional planning, the area might never realize its full potential as a national tourist attraction. Among the commission's first tasks, Love determined, the FCRPC should project a long-range master plan for the period between 1970 and 1985 to identify transportation needs, proposed routes, and cost estimates for improvements within the Four Corners.[21]

If the FCRPC committee members expressed an interest in transportation improvements, they were resolute in their commitment to devise a regional plan to promote tourism. Not surprisingly, state governors saw a direct correlation between adequate transportation and a successful tourist industry. "The tourism industry, now in its infancy in the Four Corners region, represents perhaps one of the commission's greatest challenges for improving the economic stature of the region's inhabitants," read the opening statement of the plan. Still, committee members agreed that full utilization of the region's scenic amenities would be slow to develop because of the absence of good highways. "The scenic wonders in the Golden Circle would be less than a half-day apart if there were adequate access and connecting roads," the report summarized. All agreed that inaccessibility to regional parks and recreational areas precluded the growth of tourism in the Four Corners.

Notably, FCRPC committee members referred to tourism as an "import" industry. By the term "import" the governors meant the exchange of the Four Corners' goods and services—in this case, scenic attractions—for outside income. Besides attracting new income, the tourist and recreation industry, with its ability to lure the customer to the resource, offered excellent potential to reduce unemployment. Inasmuch as the commission cited unemployment and economic underdevelopment as targets for improvement, the governors concluded that a well-conceived plan for tourist development should be given the highest priority. Similarities in topography, natural resources, and economic conditions, furthermore, provided an especially good climate for interstate cooperation. "We can, and should, assist each other in promoting tourism in a spirit which is not entirely self-contained," the governors declared, "The economic benefits to all states, already immense, are potentially beyond reckoning."[22]

Accordingly, the final draft of the FCRPC plan stressed the growth of national parks and recreation areas. It acknowledged the importance of the more than forty national parks, monuments, and forest recreational areas contained within the so-called "Golden Circle." In November 1970 members authorized the commission's first official expenditure of $75,000, awarded to an Albuquerque marketing firm for a feasibility study of tourism development potential along the Navajo Highway.

Further, the FCRPC encouraged the promotion of skiing as essential to the idea of a comprehensive, year-round tourist industry. They recognized that the number of ski areas constructed in the Four Corners area between 1950 and 1965 had jumped 626 percent, while the number of visitors to those areas had also increased. Most of these ski facilities, however, had not realized their full potential because of inadequate air service and the absence of all-weather highways to and from their remote mountain locations. Accepting the challenge put forth in Salt Lake City just one year earlier, the governors of Arizona, Colorado, New Mexico, and Utah seized an opportunity at their first organizational meeting in Cortez to endorse a cooperative interstate approach toward improving the subregional economy.[23]

On the whole, the governors worked together in their efforts to promote interstate cooperation through the FCRPC. But they were not always in accord, especially in deciding the location of commission headquarters. All agreed that the FCRPC offices should reside in one of the southwestern states; however, each governor hoped to host the new planning agency. At the same time, the Four Corners cities competed vigorously for consideration as the new headquarters site.

Northern Arizona University in Flagstaff, for example, placed all of its computer and technical research facilities at the disposal of the FCRPC. Moab and Durango, on the other hand, offered advantages such as "quality of life" and "a pristine environment," amenities while perhaps less practical were nonetheless valued among prospective residents. In the end, the commission selected Farmington as its headquarters site. Justifying the selection, federal cochairman Orren Beaty noted that Farmington was the geographic center of the Four Corners. On a more practical level, Farmington offered the most up-to-date airport in the area plus easy all-weather highway access to Albuquerque, Salt Lake City, Denver, and Phoenix.[24]

For all of its lofty ideals, the nation's newest planning agency enjoyed a brief and rather uninspired history. During the first two years of operation, the agency expended most of its limited budget funding a barrage of feasibility studies. FCRPC officials anticipated the studies would provide important data as well as workable solutions to specific problem areas noted in the Four Corners economy. This much, at least, was accomplished as each study meticulously identified areas needing improvement, then outlined in detail an appropriate "action" plan. In theory, the FCRPC spent its first years defining ways to redress economic deficiencies in agriculture, mining, manufacturing, and the recreation industries. In practice, however, little "action" ever took place.

Critics of the planning commission's failure to achieve more in its first years of operation were vocal and uncompromising. One of the most outspoken was Senator Joseph Montoya of New Mexico. During formal congressional hearings in Albuquerque to evaluate the early progress of the FCRPC, Montoya told the press that the agency failed to formulate and implement a comprehensive regional plan. "As of this moment the commission doesn't have a comprehensive plan that the law requires for expanded funding." Montoya added, "The Four Corners Regional Commission is still far behind the rest of the commissions in technical research and program planning." The disgruntled senator next blamed the various governors of the Four Corners states for their hesitancy in demanding a more strenuous implementation of the projects. "If I were a member of the regional commission, I'd certainly be on top of that staff and see that it was doing its job or I'd see some firing," Montoya declared.

In response to such acrimony, federal cochairman-designate, L. Ralph Mecham, who assumed the position upon Orren Beaty's resignation in April 1969, defended the agency's unimpressive record. Mecham, a lifetime resident of Utah and former vice president for economic and community development at the University of Utah, argued that it was unrealistic to compare the Four Corners Planning Commission with those located in other regions. In the first place, the Four Corners represented the largest of all seven economic development regions with an area approximating 288,000 square miles. Yet, while nearly twice the size of its counterparts, federal appropriations assigned to the FCRPC equalled about 30 percent of the total budget allocated for Appalachia.

In Mecham's view, the cultural makeup of the Four Corners created administrative problems unique to the FCRPC. Finally, more than 60 percent of the total land area in the Four Corners fell under federal ownership; thus the incentive for public and private investors to engage in profit-making enterprises proved negligible. "The region is, in many respects, a colony of the federal government," Mecham argued. "In terms of income, a substantial part arises from federal activities. Add to that dependency a further constraint in the area of manufacturing where earnings from this sector account for only 8 percent of the total personal income." In a feeble attempt to support Mecham's testimony, Governor David Cargo of New Mexico later commented that from the time of President Johnson's authorization of the agency it took the FCRPC nearly a year to become operational.[25] While Senator Montoya emphasized lack of a comprehensive plan as key to the FCRPC's inability to meet its objectives, the failure of the commission to implement its plans was more the issue.

The FCRPC's Second Annual Report, released in June 1969, revealed a total expenditure of $2.8 million for development projects for the entire four-state region. In keeping with organizational goals, the commission stressed highway improvements. The FCRPC authorized $100,000 to pave 25 miles of highway from Durango to the upper portion of Navajo Dam, located on the Southern Ute Reservation in Colorado. Similarly, the commission allotted $310,000 to build a road from Moab to the newly dedicated Glen Canyon National Recreation Area. Industrial development, on the other hand, was limited to construction of water and sewage treatment facilities in each of the four states. With the exception of its assistance to fund an expansion of the airport in Flagstaff, there were no other civic improvement projects noted in the annual report.

More revealing were the administrative and technical assistance expenditures for the commission's first two years of operation. The FCRPC allocated nearly one-third of its total budget in fiscal 1969 to planning studies and operational costs. In his preface to the report, newly appointed state cochairman Governor David F. Cargo of New Mexico attempted to assuage critics of the FCRPC with words of encouragement: "You can clearly see that the atmosphere of cooperation is excellent and that the goals of the Commission are coming closer to reality." Then, he cautioned, "Limited federal funds naturally limit the pace of our growth and the states continue their struggle to meet their portion of commitments." By federal cochairman Mecham's own reckoning, in its first two years of existence the FCRPC had provided "just over half of one percent" of the total federal outlay needed to substantially reduce unemployment. In 1970 unemployment in the Four Corners, which by now had risen to nearly 7 percent, still exceeded the national average. Government investigations, moreover, determined the Four Corners to be the least industrialized subregion in the United States.[26]

Despite some obvious limitations, the FCRPC remained operational, but with few notable achievements except in the area of vocational education. Under the aegis of the planning commission, state officials sanctioned the placement of vocational training facilities near Durango and Cortez and authorized construction of community colleges in Farmington and the Arizona portion of the Navajo Reservation. In March 1970, perhaps in response to Senator Montoya's allegations that the agency was too isolated from the centers of state government to operate effectively, the governors of the Four Corners states voted 3 to 1 to relocate the regional office from Farmington to Albuquerque. The FCRPC remained in Albuquerque, far removed from the economic problems that it was initially empowered to correct, until President Nixon ordered its dissolution in 1974.[27]

Although the notion of cooperative regional planning was well received among the leaders of the Four Corners states in attendance at the Salt Lake City Governor's Conference in 1966, their ability to maximize the resources available to them through the FCRPC fell well short of expectations. Congressional leaders and a new Republican administration in the White House looked unfavorably on the meager results of the FCRPC. Lyndon Johnson, who believed federal and state cooperative planning was a panacea to national economic ills, tolerated the ineffectiveness. But President Richard Nixon viewed cooperative regional organizations as essentially a failed experiment. In keeping with his proposed "New Federalism," Nixon insisted that states become less dependent on the federal government and take more initiative to fund solutions for economic development within their own regions. In 1971, just two years after assuming office, Nixon tried to terminate federal support of all regional planning commissions authorized under Title V of the Public Works and Economic Development Act. Opposition to the decision, particularly among congressional representatives from Appalachia, forced him to delay action on his order until the end of his second term.[28]

There is little documented evidence to suggest that the accomplishments of the FCRPC were notably outstanding. Because of its failure to initiate plans, the overall contributions of the agency toward the enhancement of the Four Corners economy must be judged mediocre at best. Nevertheless, the intent of the FCRPC to promote economic revitalization through interstate cooperation warrants praise. While the accomplishments of the federal agency itself were on the whole unimpressive, the spirit of cooperation it instilled among the four state governors continued beyond the political life of the FCRPC. Each governor remained resolute in his commitment to the interstate promotion of tourism. In their determination to elevate tourism from a local undertaking to a regional industry, the governors of Arizona, Utah, Colorado, and New Mexico placed total confidence in the scenic and recreational potential of the Four Corners.

SEVEN

The Inexhaustible Resource

In the wake of the FCRPC's failure as the chief arbiter of a planned regional approach to economic depression in the Four Corners, the commitment among western governors at the Salt Lake City conference in 1966 was a pivotal decision. At that time, leaders of the Southwest and Rocky Mountain states issued forth unanimous approval of the proposal for interstate cooperation in the promotion of tourism. For some states like Utah, host of the second annual event, the resolution culminated efforts to sponsor the idea. In the fall of 1965, Governor Calvin Rampton had already set the standard for a regionwide tourism campaign in his keynote address before the Western States Tourist Development Task Force in Carson City, Nevada.

Impressed with the achievements of America's Apollo Space Program, Governor Rampton entreated his listeners to imagine a view of the United States from the vantage point of the nation's astronauts. Clearly visible was a landmass of 3.6 million square miles, inhabited by 180 million people. An orbital view of the nation's topography revealed further that 85 percent of the American population lived in urban areas located east of the Rocky Mountains. Also distinguishable were the vast open spaces between the Rockies and the Pacific Coast, an area which, according to Rampton, held 72 percent of all recreation acreage and 90 percent of all public domain in the United States. Contained within the seemingly boundless acreage of the Rocky Mountain West were more than half of the nation's national parks and hundreds of designated recreation areas. "It is as if Mother Nature herself decided that the Great American West would be America's playground," Rampton said.

The natural amenities of the American West were, in Rampton's view, destined to become the economic salvation of not only Utah but also its neighbors, all of whom had experienced similar economic misery in the mid-1960s. Echoing Lyndon Johnson's concern for the nation's trade deficit with Europe, Rampton argued that a greater percentage of the $1 billion spent in overseas travel could be diverted to the West via a more aggressive tourism promotion campaign. The Utah executive stressed limited industrial development of the West and insisted that the tourist industry—one of few industries compatible with the natural environment—would enhance the economies of the western states through the attraction of tourist dollars.

The main thrust of the proposed tourism program was not limited to Europe and the East Coast. Indeed, Rampton targeted metropolitan capitals of the West as the chief suppliers of vacationers. The governor noted that at their current rate of expansion, eleven western states would increase in population to more than 40 million in 1975, approximately 27 million more than in the 1960 census. As population density increased, residents of western cities would no doubt hunger for the great outdoors. "We must stimulate our economy by utilizing every natural resource and asset at our command," Rampton urged. "The asset which we in the West are most bounteously endowed is scenery." In dramatic fashion, Rampton concluded that the governors of the western states were morally obligated to the region and the nation to pledge their state's recreational amenities to the touring public.

What Calvin Rampton proposed in 1965 was that tourism offered an unprecedented opportunity as an import economy to the interior West—an economy that would, in effect, reverse the colonial pattern characteristic of the region since the late 1800s. That Rampton recognized the urban West as a primary target for tourism promotion is significant. Generally speaking, most visitors to the Four Corners traveled less than a thousand miles to enjoy its scenic attractions. During the 1960s, the area's national parks and monuments, recreational areas, and ski resorts enjoyed their heaviest visitations from Denver, Phoenix, Los Angeles, Dallas, and similar western capitals. Unlike in previous decades, when local communities thrived on the extraction of petroleum and energy-rich mineral reserves, modern Four Corners' communities reaped handsome profits due to the increased dependency of urban populations on the scenic and recreational pleasantries surrounding them.[1]

At the Rocky Mountain Governors Conference in Salt Lake City, Governor Rampton applauded D. Howe Moffat's appeal for regional cooperation in the promotion of tourism. Although he recognized Utah as a comparative newcomer in the industry, Rampton noted that tourism already had contributed an estimated $132 million to the state treasury since 1962. Colorado, whose reputation as a vacation wonderland was more widely recognized, nearly doubled Utah's tourist dollar earnings for the same period. New Mexico and Arizona, Rampton observed, also demonstrated tremendous potential to increase state revenues through tourism. Reiterating his belief that western cities should be earmarked as early targets for an intensive regional campaign, the Utah governor remarked: "At the present time, most of us are spending our tourist promotion dollars to attract visitors from our neighboring western states."

Still, the spokesman for four adjoining states did not exclude the possibility of making the West attractive to visitors east of the Mississippi. In fact, Rampton recognized both national and international markets as long-term goals of the regional tourism campaign. He acknowledged potential markets in Canada and Mexico as well as the teeming urban communities of Europe and Asia, whose ever-growing populations were enjoying incomes that enabled frequent travel to the United States. "Any effort which the West can undertake to promote travel from Europe, Canada, Japan, and other Eastern nations," Rampton declared, "will not only benefit the West, but our nation's balance of payments." Importantly, the governor's plans to develop tourism on the regional level conformed to national goals to promote the scenic attractions of the United States as an alternative to overseas travel.

In one final appeal for interstate cooperation, Rampton urged governors of the Four Corners states to unite in a concentrated effort to attract vacationers from the heavily populated cities of the region, the nation, and the world. Cognizant that a number of natural vacation resources in the Four Corners crossed state borders, Rampton urged his political colleagues to create "a picture of the 'Great American West' in the mind of our potential customer that has no state borders confusing the image." Colorado, Utah, Wyoming, and Montana had already established a precedent for interstate cooperation in travel promotion in 1961 with the creation of a loose-knit organization known as the Rocky Mountain West Group. Using this organization as a vehicle for tourism promotion, each state had contributed $5,000 to place full-page advertisements in the *New York Times* and *National Geographic*.

At the 1966 convention, Rampton appealed to New Mexico and Arizona to follow suit. The image of a scenic and nostalgic West would, in the governor's view, become a unifying theme among the Four Corners states.

A crucial step toward the attainment of the goal of subregional cohesiveness was "the commitment of each state in the Four Corners to participate
for the common good of all." In a stirring conclusion that rallied the
attending governors around the idea of interstate cooperation toward a
regional tourist industry, Governor Rampton implored:

> The challenge that I hold out to each state is this: To take advantage
> of your state's natural resources for vacation travel to the fullest
> extent possible and to the greatest economic benefit to your people.
> To open the doors of the Great American West's playground to all
> people of the nation and the world by informing them of what we
> have to offer. To break down all barriers of self-interest and isolation
> between us for the greater development of our recreation resources
> for both visitors and those at home.[2]

Inasmuch as Calvin Rampton assumed a leading role in promoting
tourism among the Four Corners states, it was not surprising that the
residents of Moab were equally pledged to a full-scale campaign to attract
tourists to southeastern Utah. The hopes of the tiny Mormon community
rested upon the newly established Canyonlands National Park. The subject of a heated debate among the members of the Senate Committee on
Interior and Insular Affairs, Canyonlands National Park, the last link in
Interior Stewart Udall's proposal for a "Golden Circle" of national parks,
became operational on September 3, 1964.

The addition of the massive 330,000-acre national park promised Moab
residents a significant boost to their ailing economy. One university study
projected that the development of the nation's newest park, coupled with
the completion of Glen Canyon Recreation Area in northern Arizona and
major improvements to surrounding highways, would increase tourist visitations to the Moab area an estimated 60 percent. "If the new park is
created, total visits in 1980 should approximate 10.5 million visitors," read
the report.

Although these early projections proved too optimistic, Canyonlands
did bring ample tourism dollars into the economy during its first two years
of operation. Park visitations averaged around 25,000 people per year in
1965 and 1966. The Bureau of Reclamation predicted that in response to
National Park Service improvements—new campgrounds, groomed hik-
ing trails, and other recreational amenities—attraction to the park would
increase markedly in future years. Notably, both the university and the
agency studies identified the western states as the point of origin for most

of the early visitations to Moab. Arizona, California, Colorado, New Mexico, and Utah provided 75–80 percent of Canyonlands' first tourists.

Clearly, the "Golden Circle" of national parks and monuments offered the congested and densely populated centers of the West myriad opportunities for escape. Contained within the circle were some of America's most breathtaking natural wonders as well as some of its most cherished cultural treasures. Besides Canyonlands, other Utah attractions included Bryce and Zion National Parks, and Arches, Capitol Reef, Cedar Breaks, Natural Bridges, Rainbow Bridge, and Hovenweep National Monuments. Collectively, these represented an awesome collection of prehistoric ruins, cliff dwellings, and scenic rock formations.

In 1961 Utah's federal parks and monuments combined to attract 2,876,600 visitors to the state. That these recreation areas were located, on the average, only 568 miles from major western population centers like Phoenix, Tucson, Los Angeles, San Francisco, Denver, Albuquerque, and Salt Lake City made the Four Corners especially attractive to residents of the West. Improvements to federal highways and the completion of the Navajo Trail across northern Arizona in 1962 made a three-day excursion from most western departure points to the Four Corners a fairly simple undertaking. Regular air service to the once-isolated communities eased travel to Durango, Moab, Farmington, and Flagstaff even more.[3]

Not unlike its neighbor to the west, Durango invested heavily in its natural landscape to attract tourists. As in earlier years, Mesa Verde loomed as the capstone of the national park scheme in southwestern Colorado. Both the Mission 66 and the Wetherill Mesa Projects elevated Mesa Verde's popularity from a strictly local to a national attraction. "The opening of the new archeological area came none too soon," noted historian Duane Smith in his study of the federal preserve. "Crowds literally overran the park during the peak days of the summer season." Indeed, every room at the recently constructed Spruce Tree Lodge and all of the campsites furnished as a result of the Mission 66 improvements project had been full each evening since the opening of Wetherill Mesa to sightseers in June 1963. It was common practice for park rangers to turn away an estimated 200–300 cars daily.

In July 1965 Superintendent Chester Thomas voiced alarm over the adverse impact of increasing visitations to the archeological resources at Mesa Verde. What constituted a standard-sized tour group of forty to fifty visitors to the famous Cliff Palace represented, in Thomas's view, "a potentially dangerous situation from the standpoint of the damage to the ruin and the risk of human life from overcrowding." Monthly visitor figures, in fact, exceeded 100,000 for the first time in the park's history. Ironically, the throngs of visitors who converged upon the famous southwestern attraction brought needed revenues, while at the same time they threatened the 1,000-year-old resources the National Park Service was pledged to preserve.

As in the case of southeastern Utah, most of the early tourists to Mesa Verde and the Durango area originated in the West. With the completion of a shorter, all-weather route across the Navajo Reservation, Los Angeles and San Diego supplied the highest percentage of tourists to Mesa Verde. Arizona's Phoenix and Tucson were second, followed by Denver, Albuquerque, El Paso, Dallas, and Salt Lake City. In addition to the western states, the central plains states of Kansas, Missouri, Nebraska, and Oklahoma furnished many park visitors during these years. Because of its early establishment and its unique cultural appeal, Mesa Verde, unlike Canyonlands and other developing parks in the Southwest, also attracted foreign visitors early on. By the early 1960s, interpretation and information handouts were published in German, French, Spanish, and Japanese to accommodate the "literally hundreds of requests" from overseas tourist bureaus. Cumulative visits to the park for the years 1965–1970 averaged 471,229 visitors annually.[4]

As the Anasazi ruins of Mesa Verde lured tourists by the thousands to southwest Colorado, Durango's famous narrow gauge train routinely whistled the return of hundreds of jubilant passengers from historic Silverton, Colorado. The so-called "Trip to Yesterday" gained such popularity over the years that the Denver & Rio Grande Western Company added a second train in the summer of 1963 to accommodate ever-increasing numbers of enthusiasts. With the addition of a second train, the number of riders increased from 37,855 to 50,988 in one summer season. By the end of the decade, the local newspaper boasted the train's first 100,000-passenger season.

Durango residents correctly acknowledged tourism as the key to the town's economic salvation in the late 1960s. Conservative estimates placed tourist expenditures at $50,000 per day during the summer months. For this reason, both railroad officials and local businessmen willingly committed to the industry's continued success. Durango's south side, now known as "Rio Grande Land," assumed a new look as railroad officials encouraged the purchase of old buildings and land near the train depot for conversion into charming restaurants, gift shops, and a restored hotel.

Publication of the town's first comprehensive plan for urban development in February 1970 further testified that city mayor and local motel owner Mel Flock anticipated years of healthy, prosperous growth. Chamber of Commerce President John McDermott took pride in the fact that a city of only 12,000 people supported two hospitals fully staffed with nearly thirty medical and surgical professionals, seven public schools, three parochial institutions, one accredited liberal arts college, and three banks with deposits totaling $25,000,000. A newspaper editorial on the proposed plan argued that because of its social and economic diversity Durango was "urban" in every sense of the term, although it housed a relatively small population when compared with Denver, Colorado Springs, Pueblo, and other Eastern Slope cities. The challenge to Durangoans, according to editor Ian Thompson, was "whether we let change shape us or whether we will shape the change." Adoption of the comprehensive plan offered one method by which Thompson's public appeal to establish control over the future growth could be met.[5]

If Durango harbored any hope of perpetuating an "urban" image within the Four Corners, it must somehow extend the tourist industry beyond the normal three-and-one-half month season. The ski industry and proposed development plans for Purgatory Winter Sports Area, twenty five miles north of the city, promised the realization of a long-time dream to make Durango a year-round tourist attraction. In 1964 Chet Anderson, an employee of the U.S. Forest Service, San Juan District, submitted his report on the feasibility of a winter sports recreation area near Durango. The report noted that the average snow depth of the proposed site was sufficient to ensure optimum seasonal ski conditions from approximately November 15 to April 15. Once cleared of timber, the terrain would make available acres of open-slope powder skiing for its visitors. The proposal to construct 15 percent of its trails for beginners, 60 percent of the slopes for intermediate skiers, and 25 percent for advanced skiing promised to make Purgatory competitive with other major ski areas in the West. Important, too, was the recommendation that Purgatory, because of its spectacular view of the San Juan Mountains, would be popular to summer tourists as well; chair lifts could be left operational year-round for this purpose.

The report indicated that a ski area in the southwestern portion of Colorado would be especially attractive to the so-called "sunbelt" states located near the Four Corners. "We believe that the ski area will certainly attract people from Albuquerque and other points in the Southwest and West," Anderson predicted. "The town of Durango itself will provide a very enthusiastic core of skiers to use the area, and the potential of the tributary ski population has not even been scratched." In addition to attracting skiers from neighboring towns in southwest Colorado, marketing targets for the proposed ski resort were cities located in New Mexico, Texas, southern California, and Arizona. Anderson estimated these target areas would provide Purgatory with 20,000 skiers in its first year of operation. "Centers of population such as Albuquerque, Santa Fe, Amarillo, Flagstaff, Tucson, and Phoenix can be expected to contribute more and more skiers as the facilities and the area are publicized."[6]

The driving force behind the development of Purgatory Ski Resort was neither a Colorado native nor a lifetime skier. Rather, he was an Illinois oil executive whose professional interests had brought him to Durango in 1958. A 28-year-old Notre Dame graduate and Marine Corps veteran, Raymond T. Duncan had been weaned on the oil business that his father, financier Walter Duncan, started in the 1940s. As oil activity declined in the Midwest, Ray Duncan sought new opportunities in the Four Corners, which at the time was enjoying an enormous boom in oil exploration and production. "I visited Albuquerque, Salt Lake, Denver, Casper, Billings, Farmington, and Durango," Duncan later mused. "My wife, Joan, and I selected Durango as the place to come to." Durango, a bustling town filled with petroleum engineers and other young professionals in the late 1950s, was a pristine mountain hamlet enveloped in the scenic surroundings of the San Juan Basin. Ray Duncan, one of the first wave of postwar, affluent Americans to arrive in the southwest Colorado community, early recognized its potential for economic growth.

"Durango suffers from seasonal ups and downs with summer tourist traffic straining the town's facilities to the utmost, while the winter months see these same facilities begging for trade," Duncan remarked to a room full of curious onlookers gathered at the Strater Hotel in late January 1965. Duncan's audience—local businessmen, professionals, and civic leaders who not only wanted to hear more about the proposed ski development but who were themselves avid skiers—listened as the local oilman outlined his ideas. Duncan's presentation called for a ski resort that would, in time, rival Colorado's most famous winter recreation facilities— Aspen, Vail, and Breckenridge. Although the plans for the new ski area were impressive, Purgatory was clearly a costly venture requiring creative financial planning and an unfaltering commitment from the Durango business community.[7]

Inasmuch as the initial ten-year phase of the proposed ski area did not include on-site sleeping accommodations, Purgatory would be completely dependent upon the city of Durango or the remote mountain town of Silverton, twenty miles north of the ski area, to provide lodging and entertainment for weekend skiers. Thus, Durango residents saw a vested interest in the proposed resort because it promised to attract thousands of tourist dollars into the town during the long, dreary winter. Duncan proposed the creation of the San Juan Development Company, a promotional and fund-raising organization comprised mostly of local businessmen and other interested citizens. Former Durango mayor Robert Beers remembered, "Ray had looked into financing to some degree and came to us with the idea that a development company could, under the Small Business Administration 502 Program, secure a loan to get the project off the ground." The dozen or so founding members of the San Juan Development Company each contributed $1,000 to form the nucleus of the organization.

Next, they undertook the sale of stock at $100 per share in an effort to raise an additional $100,000 for the project. "The stock was in the development company, not in Purgatory," Beers explained, "The community had to show an interest before you could secure an SBA loan." The grass-roots campaign raised just under $90,000; coupled with an additional $350,000 granted from the Small Business Administration, Duncan's newly formed Durango Ski Corporation was, therefore, capitalized at approximately $450,000. Meanwhile, on February 3, 1965, San Juan Forest Supervisor Rod Blacker announced his agency's decision to approve the Durango Ski Corporation's application for 1,500 acres of land to initiate the first phase of development. That spring, the corporation purchased the land, located deep in the heart of the San Juan Range, and began construction. With the first major snowfall of winter, Purgatory Ski Area officials placed chair lifts No. 1 and No. 2 into operation for the grand opening on December 4, 1965.

From its inception, Purgatory appeared to be the financial success everyone dreamed it would be. During the first month of operation, President Ray Duncan reported to his stockholders that 6,000 skiers visited the resort, mostly from Texas, New Mexico, and Oklahoma. Based on this information, the Durango Chamber of Commerce participated in travel shows held in Dallas and San Francisco in order to promote the West's "hottest" new ski resort. "Purgatory: New Alpine Area in the Bold High Country of the Colorful San Juan Mountains—the Switzerland of America," proclaimed brochures intended to entice ski-lovers to southwest Colorado. In its first season, Purgatory serviced 28,000 skiers. Durango residents were ecstatic and immediately undertook the expansion of housing, restaurant, and motel facilities to accommodate visiting skiers, as well as the anticipated service industry work force the facility was certain to attract. Civic leaders optimistically anticipated that Durango's population would increase by 5,000–10,000 people in a single decade in response to the new ski industry.[8]

The establishment of a major ski resort in the southwestern part of Colorado was indeed timely. The promotion of winter recreation in the western United States mirrored President Johnson's personal commitment to a "Discover America" campaign. In an address given in 1964, Johnson said: "I would urge that Americans enjoy the recreational opportunities which this country offers. Life is at its best when balanced between work and play, and our land provides limitless opportunities for both."

In the president's view, the ski industry offered the nation's tourists a new and exciting recreational pastime while it accommodated the principles set forth in the Multiple Use Act of 1960. According to the Act, which President Eisenhower signed into law before leaving office, the nation's forests were to be administered for five basic uses—range, timber, watershed, wildlife activities, and outdoor recreation. With regard to the winter sports industry's potential to keep American travelers at home, Vice President Hubert Humphrey, head of the White House Task Force on Travel, assured western governors that the federal government was prepared to invest millions of dollars to promote tourism in general and the ski industry in particular across the nation in conjunction with its "Discover America" theme.

On the local level, Colorado Governor John Love initiated a program intended to publicize skiing as the newest and most successful industry in the western region. First organized in 1963, "Colorado Ski Country—U.S.A." advertised Colorado and New Mexico ski facilities among the "relatively untouched markets" of the East through ski shows, winter sports festivals, poster advertisements, and mass media campaigns. In 1966 John Love, perhaps inspired by Calvin Rampton's call to unite in a regionwide effort to promote tourism, doubled the state's budget for ski advertisement. This funding increase enabled the "Colorado Ski Country—U.S.A." organization to market southwestern ski resorts in Boston, New York, Chicago, Detroit, Los Angeles, Seattle, Houston, Dallas, and San Francisco. Eager for inclusion in the promotional campaign, Purgatory Ski Resort, Colorado's youngest ski facility, became a member of the "Colorado Ski Country—U.S.A." organization.

The long-term ambitions of John Love and companion southwestern governors went beyond mere advertisement of the region's winter recreational capabilities. In 1966 at the Summer Olympic Games in Rome, the Colorado Olympic Commission made its bid to host the 1976 Winter Olympic Games. In a letter to Governor Love dated December 19, 1967, Governor Rampton pledged his support for Colorado's bid for the Winter

Olympics because it assured economic benefits to the entire region. "In terms of the development of skiing, I would hope that it might be possible to continue working with the Denver organizing committee in the securing of regional support in connection with the Winter Olympics of 1976," Rampton wrote. With more than one million skier-visits and reported expenditures of $65,800,000 on resort facilities during the 1965 season, Colorado was the uncontested frontrunner among the Four Corners states as the candidate for the Winter Games. Unlike Flagstaff's earlier offer to host the event, Colorado's bid received serious attention.[9]

Officials at Purgatory Ski Resort, anticipating Colorado's selection as the site for the games, did their part to promote the ski industry. During its first five years of operation, the southwestern resort registered a total of 178,931 skiers, 40 percent from Texas, Oklahoma, southern California, and New Mexico, and the remaining 60 percent from neighboring towns in Colorado. Durango residents were jubilant since it appeared that the town had finally created a viable "import" economy to attract tourist dollars into the Four Corners. Early reports indicated that visitors from the metropolitan centers of the West were in seemingly inexhaustible supply; Durango businessmen were eager to capitalize on these human resources for years to come. The Olympic fervor increased with the prospect that Colorado's ski industry would achieve instant international acclaim. For its part, Purgatory Ski Area hosted the Junior National Ski Championships in March 1970. Meanwhile, in May of that year the International Olympic Committee met in Amsterdam and announced Denver as the site of the XIIth Winter Olympics.[10]

Not unlike Durango, the northern Arizona mountain community of Flagstaff also aspired to create a year-round recreation industry. As in the case of its Colorado neighbor, Flagstaff's hopes for achieving this goal depended upon improvements to existing ski facilities. In the fall of 1970 city council members supported a proposal from Summit Properties, a Texas-based land development corporation, to purchase the Snow Bowl, a popular local ski area located in the heart of San Francisco Peaks. During the 1940s and 1950s the U.S. Forest Service initiated fundamental improvements to the area in an effort to increase accessibility. In response to the increasing popularity of skiing as a recreational sport in the mid-1960s, the Arnal Corporation, a loose-knit organization comprised primarily of members of the Flagstaff Ski Club and other investment speculators, widened and expanded trails, installed a small chair lift, and built a new lodge and restaurant for local ski use. It appeared, however, that the corporation had no master plan for expansion beyond these rudimentary improvements.

On the other hand, Bruce Leadbetter, president of the Summit Prop-

erties Real Estate Development Corporation, proposed a grandiose scheme
to build a condominium complex and golf course on 325 acres of private
land purchased in nearby Hart Prairie. According to Leadbetter's presentation before the Flagstaff City Council, the Summit Properties development could be linked to the Snow Bowl, which they now also owned, by
a chair lift across U.S. Forest Service land to the base of the ski area.

The council's tentative approval of the plan, however, became the focus
of controversy among members of the northern Arizona community. First,
the U.S. Forest Service argued that expansion of any kind across government land required a comprehensive environmental assessment, which
could not be undertaken until the agency's completion of the *San Francisco
Peaks Land Use Plan*. In effect, federal opposition to Summit Properties'
proposal to expand beyond the limits of its private holdings killed the
attempt to link the development complex to the ski facility.

Additional pressure to veto the expansion scheme came from leaders of
the Navajo–Hopi reservations. In a U.S. Forest Service hearing held in
Flagstaff, Tsinnijinnie Singer, a Hopi medicine man, led a coalition of
American Indians, Northern Arizona University students and faculty, and
local conservationists in opposition to the proposed Summit Properties
development plan. The Navajos and the Hopis had for centuries wor-
shipped Humphrey Peak as one of their sacred mountains. Both tribes
considered the plan to expand the ski industry in northern Arizona a
violation of the sanctity of their ancestral homeland. According to the
medicine man, the skyline of the peak provided a cultural and agricultural
timetable for a calendrical system around which all Hopi religious and social
activities revolved. In support of the Navajo–Hopi cause, political scientist
John M. Ostheimer of Northern Arizona University testified that continued intrusion upon the sacred lands of the Arizona tribes would hasten the
ongoing "loss of contact with their traditional native culture." Navajo and
Hopi tribal members displayed an uncharacteristically unified position in
counteracting the development project in the San Francisco Mountains.

During the ensuing years, Summit Properties tried in vain to circum-
vent opposition to its recreational complex. Frustrated by its failure to win
public support for the expansion, the Texas firm sold back the Hart Prairie
property to the Forest Service, and the Snow Bowl ski area to Northland
Recreation, Inc., a Flagstaff-based operation. While the new owners made
substantial improvements to the facility, the Snow Bowl never became the
regional winter attraction that Flagstaff community leaders hoped for.
The facility attracted 27,500 skiers from 1970 to 1975, a paltry showing
when compared to figures for Purgatory and other Colorado ski resorts for
the same period. Of greater consequence was the defeat of the Texas real

estate developers in northern Arizona, which produced a "ripple effect" evidenced not only in the Four Corners but throughout the entire western region. The success of the coalition of conservation-minded citizens in Flagstaff against Summit Properties in 1971 mirrored an emerging regional and national environmental protectionist movement that determined the course of future land use in the West for the remainder of the decade.[11]

Ironically, the austere backdrop of the Navajo–Hopi reservations proved to be the key element in attracting tourists to northern Arizona. By virtue of its location at the crossroads of three of the nation's major interstate highways, Flagstaff reaped enormous financial rewards as a result of the nation's love affair with "Navajo Country." Contained within the approximately 25,000 square miles comprising the Indian reserve are some of the world's least disturbed scenic and cultural wonders. The target of numerous government geological and archeological investigations since the 1930s, the canyonlands of the Four Corners subregion were early acknowledged for their ability to lure sightseers. Secretary of the Interior Udall's inclusion of the Navajo Reservation in the so-called "Golden Circle" in 1963 was in effect an official endorsement of the area's potential as a scenic and recreational area of the American Southwest. Udall saw an opportunity to link his personal goal of greater economic self-sufficiency among the Indian tribes of northern Arizona with western boosterism.

The national parks and monuments—that Congress created and the National Park Service managed—were central to the success of the "Golden Circle" concept. The Navajo–Hopi Rehabilitation Act of 1950, which Udall helped orchestrate as a young Arizona legislator, hastened the completion of the Navajo Trail, a vital transportation link that placed all of the cultural resources of the Navajo–Hopi reservations at the disposal of average motorists. Additionally, the Mission 66 Program authorized the expenditure of millions of taxpayer dollars for the improvement of Indian theme parks and monuments to accommodate increased visitor use. The Grand Canyon and Glen Canyon National Recreation Area, on the Colorado River near the present-day town of Page, were perennially cited as the most popular natural attractions in northern Arizona. A National Park Service survey published in 1970, however, noted a phenomenal percentage increase in tourist visitations to lesser-known archeological sites on the Navajo Reservation. For example, visits to Navajo National Monument, once considered virtually inaccessible, increased an astounding 1,317 percent between 1964 and 1970.[12]

Although the scenic amenities of the Navajo Reservation clearly attracted national attention by the 1970s, the densely populated centers of the West supplied most of northern Arizona's early excursionists. A survey prepared for the Office of Economic Planning and Development in 1976 cited tourism as a billion dollar industry in Arizona, claiming that the state ranked among the leaders in the West in tourism and travel-related income. Based on statistics gathered among all of the Arizona ports-of-entry from 1970 to 1974, the survey revealed that most vehicular traffic bound for either the Navajo Reservation or the Flagstaff vicinity originated in the West. California alone provided 30 percent of the state's visitors during these years, followed by Texas with 16 percent, 6.4 percent from New Mexico, and Colorado's 4.2 percent. "The visitor to Arizona who travels by motor vehicle typically comes from the Western United States, most often California," the report concluded. "This tourist spends most of his time in northern Arizona visiting such places as Flagstaff or the Grand Canyon."

Indeed, tourists listed Flagstaff as the city in Arizona most often visited. Perhaps the alpine environment of the northern community appealed more to "sunbelt" city dwellers from other parts of the West than the desert landscape common to Phoenix and Tucson. For whatever reason, these statistics, coupled with those cited earlier, indicate that the Four Corners states had successfully created an "import" tourism economy by the early 1970s. Unquestionably, the tourist industry enabled the Four Corners communities to reverse in part the age-old colonial pattern of hinterland dependency upon the metropolitan capitals for their economic livelihood. The relationship between the interior communities and the metropolitan West had become for all intents and purposes symbiotic.[13]

In startling contrast to Moab, Durango, and Flagstaff, Farmington harbored neither national preserves nor a promising ski industry to boost its local economy. In fact, a survey of New Mexico taken in 1965 identified nine National Monuments, but only one National Park in the entire state. Aztec Ruins National Monument, located about 15 miles northeast of Farmington, could hardly compete with Mesa Verde in the quality of its cultural resources or with the Grand Canyon in the number of annual visitations. The state's best-known archeological site, Chaco Canyon National Monument (named a National Historic Park in June 1980), while it included several well-preserved prehistoric ruins, was too inaccessible and undeveloped in 1965 to elevate Farmington to the status of a major tourist community.

Tourism in Farmington, such as it was, centered chiefly upon the water-related sports—boating, water skiing, and fishing—made possible with the creation of Navajo Dam State Park in September 1963. A byproduct of the

Upper Colorado River Storage Project and New Mexico's commitment to channel water from the San Juan and Chama Rivers to Albuquerque and Santa Fe through a transmountain diversion tunnel, Navajo Dam attracted upwards of 75,000 visitors per year to Farmington. Such numbers encouraged local boosters to advertise Navajo Lake plus a boat as "a natural recipe for enjoyment." One public commercial read: "Water literally means the difference between life and death here in the Southwest—and also means recreation and enjoyment. Navajo lake, with its miles of shoreline, is a mecca for fishing and boating enthusiasts." It appeared that Farmington hoped to dispel its image as a desert community through the promotion of its lone recreational facility.

In an attempt to keep pace with other southwestern states, New Mexico, too, boasted a successful ski economy in 1970. The new industry had limited impact on Farmington, however, inasmuch as most of the ski resorts were located hours away in the Sangre de Cristo Mountains of the north-central portion of the state. In his inaugural address on January 1, 1965, Governor Jack Campbell acknowledged the importance of skiing and the tourist industry to the state economy and promised to authorize the construction of a northern thoroughfare that would link all of New Mexico's major tourist attractions from Raton to Farmington. Two years later, after the completion of State Highway 64—nicknamed the "Golden Avenue"—civic officials in Farmington expressed optimism that their city would no longer be viewed as "off the main traffic corridor" to travelers crossing northern New Mexico en route to ski resorts in neighboring Colorado. During the dedication of the road in September 1967, Senator Joseph M. Montoya applauded its completion because it opened the Four Corners to "greater regional development."[14]

Like his counterparts John Love of Colorado and Calvin Rampton of Utah, Jack Campbell was not only a progressive-minded leader, but an avid proponent of interstate cooperation in the promotion of tourism. One year after assuming office, Campbell tripled the state budget for tourism advertising. With the aim of promoting northern New Mexico and southern Colorado as a "skier's paradise," the governor launched the most effective advertising effort his state had ever known. Similar to Colorado Governor Love's approach, the Campbell program targeted the oil-rich states of Texas and Oklahoma in addition to Arizona and southern California. In his first report to the New Mexico legislature on October 1, 1966, Campbell announced the tourist industry had attracted 14 million visitors and $300 million in revenues, more than 50 percent of the state's total revenue from mineral production in 1965.

Former state dignitaries and weekend ski enthusiasts alike expressed their approval of Campbell's efforts to revitalize the economy. One letter of support came from Robert Brierly, a self-professed ski lover and sales manager for Shamrock Oil and Gas Corporation of Amarillo, Texas, who thanked the governor for the benefits he had personally derived from the stepped-up tourism campaign. "Your state is fortunate to be blessed with snow, mountains, and sunshine," his letter began. "As you know, we poor Texans are lacking in ski areas, but we are fortunate in living close enough to New Mexico to be able to visit your state on weekends." Tom Bolack, former mayor of Farmington, former state governor, and owner of a world-wide travel agency in Albuquerque, credited Jack Campbell for New Mexico's improved national image.

While Farmington benefitted indirectly from Campbell's tourism promotion efforts, it struggled to establish a clear identity as a tourist town. Encumbered by the lack of natural amenities, Farmington relied—as it always had—upon its industrial base for economic enhancement. Limited tourism capabilities notwithstanding, Farmington's self-image was, on the whole, positive. A city of nearly 50,000 people in 1970, the largest population among the Four Corners municipalities, Farmington envisioned itself as the hub of all regional activity. Civic leaders appeared unconcerned that Farmington itself had few scenic pleasantries to offer visitors. Chamber of Commerce brochures, in fact, listed the city's qualifications as a regional convention center while at the same time noting that Farmington was located "minutes away" from Mesa Verde National Park and Purgatory Ski Resort. No doubt the Durango Chamber of Commerce appreciated the free plug from its southern neighbor. In a 1976 centennial profile entitled "Fabulous Farmington," an unidentified author summarized the basis for the city's historic progress while predicting the formula for future economic success: "While the crest of the oil and gas exploration is past, the primary economy of the area remains based on the development and operation of vast petroleum resources."[5]

To be sure, the attitudes of some Four Corners residents toward tourism, especially those who marvelled at the dynamic growth of the subregion in response to the energy resource booms of earlier decades, were slow to change. To others, however, the seemingly endless stream of visitors—armed with cameras and camp gear—who poured into the once-provincial communities of the Four Corners suggested that a new dawn of expansion and economic prosperity was upon them.

EIGHT

The Fabulous Four Corners

The exigencies of the Second World War hastened America's need to exploit the vast, undisturbed energy resources buried deep beneath the surface of its western hinterlands. Before 1941 the area designated as the "Colorado Plateau" on U.S.G.S. Survey maps remained for the most part a scientific curiosity. Except for a handful of petroleum geologists, few visitors to the area found redeeming value in the arid, sparsely inhabited wasteland known simply as the Four Corners. Government agents who traveled to the area in these early years did so more out of necessity than enjoyment.

The fast-paced developments of the war years, in particular the military's insatiable appetite for fissionable material and petroleum resources, elevated the strategic importance of the subregions of the interior West. Among the states to receive exhaustive national attention during wartime were those of the Four Corners. Scientific reports from the 1930s showed that the uncharted backcountry of northwestern New Mexico, southwestern Colorado, northeastern Arizona, and southeastern Utah held seemingly boundless energy reserves. The federal effort to exploit the subsurface richness of the American Southwest during and after the war precipitated a social and economic transformation that effected long-term, irreversible change among four small communities in the southwestern heartland.

Although Durango, Flagstaff, Farmington, and Moab displayed unique cultural and topographical characteristics, the pattern of their historical development and economic growth was strikingly similar. Each evolved in a manner not unlike that of most western frontier towns. Railroads, ranch-

ing, and romantic "wild west" episodes typified their slow but steady
transition into the modern age. Consistent throughout was the presence of
a colonial economic relationship between local mining and agricultural
producers and a bulging network of eastern consumers. The unparalleled
consumption of natural and energy resources extracted primarily from the
interior subregions of the West during World War II stimulated an appreciable—although not altogether different—change in the traditional
colonialism paradigm that predated 1945.

Global war accelerated the independent growth of the West enabling
the region to develop a consumer economy. "The colonial economy had
been liberated; the foundations for another great population boom had
been laid; sleepy western towns were transformed into teeming cities. . . .,"
summarized historian Gerald Nash.[1] The virulent growth of the postwar,
metropolitan West consummated its economic independence from the
eastern capitalists. As for its hinterland subregions, the continuing dependency upon natural and mineral resources merely transferred from the
industrialized East to an expansionist West. Uranium, coal, timber, natural gas, petroleum, and water became coveted necessities of western sub-
urbanites who competed for their use.

Meanwhile, the Four Corners communities, mindful of the opportunity
to remove the stigma of geographic isolation and economic stagnation
through a direct link to the urbanized West, hastened the extraction of
their abundant resources. Regional preeminence and rapid municipal
growth were the benchmarks of the late 1950s and early 1960s, as each city
forged a discernable urban identity. Flagstaff emerged as a premier lumber
and timber producer; Farmington an oil town; Moab's fame derived from
its production of uranium—a byproduct of the atomic age; while Durango
fancied itself a "white collar" professional community possessing incomparable scenic ambience. As postwar expansion of the West accelerated,
metropolitan boundaries bulged to accommodate ever-increasing populations. The aggrandizement of extractive resources found mostly in the
hinterlands increased proportionately. In short, the "plundered" West fell
victim to its own unwieldy growth.

Accessibility to hinterland resources was paramount to the objectives of
the industrial modernization of the West. Toward this end, the Atomic
Energy Commission, the Bureau of Indian Affairs, and other federal agencies with a vested interest in the Four Corners, commissioned a crude
network of secondary roads linking the Southwest to the larger corpus of
American society. Massive federal spending and strident commitments to
enhance national mobility in the mid-1950s produced an interstate system

of highways that fostered geographic cohesion among the Four Corners states. The flurry of federal highway projects in the West in subsequent decades, climaxed by the completion of a major all-weather route across the Navajo Reservation, forecast unlimited opportunities for internal growth and subregional independence.

With the arrival of thousands of motorists to the adjoining southwestern states, prospects for a sound economic future derived from one seemingly inexhaustible resource—the American tourist. Paved interstate highways, air-conditioned vehicles, and jet transportation belayed the long-standing fear of aridity and desolation in the mind of the average traveler. Correspondingly, the romantic image of the brawling frontier towns in Colorado, Arizona, Utah, and New Mexico piqued the imagination of would-be cowboys who flocked to the dude ranches and abandoned mining camps of the Four Corners in a desperate attempt to recapture the flavor of the "Old West." While a good number of these early visitors were easterners, most embarked from leading western capitals—Denver, Phoenix, Houston, Los Angeles, Albuquerque, San Diego, San Francisco, and Salt Lake City. All sought an escape from the hectic, fast-paced lifestyle of the city to the solitude and scenic grandeur of remote interior communities.

As the energy boom town era approached its nadir in 1965, it was tourism that offset economic disaster. While Farmington and Flagstaff retained a strong industrial base, Durango and Moab pledged forthright commitments to service industries as their main endeavor. National parks and state and federal recreational areas were the backbone of the western tourism economy. Accordingly, the federal government exhausted millions of taxpayer dollars toward improvement of the national parks system in its effort to dissuade Americans from traveling abroad. Promotion of the Four Corners as a scenic wonderland enhanced its attractiveness to western city-dwellers who, abandoning their high-pressure jobs, spent greater vacation time there.

The emergence of skiing as a favorite winter recreational pastime transformed tourism in the Four Corners from a seasonal occurrence into a billion dollar, year-round enterprise. No longer did the first snowfall mark the end of the visitor season; on the contrary, winter heralded the arrival of a new generation of pleasure seekers. In the process, skiing dispelled the image of the arid West in the American mentality. That Purgatory Ski Resort elected in 1983 to advertise their facility nationwide as the "Hottest Skiing in the West" underscored the acceptance of a new recreational direction for the American Southwest.[2]

Significantly, the establishment of a year-round tourist industry reversed the colonialism pattern in which the small town was exclusively dependent upon its metropolitan neighbor for economic sustenance. After 1965 the economic relationship between the city and the hinterland communities, if anything, became more symbiotic. Visitor statistics and annual expenditures suggest that urbanites, many of whom originated in the major cities of the West, were increasingly dependent upon the scenic and recreational amenities of the Four Corners for refuge and relaxation. By 1970 the economies of Flagstaff, Moab, Farmington, and Durango were no longer exclusively "export" in character. In the view of local businessmen, tourists were "import" commodities, eager to exchange dollars for local amusements, scenic attractions, and recreational activities.

The commitment to lure more visitors to the Four Corners through a cooperative promotional campaign encouraged long-range planning among the business-minded executives of the various southwestern states. In their view, the monetary benefits derived from tourism outweighed lingering political differences. Unlike earlier decades when Arizona, New Mexico, Colorado, and Utah asserted economic individualism, leaders of the 1960s placed confidence in interstate cooperation to address regional needs. While state governors consolidated their energy to promote the Four Corners as a national scenic and recreational playground, city planners and federal administrators forged a subregional ethos in which all southwestern municipalities could identify. Though essentially a failed experiment, the Four Corners Regional Planning Commission was the first conscientious attempt to define the Four Corners as a distinct subregion of the West based upon geographic and economic similarities.

The so-called "Golden Circle" was yet another concept designed to convey the impression of a single scenic and recreational entity unencumbered by political demarcation. Curiously, the merging of state boundaries into a common border symbolically underscored the commitment of Four Corners' leadership to the call for interstate cooperation and subregional unity. That local inhabitants invariably refer to themselves as "Four Corners" residents rather than affiliates of a particular state further testifies to a maturing regional consciousness.[3] In a sense, no clear delineation of boundaries separates the residents of these four states. Durangoans, for example, are annually bombarded with media campaigns in support of New Mexico politicians, though they cannot vote for them. Conversely, the Farmington Opera Company stages most of its performances in southwest Colorado. Similarly, the bonds of Mormon kinship prevalent throughout southeastern Utah and northern Arizona remain virtually unsevered despite geographic separation.

Thus, by 1970 the cultural subregion of the Four Corners appeared securely tied to the larger western community. Rising tourism, moreover, ensured a healthy economic prognosis for all municipalities. Nonetheless, polemic issues of the decade tempered the euphoria that pervaded the Four Corners during these prosperous times. Amid the backlash of the environmental protection movement, conservation-minded westerners asserted themselves. Fueled by the antigrowth sentiment of Richard Lamm, who referred to the impending Olympic Games as "an environmental Vietnam" during his 1972 gubernatorial campaign, Colorado residents voted three-to-two against hosting the international event. "That was a serious blow to the Colorado ski industry," Mike Elliott, former Nordic Olympian and sales manager for Purgatory Ski Corporation, criticized. "I will never forgive Governor Lamm or the State of Colorado for that."[4]

No less disturbing to Four Corners inhabitants were the effects of the Arab oil embargo of 1973. In response to the crisis, American oil producers hoped to assuage the impact through renewed oil and gas explorations. "The resurgence of the petroleum industry was brief," remarked independent oilman Tom Dugan of Farmington. "While some of the independents invested heavily in new exploration, the major producers refused to spend much money other than to uncap old wells." The consequences of the oil crisis were staggering, however. In the 1990s the Four Corners communities still endure the strain of economic recession. The reduction of oil dollars in Texas, California, and Oklahoma has resulted in a significant decline in tourism revenues all through the Four Corners. One Durango newspaper ominously projected that condominium sales and housing construction had reached their limits.[5]

It appears, then, that the "golden age" of municipal growth and economic prosperity in the Four Corners were the years 1945 to 1970. While recent trends forecast some resurgence of growth for these interior communities, they remain inextricably linked to the currents of the western region as well as the nation. Perhaps future studies of this and other subregions will serve as a basis for understanding the more complex developments of a post–World War II West. The Four Corners in many respects represents the urban West in microcosm. For the nearly three decades examined here, and continuing to the present day, the inhabitants of this dynamic subregion have proudly resolved to live up to the region's self-proclaimed epithet, the "Fabulous Four Corners."

Abbreviations Used in Notes

AEC   Atomic Energy Commission Records, Grand Junction Operations Office, Grand Junction, Colorado

ATL   Arizona Timber and Lumber Company Papers, University of Northern Arizona Library, Flagstaff, Arizona

AW   Arthur M. Wyatt Papers, Fort Lewis College Library, Durango, Colorado

CPA   Clinton P. Anderson Papers, Manuscript Division, Library of Congress, Washington, D.C.

CTH   Carl T. Hayden Papers, Special Collections, Hayden Library, Arizona State University, Tempe, Arizona

DFC   David F. Cargo Papers, New Mexico State Records Center and Archives, Santa Fe, New Mexico

ELM   Edwin L. Mechem Papers, New Mexico State Records Center and Archives, Santa Fe, New Mexico

JAL   John A. Love Papers, Division of Colorado State Archives and Public Records, Denver, Colorado

JB   John Burrows Papers, New Mexico State Records Center and Archives, Santa Fe, New Mexico

JMC   Jack M. Campbell Papers, New Mexico State Records Center and Archives, Santa Fe, New Mexico

JMM   Joseph M. Montoya Papers, Special Collections, University of New Mexico, Albuquerque, New Mexico

LBJ   Lyndon Baines Johnson Papers, Lyndon Baines Johnson Presidential Library, Austin, Texas

MG   Morris Garnsey Papers, Western Historical Collection, Norlin Library, University of Colorado, Boulder, Colorado

SLRM   Stephen L. R. McNichols Papers, Division of Colorado State Archives and Public Records, Denver, Colorado

SLU   Stewart L. Udall Papers, Special Collections Library, University of Arizona, Tucson, Arizona

SML   Saginaw and Manistee Lumber Company Records, Special Collections, University of Northern Arizona, Flagstaff, Arizona

WA   Wayne Aspinall Papers, University of Denver, Denver, Colorado

Notes

INTRODUCTION

1. Neil R. Peirce, *The Mountain States of America: People, Politics, and Power in the Eight Rocky Mountain States* (New York, 1972); Governor Anderson's quote cited in William G. Robbins, "The 'Plundered Province' Thesis and the Recent Historiography of the American West," *Pacific Historical Review* 54 (1986): 586–87; F. Alan Coombs, "Twentieth-Century Western Politics," in Michael P. Malone and Rodman W. Paul, *Historians and the American West* (Lincoln, 1983), 303.

2. Some of the more important early works on the theme of colonial dependency in the hinterland regions include Bernard De Voto, "The West Against Itself," *Harper's Magazine* 194 (January 1947): 1–13; Carey McWilliams, *Southern California Country: An Island on the Land* (New York, 1946); Ray B. West, ed., *Rocky Mountain Cities* (New York, 1949); Morris E. Garnsey, *America's New Frontier: The Mountain West* (New York, 1950); and Carl Frederick Kraenzel, *The Great Plains in Transition* (Norman, 1955).

3. Neil R. Peirce, *The Pacific States: People, Politics, and Power in the Five Pacific Basin States* (New York, 1972); Peirce, *The Great Plains States of America: People, Politics, and Power in the Nine Great Plains States* (New York, 1973). Historian Richard W. Etulain presents a concise and thoughtful analysis of Peirce's contribution to the field of western history in his "Prologue," in Gerald D. Nash and Richard W. Etulain, eds., *The Twentieth-Century West* (Albuquerque, 1989), 22–23.

4. Urban historian Carl Abbott coined the term "metropolitanization" to refer to the phenomenal urban expansion of the West since 1940. See "The Metropolitan Region: Western Cities in the New Urban Era," in *The Twentieth-Century West*, 72; see also Robbins, "'Plundered Province' Thesis," 582.

5. Works on individual cities include David McComb, *Houston: The Bayou City* (Austin, 1969); Roger Sale, *Seattle: Past and Present* (Seattle, 1976); Lyle Dorsett, *The Queen City: A History of Denver* (Boulder, 1977); C. L. Sonnichsen, *Tucson: The Life and Times of an American City* (Norman, 1982). Among the comparative works

are Carl Abbott, *The New Urban America: Growth and Politics in Sunbelt Cities* (Chapel Hill, 1981); Bradford Luckingham, *The Urban Southwest: A Profile History of Albuquerque—El Paso—Phoenix—Tucson* (El Paso, 1982); and Richard Bernard and Bradley Rice, eds., *Sunbelt Cities: Politics and Growth since World War Two* (Austin, 1983). Works on subregional topics include Duane Vandenbusche and Duane A. Smith, *A Land Alone: Colorado's Western Slope* (Boulder, 1981); and Roger M. Olien and Diana Davids Olien, *Oil Booms: Social Change in Five Texas Towns* (Lincoln, 1982).

6. Carey McWilliams, introductory notes to Ray B. West, ed. *Rocky Mountain Cities* (New York, 1949): 7–28.

PROLOGUE

1. Henry P. Walker and Don Bufkin, eds., *Historical Atlas of Arizona* (Norman, 1979); Jerry L. Williams, ed., *New Mexico in Maps*, 2nd ed. (Albuquerque, 1986); Gregory Crampton, *Standing Up Country: The Canyon Lands of Utah and Arizona* (New York, 1964).

2. Faun McConkie Tanner, *The Far Country: A Regional History of Moab and La Sal, Utah* (Salt Lake City, 1976), 13–14.

3. Philip L. Fradkin, *A River No More: The Colorado River and the West* (1968; reprint, Tucson, 1984), 30–31, 41–53.

4. The Anasazi were the prehistoric ancestors of the modern-day Pueblos. The term "Anasazi" is from the Navajo and means "the ancient ones."

5. Archeological discoveries have shown that other cultural groups, such as the Fremont, Mogollon, and Hohokam, preceded the Anasazi into this region of the Southwest. Comparatively fewer archeological ruins exist to verify the presence of these earlier peoples, however.

6. David Grant Noble, *Ancient Ruins of the Southwest* (Flagstaff, 1981), 25–29, 47–48, 101–3.

7. Noble, *Ancient Ruins*, 31–35; 77–82; Olmstead's comments cited in Superintendent's Monthly Report, September 13, 1945, Research Center, Mesa Verde National Park, Colorado; see also Duane A. Smith, *Mesa Verde National Park: Shadows of the Centuries* (Lawrence, 1988), 149–50.

8. Alfred W. Yazzie, *Navajo Oral Tradition*, vol. 2 (Rough Rock, AZ, 1984), 29–31; Walker and Bufkin, *Historical Atlas of Arizona*, 3–5.

9. *Between Sacred Mountains: Stories and Lessons from the Land*, n.a. (Chinle, AZ, 1984), 2–4; Yazzie, *Oral Tradition*, 29–31.

10. Garcés quote cited in Stephen J. Pyne, *Dutton's Point: An Intellectual History of the Grand Canyon* (Grand Canyon, AZ, 1982), 6; Walker and Bufkin, *Historical Atlas of Arizona*, 13; on the Domíguez–Escalante expedition see Walter Briggs, *Without Noise of Arms: The 1776 Domínguez-Escalante Search for a Route from Santa Fe to Monterey* (Flagstaff, 1976).

11. Pyne, *Dutton's Point*, 4–7; John Kessell, *Kiva, Cross, and Crown: The Pecos*

Indians and New Mexico, 1540–1840 (1979; reprint, Albuquerque, 1987), 18–19; David E. Miller, *The Route of the Domínquez–Escalante Expedition, 1776–77* (Durango, 1976), 46–49, 177–82; Briggs, *Without Noise of Arms.*

12. James H. Simpson, *Journal of a Military Reconnaissance from Santa Fe, New Mexico to the Navajo Country Made with the Troops under Command of Brevet Lieutenant Colonel John M. Washington, Chief of the Ninth Military Department and Governor of New Mexico, 1850,* 31st Cong., 1st sess., Senate Exec. Doc. 64, 55–168; for the best overall account of the military reconnaissance of the American Southwest, see William H. Goetzmann, *Army Exploration in the American West, 1803–1863* (New Haven, 1959); see also David J. Weber, *Richard Kern: Expeditionary Artist in the Far Southwest, 1848–1853* (Albuquerque, 1985).

13. Captain Lorenzo Sitgreaves, *Report of An Expedition Down the Zuni and Colorado Rivers,* 1853, 32nd Cong., 2d sess., Senate Exec. Doc. 59, 244–45; Grant Foreman, *A Pathfinder in the Southwest: The Itinerary of Lt. A. W. Whipple during His Explorations for a Railway Route from Ft. Smith to Los Angeles in the Years, 1853–1854* (1941; reprint, Norman, 1968), 30–31; Ives quote cited in Lieutenant John C. Ives, *Report Upon the Colorado River of the West,* 1858, 36th Cong., 1st sess., Senate Exec. Doc. 90, 45; Capt. Beale's comments cited in Platt Cline, *They Came to the Mountain: The Story of Flagstaff's Beginnings* (Flagstaff, 1976), 33–37.

14. Goetzmann, *Army Explorations,* 377–94; Captain John N. Macomb, *Report of the Exploring Expeditions from Santa Fe, New Mexico to the Junction of the Grand and Green Rivers of the Great Colorado of the West in 1859* (Washington, D.C., 1876), 53–55, 77–79.

15. Macomb, *Report,* 88–94.

16. Ibid., 54–55

17. Leonard J. Arrington, *Great Basin Kingdom: Economic History of the Latter-day Saints, 1830–1900* (1958; reprint, Lincoln, 1966), 84–85; Tanner, *The Far Country,* 90–91; Charles S. Peterson, "San Juan: A Hundred Years of Cattle, Sheep, and Dry Farms," in Allen Kent Powell, eds., *San Juan County, Utah: People, Resources, and History* (Salt Lake City, 1983), 171–203; Cline, *They Came to the Mountain,* 106–12; Donald Paul Shock, "The History of Flagstaff" (Master's thesis, Arizona State University, 1950), 30–34; Charles S. Peterson, *Take Up Your Mission: Mormon Colonizing Along the Little Colorado River, 1870–1900* (Tucson, 1973), 24–27.

18. Duane A. Smith, *Rocky Mountain Boom Town: A History of Durango* (Albuquerque, 1980), 6–7; Paul M. O'Rourke, *Frontier in Transition: A History of Southwestern Colorado* (Denver, 1980), 59–67; Garrick A. Bailey and Roberta G. Bailey, *Historic Navajo Occupation of the Northern Chaco Plateau* (Tulsa, 1982), 70–79; Williams, *New Mexico in Maps,* 102.

19. Quotes on Flagstaff cited in Cline, *They Came to the Mountain,* 252; *Farmington Times Hustler,* June 7, 1906; Smith, *Rocky Mountain Boom Town,* 26–28.

20. Gary L. Shumway, "Uranium Mining on the Colorado Plateau," in Powell, *San Juan County, Utah,* 265–82; Holger Albethsen, Jr. and Frank E. McGinley, *Summary History of Domestic Uranium Procurement under U.S. Atomic Energy Com-*

mission Contracts: Final Report (U.S. Department of Energy (DOE), Grand Junction Regional Office, 1982), A10–11; Howard W. Balsley interview with Nancy J. Taniguchi, May 7, 1979, transcript, Moab Public Library, Moab, Utah; William L. Chenoweth, "Early Vanadium–Uranium Mining in Monument Valley, Apache, and Navajo Counties, Arizona, and San Juan County, Utah," (DOE, Grand Junction Regional Office, 1984), 2–7.

21. A. L. Kroeger, "A Report on That Portion of the Durango, Colorado, Coal Field Comprising the La Plata River Watershed," Fort Lewis College, Center for Southwest Studies, Durango, n.d., 1–10; Smith, *Rocky Mountain Boom Town*, 78–79; Eleanor Davenport MacDonald and John Brown Arrington, *The San Juan Basin: My Kingdom Was a County* (Denver, 1970), 173–91.

22. John Franklin Palmer, "Mormon Settlements in the San Juan Basin of Colorado and New Mexico" (Master's thesis, Brigham Young University, 1967), 74; Emory C. Arnold and Thomas A. Dugan, "Hogback Discovery in San Juan County Was New Mexico's First Oiler in 1922," *Western Oil Reporter* (August 1971): 17–18; *Farmington Times Hustler*, April 27, 1923; Marvin L. Matheny, "A History of the Petroleum Industry in the Four Corners Area" (El Paso Natural Gas Company, Farmington), 19; Gary Bilodeau, "A Look at the Good Old Days in the San Juan Basin," *The Pipeliner* 40 (April 1977): 24–27.

23. Frank C. Lockwood, *The Life of Edward E. Ayer* (Chicago, 1929), 95–114; Cline, *They Came to the Mountain*, 193; on the Riordan family's rebuilding of the AL&T sawmill, see Timothy Riordan to Denis Riordan, July 17, 1887; and Timothy Riordan to M. Garland, March 30, 1888, Letters 1887–88, Arizona Timber and Lumber Company Records, Special Collections Library, Northern Arizona University, Flagstaff; see also Robert L. Matheny, "The History of Lumbering in Arizona Before World War II" (Ph.D. diss., University of Arizona, 1975), 56–111, 144–55.

24. Earl Pomeroy, Jr., *The Pacific Slope: A History of California, Oregon, Washington, Idaho, Utah, & Nevada* (New York, 1965); see also Pomeroy, "Toward a Reorientation of Western History: Continuity and Environment," *Mississippi Valley Historical Review* 41 (1955): 579–600; followers of Pomeroy's thesis of an imitative urban West include Lawrence Larsen, *The Urban West at the End of the Frontier* (Lawrence, 1978).

25. Gerald D. Nash, *The American West Transformed: The Impact of the Second World War* (Bloomington, 1985).

CHAPTER ONE

1. President Truman's message, August 6, 1945, in *Public Papers of Harry S. Truman 1945* (Washington, D.C., 1952), 196–200; on the development of the atomic bomb, see Richard G. Hewlett and Oscar E. Anderson, Jr., *The New World 1939–1947: A History of the United States Atomic Energy Commission* (University Park, 1962); Stephane Groueff, *Manhattan Project: The Untold Story of the Making*

of the Atomic Bomb (Boston, 1967); Ferenc Morton Szasz, *The Day the Sun Rose Twice: The Story of the Trinity Site Nuclear Explosion, July 16, 1945* (Albuquerque, 1984); Henry DeWolf Smyth, *Atomic Energy for Military Purposes: The Official Report on the Development of the Atomic Bomb under the Auspices of the United States Government, 1940–1945* (Princeton, 1947).

2. Martin V. Melosi, *Coping with Abundance: Energy and Environment in Industrial America* (Philadelphia, 1985), 199–273; Gerald D. Nash, *The American West Transformed: The Impact of the Second World War* (Bloomington, 1985).

3. President Truman's State of the Union message, entitled "From War to Peace—The Year of Decision," in *Public Papers of President Harry S. Truman, 1946*, 38–87.

4. Nash, *The American West Transformed*, 17–36; see also Gerald D. Nash, *The American West in the Twentieth Century: A Short History of an Urban Oasis* (1973; reprint, Albuquerque, 1977), 191–212; Leonard J. Arrington, *The Changing Economic Structure of the Mountain West, 1850–1950* (Logan, 1963) 9–21; *Report and Audit of Reconstruction Finance Corporation and Affiliated Corporations as of June 30, 1945: Defense Plant Corporation*, 80th Cong., 1st sess., H. Doc. 474, 1945.

5. President Truman's address to Congress, October 3, 1945, *Congressional Record*, 79th Cong., 1st sess., 9322–23; Hewlett and Anderson, *The New World*, 423–27; Harry S. Truman, *Memoirs* (New York, 1955), vol. 1, *The Year of Decisions*, 530–33.

6. Hewlett and Anderson, *The New World*, 408–18, 428–55; Leslie R. Groves, *Now It Can Be Told: The Story of the Manhattan Project* (London, 1963), 389–93; U.S. Congress, House, Committee on Military Affairs, *Atomic Energy; Hearings on H.R. 4280*, 79th Cong., 1st sess., October 9–18, 1945, 4–10, 13, 29, 35–39, 51–52, 70.

7. Hewlett and Anderson, *The New World*, 455–81; Groves, *Now It Can Be Told*, 389–400; Truman outlined the full details of the agreement in his news conference, November 15, 1945, *Public Papers of President Harry S. Truman, 1945*, 472–75.

8. Hewlett and Anderson, *The New World*, 431–39; U.S. Congress, Senate, Committee on Military Affairs, *Hearings on Science Legislation*, 79th Cong., 1st sess., October 8–March 5, 1945, 10, 203–4, 308–9; *Hearings on H.R. 4080*, 71–89, 100–116, 126–29; Alice Kimball Smith, *A Peril and A Hope: The Scientists' Movement in America, 1945–1947* (1965; reprint, Cambridge, 1971) 40–63; *New York Times*, October 16, 1945.

9. Hewlett and Anderson, *The New World*, 435–45; *New York Times*, October 31, 1945.

10. Hewlett and Anderson, *The New World*, 435–36, 504–30; for a full text of the McMahon bill, see U.S. Congress, Senate, Special Committee on Atomic Energy, *Hearings on S. 1717, A Bill for the Development and Control of Atomic Energy*, 79th Cong., 1st sess., January 22–23, 1946, 1–9; *New York Times*, August 1, 1946; *Congressional Record*, 79th Cong., 1st sess., 8362–63, 9400–02.

11. Early reports on the potential for uranium mining in southeast Utah and southwest Colorado include Robert K. Kirkpatrick, "Field Survey of Monticello (Dry Valley) District, Green River Desert Area, Utah-Colorado: Union Mines Development Corporation," AEC Report, Regional Area Office, Grand Junction, Colorado, 1944; C. W. Livingston, "Report on the West Paradox District, Dolores Plateau Area, Colorado-Utah: Union Mines Development Corporation," AEC Report, Grand Junction, 1946; Benjamin N. Weber, "Geology and Ore Resources of the Uranium-Vanadium Depositional Province of the Colorado Plateau Region: United Mines Development Corporation Final Report," AEC Report, Grand Junction, 1947; *The Journals of David E. Lilienthal* (New York, 1964), vol. 2, *The Atomic Energy Years, 1945–1950*, 128–48.

12. Leonard J. Arrington and Anthony T. Cluff, *Federally Financed Industrial Plants Constructed in Utah During World War II* (Logan, 1969); Nash, *The American West in the Twentieth Century*, 200–206; Gary Lee Shumway, "A History of the Uranium Industry on the Colorado Plateau" (Ph.D. diss., University of Southern California, 1970), 99–118; "Uranium Exploration on the Colorado Plateau," AEC Report, Grand Junction, 1951, 12–19; milling activity in southwest Colorado during World War II summarized in *Durango Herald-Democrat*, June 17, 1948.

13. Weber, "Geology and Ore Resources of the Colorado Plateau Region," 14–19; William L. Chenoweth, "Historical Review of Uranium-Vanadium Production in the Eastern Carrizo Mountains, San Juan County, New Mexico, and Apache County, Arizona," New Mexico Bureau of Mines and Mineral Resources Report, Santa Fe, New Mexico, 1984, 11–12; William L. Chenoweth, "Uranium Deposits of the Canyonlands Area," *Four Corners Geological Society Guidebook* 4 (1975): 253; on the significance of uranium ore imported from the Belgian Congo and Canada, see Groves, *Now It Can Be Told*, 33–37; Lilienthal, *Journals*, vol. 2, 175–76, 437–38.

14. AEC circular, April 11, 1948, published in U.S. Atomic Energy Commission, *Atomic Energy Development, 1947–1948* (Washington, D.C., 1948), 160–63; Shumway, "History of Uranium Industry," 176–78; R. E. Cohenour, "History of Uranium Development of Colorado Plateau Ores with Notes on Uranium Production in Utah," *Guidebook to the Geology of Utah* 20 (1967): 17–18; Neilsen B. O'Rear, "Summary and Chronology of The Domestic Uranium Program," Department of Energy Report, DOE, Division of Raw Materials, Grand Junction, Colorado, 1966, 1–8; William L. Chenoweth, "Historical Review of Uranium-Vanadium Production in the Eastern Carrizo Mountains," 2–14; *Moab Times Independent*, May 13, June 3, 1948.

15. O'Rear, "Summary Domestic Uranium Program," 13–17; Albrethsen and McGinley, "History of Domestic Uranium Procurement," 8–10, Appendices B-3–B-5; Duane A. Smith *Rocky Mountain Boom Town: A History of Durango* (Albuquerque, 1980), 153–71; *Durango Herald Democrat*, May 23, June 17, and July 25, 1948; Dr. Leo W. Lloyd interview with Duane A. Smith, November 8, 1976, Fort Lewis College Library, Durango, Colorado.

16. Eleanor Davenport MacDonald, *I Remember Old MacDonald's Farmington* (Santa Fe, 1975); Garrick A. Bailey and Roberta G. Bailey, *Historic Navajo Occupation of the Northern Chaco Plateau* (Tulsa, 1982); *Farmington Times Hustler*, February 21, June 20, 1947; July 23, 1948; *Albuquerque Tribune*, December 17, 1948; Wayne Dallas interview with Tom Dugan, April 10, 1981, Farmington Public Library, Farmington, New Mexico.

17. Platt Cline, *They Came to the Mountain: The Story of Flagstaff's Beginnings* (Flagstaff, 1976); Robert L. Matheny, "Lumbering in the White Mountains of Arizona," *Arizona and the West* 18 (Autumn 1976): 237–56; *Coconino Sun*, August 17, 1945; *Arizona Daily Sun*, January 17, 1947; March 19, 1948.

18. Raymond W. Taylor and Samuel W. Taylor, *Uranium Fever or No Talk Under $1 Million* (New York, 1970), 84–100; *Denver Post*, December 16, 1948; Lilienthal, *Journals*, vol. 2, 438–40; AEC, *Atomic Energy Development, 1947–48*, 1–8; the figure 54,000 tons is paltry when compared to the 4,500,000 tons mined a decade later; the AEC also spent $105 million in 1954 for uranium. See O'Rear, "Summary Domestic Uranium Program," 3–4.

19. Taylor, *Uranium Fever*, 84; Shumway, "A History of the Uranium Industry," 176–78; Atomic Energy Commission Circulars #1, #2, and #3 in AEC, *Atomic Energy Development*, 160–63; *Moab Times Independent*, July 28, 1949; *Rocky Mountain News*, July 29, 1949, *Durango Herald Democrat*, July 18, 1949; *Grand Junction Sentinel*, July 17, 1949.

20. Earl Pomeroy, *The Pacific Slope: A History of California, Oregon, Washington, Idaho, Utah and Nevada* (Seattle, 1965), 293–332; Nash, *The American West Transformed*, 1985; Leonard J. Arrington, *The Changing Economic Structure of the Mountain West*; Morris E. Garnsey, *America's New Frontier: The Mountain West* (New York, 1950); Carl Abbott, *The New Urban America: Growth and Politics in Sunbelt Cities* (Chapel Hill, 1981); Roger W. Lotchin, "The Metropolitan-Military Complex in Comparative Perspective: San Francisco, Los Angeles, and San Diego," in Gerald D. Nash, ed., *The Urban West* (Manhattan, 1979), 19–30.

21. L. C. Gardner, Arthur Schlesinger, Jr., and Hans Morganthau, *The Origins of the Cold War* (Waltham, Ma., 1970); Elmo Richardson, *Dams, Parks and Politics: Resource Development and Preservation in the Truman-Eisenhower Era* (Lexington, 1973), 37–40; Truman's message to Congress in *The Public Papers of President Harry S. Truman*, 728–29; Shumway, "A History of the Uranium Industry," 6–10, 11–13.

22. Frank Magan, *The Pipeliners: The Story of El Paso Natural Gas* (El Paso, 1977) 236–39; Taylor and Taylor, *Uranium Fever*, 250–53; Robert Stapp, "Can They Strike It Rich?", *Rocky Mountain Empire Magazine* 12 (August 21, 1949), 2; R. Maurice Tripp, "The Great American Sport—1955 Version," *Oil and Gas Journal* (April 1955), 160–68; *Durango Herald News*, Annual Booster Edition, May 12, 1953, April 25, 1954; Albrethsen and McGinley, "History of Domestic Uranium Procurement," B-3; "Atomic Energy Commission Report, 1959" in Stephen L. R. McNichols Papers, Colorado State Archives and Public Records, Denver, Box 27129, File 18 (hereafter cited SLRM).

23. Albrethesen and McGinley, "History of Domestic Uranium Procurement," B-3; O'Rear, "The Domestic Uranium Program," 4–8; *Moab Times Independent*, February 26, 1953; Taylor and Taylor, *Uranium Fever*, 250–53.

24. *Moab Times Independent*, January 3, 31, 1952; June 11, 1953; Ezra C. Knowlton, *History of Highway Development in Utah* (Salt Lake City, 1966); for a complete breakdown of AEC expenditures on the Access Roads Program for the years 1952–1958, see "Summary U.S. Atomic Energy Commission Access Road Program," DOE Report, Raw Materials Division, Grand Junction, 1960.

25. "Uranium Exploration on the Colorado Plateau," AEC Report, Regional Area Office, Grand Junction, 1951, 19–22; Duane A. Smith, *Rocky Mountain Boom Town*, 160–61; *Durango Herald Democrat*, June 17, July 25, 1948; *Grand Junction Sentinel*, March 16, 1949; Walter K. Gutman, "Vanadium Corporation: Rich Stake in Uranium Bolsters Its Profits," *Barron's Magazine* 23 (September 1954); 15–16; Chenoweth, "Uranium-Vanadium Production in the Eastern Carrizo Mountains," 13–15.

26. *Rocky Mountain News*, June 4, 1951; L. J. Crampton, et al., *The Economic Potential of Western Colorado: Report to the Colorado Conservation Board* (Boulder, 1953), in MG Papers, Box 5, File 22 ; *Durango Herald News*, September 14, 1953; Annual Booster Edition, April 25, 1954; *New York Herald Tribune*, August 16, 1954.

27. Howard Lamar, eminent Yale University historian, witnessed the Moab boom firsthand (Lamar conversation with Art Gomez, January 1985, New Haven) quotes as cited in *Moab Times Independent*, January 14, September 30, 1954; Elroy Nelson, "The Impact of Uranium on the Economy of the State and the Southeastern Utah Area," *Guidebook to the Geology of Utah* (1957), 102–3.

28. Marion Stocking, "Charlie Steen—Prospector," *Four Corners Geological Society Guidebook* 3 (1975): 51–54; *Denver Post*, April 23, 1954; Chenoweth, "Uranium Deposits of the Canyonlands Area," 256; Raye C. Ringholz, *Uranium Frenzy: Boom and Bust on the Colorado Plateau* (New York, 1989), 28–32; on the significance of the Mi Vida Mine discovery, see U.S. Congress, Senate, Subcommittee of the Committee on Interior and Insular Affairs, *Hearings on Stockpile and Accessibility of Strategic and Critical Materials to the United States in Time of War*, 83rd Cong., 1st and 2d sess., 59–93; *Moab Times Independent*, April 16, 1953; February 11, November 11, 1954.

29. *Moab Times Independent*, April 16, August 27, December 17, 1953; November 11, 1954; *Stockpile Hearings*, 63–66; R. E. Cohenour, "History of Uranium and Development of Colorado Plateau Ores with Notes on Uranium Production in Utah," *Guidebook to the Geology of Utah* (1967), 19–22; production statistics for 1954–1968 for the Uranium Reduction Company showed 6.3 million tons processed, compared to 1.6 million tons for the Vanadium Corporation of America (see Albrethsen and McGinley, "Summary History," B-4).

30. Jesse C. Johnson, "Summary Report Domestic Uranium Procurement Pro-

gram," Raw Materials Division, Grand Junction, 1954, 12–15; *Moab Times Independent*, December 30, 1954; Albrethsen and McGinley, "Summary History," B-3.

31. Rodman Wilson Paul, *Mining Frontiers of the Far West 1848–1880* (Albuquerque, 1974); Gene M. Gressley, *Bankers and Cattlemen* (Lincoln, 1971); Bernard De Voto, "The West: A Plundered Province," *Harper's Magazine* 169 (August 1934), 355–64. Nash, *The Twentieth Century West*, 136–212.

CHAPTER TWO

1. De Voto's essay, "The West Against Itself," in reality a rejoinder to an earlier publication entitled, "The West: A Plundered Province" (1934), appeared in *Harper's Magazine* 194 (January 1947): 1–13; for an interpretation of De Voto's application to postwar development, see Art Gómez, "The New Natural Resources Colonialism: The Small City in the West, 1945–1970," in Duane A. Smith, ed., *Natural Resources in Colorado and Wyoming* (Manhattan: Sunflower Press, 1982), 51–59.

2. Gerald D. Nash, *The American West Transformed: The Impact of the Second World War* (Bloomington, 1985), especially 17–36; Nash, *The American West in the Twentieth-Century* , 213–15; other interpretations of postwar western development include Garnsey, *America's New Frontier*; Arrington, *The Economic Structure of the Mountain West*, 22–27; and Neil Morgan, *Westward Tilt: The American West Today* (New York, 1963).

3. Melosi, *Coping With Abundance*, 254–55; Nash, *The West Transformed*, 62–63; Carey McWilliams introduction in Ray B. West, ed., *Rocky Mountain Cities* (New York, 1949), 7–28.

4. Marvin L. Matheny, "A History of the Petroleum Industry in the Four Corners Area," *Four Corners Geological Society* 8 (1978): 19; Thomas A. Dugan, "The San Juan Basin: Episodes and Aspirations," *New Mexico Geological Society Guidebook* 4 (1977): 85–86; Emery Arnold interview with Tom Dugan, January 14, 1981, transcript, Farmington Historical Museum, Farmington, New Mexico; Frank Magan, *The Pipeliners: The Story of El Paso Natural Gas* (El Paso, 1977), 79–82; *Reports of the Federal Trade Commission on Natural Gas, and Natural Gas Pipelines in the U.S.A.* (Washington, D.C., 1940), 85–89; quote cited in Gerald D. Nash, *United States Oil Policy, 1890–1964* (Pittsburgh, 1968), 209–10; Arthur M. Johnson, *Petroleum Pipelines and Public Policy, 1906–1959* (Cambridge, 1967), 353.

5. F. B. Dow, "The Role of Petroleum Pipelines in the War," *Annals of the American Academy of Political and Social Science* 230 (November 1943): 93–100; *Report on the Audit of the Reconstruction Finance Corporation*, 378–91; Nash, *United States Oil Policy*, 162–63; Johnson, *Petroleum Pipelines*, 328–29.

6. Johnson, *Petroleum Pipelines*, 330–31; Ickes to L. M. Glasco, June 3, 1944, in "Before the Petroleum Administrator for War, Application of Pacific War Emergency Pipelines, Inc., A Compendium," (Washington, D.C., 1944), 552–54; *Fuel for the Fighting Fronts via "Big Inch" and "Little Inch"* (New York, 1944), 4–8.

7. Johnson, *Petroleum Pipelines*, 330–31; *Durango Herald Democrat*, December 5, 1948, March 6, 1949; *Farmington Times Hustler*, July 4, 1947, July 16, 1948; Dugan, "The San Juan Basin," 86–87; Magan, *The Pipeliners*, 42–86; C. W. Merchison, president, Delhi Corporation, to Federal Power Commission, August 1, 1949, CTH Papers, Box 143, File 18.

8. Merchison to FPC, August 1, 1949, CTH Papers, Box 143, File 18; the years 1945–49 have been termed the most significant period of discovery in the Four Corners' petroleum history. The development of four of the region's best producing gas fields during this time ranked the Durango–Farmington area as one of the "largest continuous producers in the nation." See, Matheny, "Petroleum Industry," 19; "Among These Basins: A New Chapter in American Oil is Being Written," *Oil and Gas Journal* (October 1953): 158, 196; for production increases of natural gas in New Mexico by counties during the period mentioned, see *New Mexico Oil and Gas Production Industry: New Mexico the Energy State* (Santa Fe, 1962); *Denver Post*, October 22, 1948.

9. "Notice of Application before the Federal Power Commission in the Matter of El Paso Natural Gas Company, San Juan Pipeline Company, and Pacific Gas & Electric Company," July 15, 1948, CTH Papers, Box 143, File 18; FPC to Senator Carl Hayden, March 21, 1949, CTH Papers, ibid.

10. *Farmington Times Hustler*, June 3, 1949; Frank C. Barnes, "Developments in the San Juan Basin," *Oil and Gas Journal* (June 1949): 60–67; Vicente T. Ximenes, "The Economic Significance of the Natural Gas Industry in New Mexico" (Master's thesis, University of New Mexico, 1953), 10; *Albuquerque Tribune*, December 17, 1948; *Farmington Times Hustler*, June 20, 1947, July 23, 1948.

11. Ximenes, "Natural Gas Industry," 20–22; Dugan, "The San Juan Basin," 87; *Farmington Times Hustler*, December 17, 1948; *Farmington Daily Times*, August 1, 1949; *San Juan Valley Sun*, December 14, 1950; *Albuquerque Tribune*, February 14, 1951.

12. Statistics noted on the consumption of natural gas from 1935 to 1975 are cited in M. Elizabeth Sanders, *The Regulation of Natural Gas: Policy and Politics, 1938–1978* (Philadelphia, 1981), 58–67; Secretary of the Interior Oscar Chapman to Senator Carl Hayden, August 1, 1951, CTH Papers, Box 430, File 7; Governor Mechem's speech as cited in *Albuquerque Journal*, January 2, 1951.

13. Emery Arnold interview with Tom Dugan; Ximenes, "Natural Gas Industry," 10–12; *Albuquerque Tribune*, December 31, 1952; building permits increased in Farmington from $891,622 in 1950 to $2,473,544 in 1955. The city's population, meanwhile, rose from 3,572 in 1950 to 12,500, according to a special federal census published in 1955, "Fabulous Farmington, New Mexico: The Energy Capital of the West," Farmington Chamber of Commerce, 1961, 2.

14. *Durango Herald News*, February 3, 1953, First Annual Booster Edition, May 12, 1953; for a brief summary on the significance of the Pacific Northwest Pipeline as it applied to the resource needs of those states, see Ralph Wickburg, President, Idaho Public Utilities Commission, to Senator Warren G. Magnuson, December

8, 1966, CTH Papers, Box 320, File 165; Smith, *Rocky Mountain Boom Town*, 163; on the rivalry between El Paso Natural Gas and the Pacific Northwest Pipeline Corporation to utilize Four Corners reserves to supply the urban West, see "El Paso to Boost Gas Flow Westward," *Oil and Gas Journal* (May 1955): 83–84.

15. Matheny, "Petroleum Industry," 17–18, 21; Norman S. Morrissey, "Eight Paradox Strikes Is a Perfect '56 Score in Prospect?" *Oil and Gas Journal* (October 1956): 149.

16. C. B. Wilson to Carl Hayden, March 6, 1951; V. P. Richards to Hayden, May 30, 1951; Freeman Shultz, President, Saginaw & Manistee Lumber Company to Hayden, July 6, 1951; H. L. Hutchison, Mayor of Flagstaff to Hayden, March 31, 1951, CTH Papers, Box 430, File 7; on U.S. District Court ruling, see Magan, *The Pipeliners*, 162–66; D. M. Lyons to Senator Hayden, July 6, 1951; John Babbitt to Hayden, July 6, 1951, CTH Papers, Box 430, File 7; *Coconino Sun*, March 10, April 28, July 7, 1951.

17. *Resource Atlas of Coconino County, Arizona* (Flagstaff, 1981), 41, 55; Thomas Clifford Moses, "An Institutional and Economic Analysis of the Arizona Timber Industry" (Ph.D. diss., University of Arizona, 1981), 17–19.

18. For a good general synthesis on federal policy and the lumber industry after World War II, see William G. Robbins, *American Forestry: A History of National, State, and Private Cooperation* (Lincoln, 1985), 170–204; Minutes, Central Wooden Box Association Meeting, October 25, 1945, in SML Records, Box 7, Letters 1945; on the growth of West Coast agribusiness during the postwar period, see Nash, *The Twentieth Century West*, 236–37; National Wooden Box Association, Pacific Division report, December 18, 1945, SML Records, Box 7, Letters 1945, G. T. Gerlinger to Jack Bedford, July 25, 1945; ibid.

19. Platt Cline, *They Came to the Mountain*; Frank C. Lockwood, *The Life of Edward E. Ayer* (Chicago, 1929); Kenneth J. LaBoone, "The Arizona Lumber and Timber Company, 1881–1981" (Master's thesis, University of Northern Arizona, 1981); James McNary, *This Is My Life* (Albuquerque, 1956); Moses, "Arizona Timber Industry," 48.

20. McNary, *This Is My Life*, 181–82; "The Northern Arizona Statistical Abstract," Bureau of Business and Economic Research, Northern Arizona University, 1984, 5; *Coconino Sun*, January 10, 1947.

21. Veteran's Emergency Housing Program Order 1, March 26, 1946, in SML Records, Box 8, Letters 1946; F. H. Brundage to Sawmill Operators in Douglas Fir, Pine, and Redwood Areas, August 17, 1946, ibid.; Moses, "Arizona Timber Industry," 46.

22. A Civilian Production Administration press release issued in December 1946 reported that the supply of lumber did not yet equal active current demands; a memorandum published May 1949 noted that lumber supplies had overtaken market demands (SML Records, Box 8, Letters 1946, Box 11, Letters 1949); *Forests and National Prosperity: A Reappraisal of the Forest Situation in the United States* (Washington, D.C., 1948), 43–44; Raymond Price, U.S. Forest Service to Sag-

inaw and Manistee Lumber Co., March 1, 1949, SML Records, Box 11, Letters 1949.

23. M. E. Kuhn to Otto Lindh, Regional Forester, June 2, 1949, SML Records, Box 11, Letters 1949; *Forests and National Prosperity*, 60; *Flagstaff Federal Sustained Yield Unit: Periodic Reanalysis* (Albuquerque, 1970); Moses, "Arizona Timber Industry," 44-45.

24. Robert L. Matheny, "The History of Lumbering in Arizona before World War II" (Ph.D. diss., University of Arizona, 1975), 360-62; McNary, *This Is My Life*, 220-22. In 1965 there were twenty-five active sawmills in northern Arizona owned by twenty different operators; ten years later that number had been reduced to fourteen, nine of which were owned by four firms producing 96.3 percent of state's lumber. See *Arizona Landmarks*, vol. I (Phoenix, 1971), 49; *Coconino Sun*, January 17, 1947, March 19, 1948, November 11, 1953; "Southwest Forest Industries: A Fully Integrated Forest Products Company," *Builder Architect Contractor Engineer* 39 (August 1977): 6-7.

CHAPTER THREE

1. *Durango Herald News*, May 12, 1953, June 18, 1954, October 18, 1956; Duane A. Smith, *Rocky Mountain Boom Town: A History of Durango* (Albuquerque, 1980), 160-70; Roger Joseph Lauen, "Community Change" (Ph.D. diss., University of Colorado, 1973), 100-07.

2. Historian Arthur Schlesinger, Sr. was first to coin the term "urban imperialism" in a seminal 1940 essay. According to Schlesinger, competitive activity between America's leading cities to establish regional dominance as trade and transportation centers influenced national growth soon after independence. See Arthur M. Schlesinger, Sr., "The City in American History," *Mississippi Valley Historical Review* 27 (June 1940): 43-66.

3. Larsen, *The Urban West*, 121-24; on interregional colonialism, see Gene M. Gressley, *Bankers and Cattlemen: Politics, Investors, Operators from 1870 to 1900* (1966; reprint, Lincoln, 1971); Gerald D. Nash, *The American West in the Twentieth Century: A Short History of an Urban Oasis* (Albuquerque, 1977), chaps. 1-2; on the significance of energy resource development and the growth of the modern West, see Lynton R. Hayes, *Energy, Economic Growth, and Regionalism in the West* (Albuquerque, 1983).

4. These earnings estimates were probably exaggerated since *Barron's* based its figures on an average ore value of $40 per ton. The AEC never paid higher than $12 per ton for processed uranium during the entire procurement program. Walter K. Gutman, "Vanadium Corporation: Rich Stake in Uranium Bolsters Its Profits," *Barron's* (September 1954); 15-16; *Durango Herald News*, Second Annual Booster Edition, Spring, 1954; Holger Albrethsen, Jr., and Frank E. McGinley, *Summary History of Domestic Uranium Procurement under U.S. Atomic Energy Commission Contracts: Final Report* (U.S. Department of Energy, Grand Junction Re-

gional Office, 1982), A10–A14; Robert B. Scarborough, "Radioactive Occurrences and Uranium Production in Arizona: Final Report," (DOE, Grand Junction Regional Office, 1981), 279.

5. Smith, *Rocky Mountain Boom Town*, 169–71; Lauen, "Community Change," 105; Ralph G. Ringgenberg, "An Economic Study of the Durango Trading Area" (Boulder, University of Colorado, Department of Economics, 1965), 25–30; Lester Gardenswartz interview with Duane Smith, January 14, 1977, transcript, Center for Southwest Studies, Fort Lewis College, Durango; *Durango Herald News*, March 22, 1954.

6. U.S., Congress, Senate, Subcommittee on Minerals, Materials, and Fuels Economics, *Stockpile and Accessibility of Strategic and Critical Materials to the United States in Time of War. Hearings before a subcommittee of the Senate Committee on Interior and Insular Affairs on S. Res. 143*, 83d Cong., 1st and 2d sess., 1954, 54–90; Albrethsen and McGinley, *Summary History*, A86–A88; *Moab Times Independent*, December 10, 1953.

7. U.S. Bureau of the Census, *Census of the Population, 1960, Vol. I, part 46* (Washington, D.C., 1961) 46:19; *Moab Times Independent*, January 14, September 30, November 11, 1954; "Profile of a City," *Denver Post*, February 26, 1956; Harold W. Balsley interview with Nancy J. Taniguchi, May 7, 1979, transcript, Moab Public Library.

8. Urban historian Blaine Brownell coined the term "urban ethos" in his examination of urban expansion in the South during the 1920s. Brownell argued that small cities seek to become replicas of the larger metropolitan models through boosterism. See Blaine Brownell, *The Urban Ethos in the South, 1920–1930* (Baton Rouge, 1975), 43–50. Whereas Brownell analyzes the small city in the South, Ronald Davis makes similar comparisons about the hinterland West. Davis stresses the importance of maintaining an economic link to the larger metropolitan areas as crucial to the development of small western towns. See Ronald L. F. Davis, "Western Urban Development: A Critical Analysis," in Jerome O. Steffen, ed., *The American West: New Perspectives, New Dimensions* (Norman, 1979), 178–84.

9. Moab's total output of 38.5 million pounds of concentrate from 1957 to 1971 significantly outdistanced the Durango total of 7.85 million pounds from 1950 to 1963. See Albrethsen and McGinley, *Summary History*, A10–A12, A86–A88; *Durango Herald News*, January 3, February 27, April 6, 1958; *Moab Times Independent*, May 14, 1959, February 3, 1960; *Wall Street Journal*, August 1, 1962.

10. AEC Circulars, October 28, 1957, November 24, 1958 (DOE, Grand Junction Regional Office); President Eisenhower's speech in *The Public Papers of President Dwight D. Eisenhower, 1953*, 813–22; John A. McCone, Chairman AEC, to Senator Clinton P. Anderson, Chairman JCAE, March 24, 1959, in CPA Papers, Box 817, Project Plowshare File; Martin V. Melosi, *Coping with Abundance: Energy and Environment in Industrial America* (Philadelphia, 1985), 223–30.

11. Raymond W. Taylor and Samuel W. Taylor, *Uranium Fever or No Talk Under $1 Million* (New York, 1970), 103, 250–52; Governor McNichols statement

in "Summary: Western Governors Conference," February 26, 1958, in SLRM Papers, Box 27135, AEC File; *Rocky Mountain News*, June 18, 1957.

12. *Durango Herald News*, February 7, 1958; Arthur A. Crevi, Sacramento Gulch Mining Company to Governor McNichols, May 19, 1959, SLRM Papers, Box 27129, File 18; "Preliminary Report on the Colorado Uranium Industry" (Grand Junction, Uranium Institute of America, 1959), 1–7, in SLRM Papers, Box 27135, AEC File; Joint Committee on Atomic Energy, *Problems of the Uranium Mining and Milling Industry*, 85th Cong., 2d sess., 1958, 27–41.

13. John A. McCone, Chairman AEC, to Senator Clinton P. Anderson, Chairman JCAE, March 24, 1959, CPA Papers, Box 817, Project Plowshare File; Lee Hydeman, Report to Senator Anderson, undated, ibid.; *Denver Post*, May 14, 1956, September 8, 1958.

14. Alice Kimball Smith, *A Peril and A Hope: The Scientists' Movement in America, 1945–47* (1965; reprint, Cambridge, 1971), 29–41, 63–71, 180–81, 272–75; S. David Aviel, *The Politics of Nuclear Power* (Washington, D.C., 1982), 15–25; Steven L. Del Soto, *Science, Politics, and Controversy* (Boulder, 1969); Melosi, *Coping with Abundance*, 226–27; George T. Mazuzan, "Conflict of Interest: Promoting and Regulating the Infant Nuclear Power Industry, 1954–1956," *The Historian* 46 (November 1981): 3–10.

15. Jesse C. Johnson, "The Outlook for Uranium," in WA Papers, Box 106, AEC File; Taylor and Taylor, *Uranium Fever*, 281–311; Albrethsen and McGinley, *Summary History*, A10, A86; *Durango Herald News*, December 9, 1958, November 20, 1962; *Denver Post*, March 11, 1959.

16. *Durango Herald News*, April 25, 1954, October 18, 30, 1956, April 8, 1959, November 14, 1961. A 45 percent increase in the number of gas wells completed in 1955 plus a major oil discovery in the Bisti area near Farmington made New Mexico the most rapidly developing petroleum reserve in the nation; see Frank C. Barnes, "The San Juan Basin Fulfills Its Promise," *Oil and Gas Journal* (February 6, 1956): 154–55; *Farmington Times Hustler*, June 18, 1954; January 6, March 21, October 8, 1955; July 25, 1956; Smith, *Rocky Mountain Boom Town*, 172.

17. Smith, *Rocky Mountain Boom Town*, 169–78; *Durango Herald News*, August 29, 1956, February 10, 1962, April 20, 1964; Arthur Atwood Ballantine, interview with David McComb, June 10, 1974, transcript, Center for Southwest Studies, Fort Lewis College, Durango; Dr. Leo W. Lloyd, interview with Duane Smith, November 8, 1976, ibid.; Eugene T. Halaas, "The Impact of Fort Lewis College on the Durango Economy" (Denver: University of Denver, Department of Economics, 1965), 1–4; Duane A. Smith, *Sacred Trust: The Birth and Development of Fort Lewis College* (Boulder: University of Colorado Press, 1991, 83–98.

18. *Durango Herald News*, August 29, 1956, April 15, 1960, *Census of the Population, 1960 Census, Vol. I, part 26* (Washington, D.C., 1961) 26:13; Eugene T. Halaas, "Economic Feasibility of the Bank of Durango," University of Denver, Department of Economics, 1965, 12–15; Ralph G. Ringgenberg, "The Durango Trading Area," 40–41. On the traditional economy of the Durango area in the

1950s, see L. J. Crampton et al., "The Economic Potential of Western Colorado" (University of Colorado, Bureau of Business Research, 1953), sec. VI–VII, in MG Papers, Box 5, File 22.

19. Smith, *Rocky Mountain Boom Town*, 167–77; Crampton, "The Economic Potential of Western Colorado," sec. VII; Earl Pomeroy, *In Search of the Golden West: The Tourist in Western America* (New York, 1957), 60–61; Duane A. Smith, *Mesa Verde National Park: Shadows of the Centuries* (Lawrence, 1988), 78–147; Vacationland Colorado Style," *Durango Herald News*, April 17, 1960.

20. *Census of Population, 1960 Vol. I, Part 33*, 33:10. Economist Ralph Ringgenberg makes statistical comparisons between Durango and other cities in the Four Corners in "The Durango Trading Area," 65–68; Eleanor Davanport MacDonald, *I Remember Old MacDonald's Farmington* (Santa Fe, 1975); *Preliminary Report, Economy, Population, Land Use, Major Thoroughfares and Central Business District: Farmington, New Mexico* (St. Louis, 1967), 30–33; Paul Harvey's comments in Valda Cooper, "The Fabulous Four Corners," *New Mexico Magazine* 48 (March 1965): 13.

21. "El Paso to Boost Gas Flow Westward," *Oil and Gas Journal* (May 23, 1955): 83–84; Frank Magan, *The Pipeliners: The Story of El Paso Natural Gas* (El Paso, 1977), 195–97, 290–92; New Mexico Oil and Gas Conservation Commission position in JB Papers, Federal Power Commission File.

22. Tom Bolack interview with Tom Dugan, January 14, 1981, transcript, Farmington Public Library; Joe Reilly, "Pacific Northwest: Pipeline Rarity," *Oil and Gas Journal* (October 1955): 118–21; excerpts of the transcript from the November 30, 1953, hearings in JB Papers, Federal Power Commission file; *Albuquerque Tribune*, June 18, 1954; *Farmington Daily Times*, April 22, 1955.

23. *Albuquerque Tribune*, July 23, 1949; Senators Clinton P. Anderson and Ernest W. McFarland to Hubert E. Howard, Chairman, Department of Defense Munitions Board, September 11, 1950, CPA Papers, Box 66, File 678; Anderson to Martin Yates, February 9, 1951, ibid.; Governor John Burroughs to Attorney General William P. Rogers, November 23, 1959, in JB Papers, Oil Conservation Committee File; Governor Edwin L. Mechem to Joseph H. Gutride, April 6, 1961, in ELM Papers, New Mexico Petroleum Industry File; R. R. Spurrier to Clinton P. Anderson, August 12, 1949, CPA Papers, Box 31, File 678; Spurrier's comments cited in *Albuquerque Tribune*, June 18, 1954.

24. Bolack to Anderson, July 16, 1949, CPA Papers, Box 31, File 678; Bolack interview with Dugan, January 14, 1981.

25. John Franklin Palmer, "Mormon Settlements in the San Juan Basin of Colorado and New Mexico" (Master's thesis, Brigham Young University, 1967), 107–08; Wayne Dallas interview with Tom Dugan, April 10, 1981, transcript, Farmington Public Library; "Oil and Gas Summary of New Mexico," 1960, JB Papers, Oil and Gas Conservation File; *Albuquerque Tribune*, July 25, 1956; *Farmington Daily Times*, April 18, 1958, January 17, 1960; "Fabulous Farmington, New Mexico: The Energy Capital of the West" (Farmington: Chamber of Commerce, 1961); *Preliminary Report: Farmington*, 33.

26. Melosi, *Coping with Abundance*, 259–66; Gerald D. Nash, *United States Oil Policy, 1890–1964: Business and Government in Twentieth-Century America* (Pittsburgh, 1958), 201–08, 233–37; for the position of one of New Mexico's congressional spokesmen on federal oil policy, see Congressman Joseph M. Montoya's speech before the New Mexico Oil and Gas Conservation Commission, September 11, 1962, JMM Papers, Box 36, File 19.

27. Melosi, *Coping with Abundance*, 259–66.; Gerald D. Nash, *United States Oil Policy*, 201–8, 233–37; Henry D. Ralph, "FPC Backs Phillips," *Oil and Gas Journal* (September 1953): 67; "A Healthy Domestic Oil and Gas Industry," October 2, 1964, JMM Papers, Box 36, File 100; Emery Arnold interview with Tom Dugan, January 14, 1981, transcript, Farmington Public Library.

28. "Project Gasbuggy: Possible Use of a Nuclear Explosive for Stimulation of a Natural Gas Reservoir" (El Paso Natural Gas Company, U.S. Atomic Energy Commission, and U.S. Bureau of Mines, 1965), 1–9, in JMM Papers, Box 159, File 26; "Gasbuggy: What's the Next Step?" *World Oil* (1965), reprint in JMM Papers, Box 127, File 5; Brig. Gen. Alfred D. Starbird to Governor Steve McNichols, January 8, 1959, SLRM Papers, Box 27129, File 18; Marling J. Ankeny, Director, U.S. Bureau of Mines to L. A. Sunkel, Atlantic Richfield Company, December 3, 1959, CPA Papers, Box 817, Project Plowshare File; John D. Kelly to Congressman Joseph Montoya, June 14, 1965, JMM Papers, Box 159, File 26; *Farmington Daily Times*, January 21, 1962.

29. *Albuquerque Journal*, November 18, 1959. The San Juan Basin produced an annual average of 12 million barrels of oil and 295 million cubic feet of natural gas in 1959 and 1960; see "Oil and Gas Summary of New Mexico, 1960," 18–20; *Census of Population, 1960, Vol. I, Part 33*, 33:10.

30. *Census of the Population, 1960, Vol. I, Part 4*, 4:7; "Arizona: Sun, Room, and Low Taxes," *Fortune Magazine* 32 (March 1958): 14–25; R. J. Gunderson, "Population Changes in Northern Arizona Counties," *Northern Arizona Economic Review* 9 (September 1982): 1–3; *Coconino Sun*, March 3, August 25, 1956, March 30, October 5, 1957; "Industrial Facts and Figures of Flagstaff, Arizona" (Flagstaff: Chamber of Commerce, 1957), 6–12; Thomas J. McCleneghan, "Flagstaff, Arizona: Planning for the Future" (Arizona State University, Bureau of Business and Public Research, Tempe, 1959), 1–8.

31. *Coconino Sun*, June 5, 1954, March 10, 1956; "Twenty-five years of Progressive and Diversified Growth," *Builder Architect/Contractor Engineer* 39 (August 1977): 12–13; Thomas Clifford Moses, "An Institutional and Economic Analysis of the Arizona Timber Industry" (Ph.D. diss., University of Arizona, 1981), 44–45, 70–71; L. D. Porter interview with Art Gómez, June 28, 1983, transcript, Arizona State University, Hayden Library, Department of Oral History, Tempe.

32. For comparisons of the lumber industry throughout the American Southwest, see John A. Guthrie and George R. Armstrong, *Western Forest Industry: An Economic Outlook* (Baltimore, 1961); Moses, "Arizona Timber Industry," 48, 72;

Pauline Hanson, "Southwest Forest Industries," *Arizona Highways* 39 (July 1964): 37–40 *Arizona Daily Star*, May 31, 1959; Porter interview with Gómez.

33. "Timber Management Plan, San Juan National Forest" (U.S. Department of Agriculture, Forest Service, Region 2, Durango, 1961), 38–39; "Annual Review: San Juan National Forest" (U.S. Department of Agriculture, Forest Service, Region 2, Durango, 1959), 2–3; Gordon S. Chappell, *Logging Along the Denver & Rio Grande* (Golden, CO, 1971), 173–74; Charlie Graves and Grace Shober interview with Art Gómez, December 9, 1986, in author's possession.

34. Moses, "Arizona Timber Industry," 76–79; *Arizona Daily Star*, October 15, 1959, January 8, 1960, September 29, 1961.

35. Henson, "Southwest Forest Industries," 40–47; *Arizona Daily Star*, February 3, 1965; "Fort Apache Indian Reservation Forest Management Plan" (U.S. Department of the Interior, Bureau of Indian Affairs, Branch of Forestry, Whiteriver, Arizona, 1985), IV, 23–26; *Southwest Forest Industries, Annual Report, 1964–65* (Phoenix, 1965), 1–4.

CHAPTER FOUR

1. Vocalist Nat "King" Cole was the first to record Troup's composition for the Decca Record Corporation of New York in 1946.

2. Among the most notable works on Route 66 are: Susan Croce Kelly and Quinta Scott, *Route 66: The Highway and its People* (Norman, 1988); Michael Wallis, *Route 66: The Mother Road* (New York, 1990); and Arthur Krim, "Mapping Route 66: A Cultural Geography," in *Roadside America: The Automobile in Design and Culture* (Ames, IA, n.d.), 198–208.

3. Quote cited in Richard O. Davies, *The Age of Asphalt: The Automobile, the Freeway, and the Condition of Metropolitan America*, ed. Harold M. Hyman (New York, 1975), 10; Mark H. Rose, *Interstate: Express Highway Politics, 1941–1956* (Lawrence, 1979).

4. Jack D. Rittenhouse, *A Guidebook to Highway 66* (1946; reprint, Albuquerque, 1988), 7, 67, 102–03; E. B. Bail, "New Mexico–U.S. 66: Albuquerque's Golden Road Born of a Farewell Gesture," in Arthur Thomas Hannett, *Sagebrush Lawyer* (New York, 1964), 277–88.

5. Rose, *Interstate*, 15–18; Wilfred Owen, "Transportation and Public Promotional Policy," in *Transportation and National Policy* (Washington, D.C., 1942), 267–76; [Wilfred Owen], "The Future Development of Highway Transportation," in *Proceedings of the Twenty-first Annual Meeting*, ed. Roy W. Crum (Washington, D.C., 1942), 16–20.

6. Rose, *Interstate*, 19–20; Thomas H. MacDonald, "The New Federal Highway Program," *American Planning and Civic Annual* 23 (1941): 51–53; Davies, *The Age of Asphalt*, 12–13; U.S. Congress, Senate, Committee on Public Works, *Federal Aid for Highways*, 80th Cong., 2d sess., 1948, 158–69; Charles A. Rasor before the Grand Junction Geological Society, September 24, 1954, in AEC Records, File 42: Access Roads Program.

7. Portions of the Highway Act of 1944 cited in *Federal Aid for Highways Hearings, 1948*, 327–28; Senator Hayden's comments cited in U.S. *Congressional Record*, 78th Cong., 2d sess., 1944, Vol. 90, 7676; Rasor to Grand Junction Geological Society, September 24, 1954, AEC Records, File 42.

8. Rose, *Interstate*, 35–39; *Federal Aid For Highways Hearings, 1948*, 158–60.

9. Charles Rasor address before the Uranium Ore Producers Association, May 12, 1956, AEC Records, File 42; U.S., Code Congressional Service, *Legislative History, Federal Aid Highway Act of 1950*, 81st Cong., 2d sess., 1952, 3660–71; John R. Nichols, Commissioner, Bureau of Indian Affairs, to Senator Clinton P. Anderson, April 18, 1950, CPA Papers.

10. "Summary U.S. Atomic Energy Commission Access Roads Program," AEC Records, File 42.

11. Jay M. Haymond, "San Juan County Roads: Arteries to Natural Resources and Survival," in Allan Kent Powell, *San Juan County, Utah: People, Resources, and History* (Salt Lake City, 1983), 233–37; *New York Times*, June 7, 1953; "National Parks and Monuments in Utah Fact Sheet," in SLU Papers, Box 93, File 2; *Moab Times Independent*, June 18, December 31, 1953.

12. *Denver Post*, January 14, 1949; "Summary Access Roads Program," AEC Records, File 42.

13. *Farmington, New Mexico: Welcome Guide* (San Diego, 1983), 4–5; "Two Years of Highway Progress, 1951–52" (Santa Fe, New Mexico Highway Department, 1953), 1–16; Eleanor MacDonald interview with Jimmy Miller, December 30, 1980, transcript, Farmington Public Library; R. W. Cook, Acting General Manager, AEC, to Senator Anderson, February 15, 1957, CPA Papers, Box 65, File 611.

14. "Durango Chamber of Commerce, Minutes, 1946–1950," Fort Lewis College Library, Durango; "History of the Navajo Trail Project," in SLRM Papers, Box 27115, File 26; *Durango Herald Democrat*, January 15, 1950.

15. John R. Nichols to Senator Clinton P. Anderson, October 18, April 18, 1949, CPA Papers, Box 65, File 611; Charles A. Rasor address before the Grand Junction Geological Society, September 24, 1954, AEC Records, File 42; J. Maughs Brown, Chief, BIA Branch of Roads, in U.S. Congress, Senate, Committee on Public Works, *Federal Aid Highway Act of 1952*, 82d Cong., 2d sess., 1952, 224–25.

16. Details of the road improvement program stipulated in the Navajo–Hopi Rehabilitation Act of 1950 in *Hearings Federal Highway Act of 1952*, 217–26; George B. Roberts, Farmington Chamber of Commerce, to Senator Anderson, March 25, 1950, CPA Papers, Box 65, File 611; *Durango Herald Democrat*, September 14, 1949; *Coconino Sun*, June 6, 1953.

17. George B. Roberts to Senator Anderson, September 30, December 12, 1949, February 20, March 25, 1950; George Lusk, Manager Albuquerque Chamber of Commerce, to Anderson, October 4, 1949; John R. Nichols, Commissioner, BIA, to Anderson, April 18, 1950; William Zimmerman, Jr., Assistant Commissioner, BIA, to Anderson, January 26, 1950, CPA Papers, Box 65, File 611.

18. Calvin Black, "San Juan County Roads and Resources," Powell, *San Juan County, Utah* 247–48; *Durango Herald Democrat*, September 14, 1949; *Coconino Sun*, April 1, August 11, 1953.

19. Davies, *The Age of Asphalt*, 6–7; Dwight D. Eisenhower, *The White House Years: Mandate for Change, 1953–1956* (New York, 1963), 548–49; Eisenhower remarks cited in Daniel Yergin, *The Prize: The Epic Quest for Oil, Money, & Power* (New York: Simon & Schuster, 1992), 207–08; Chavez's speech of February 14, 1952, in *Hearings, Federal Highway Act of 1952*, 15–16.

20. Rose, *Interstate*, 70–72; Ezra C. Knowlton, *History of Highway Development in Utah* (Salt Lake City, 1966), 520–24; U.S. Congress, Senate, Committee on Public Works, *Federal Highway Act of 1954*, 83d Cong., 2d sess., 1954.

21. *A 10-Year National Highway Program: Report to the President [Clay Committee Report]*, President's Advisory Committee on Highway Development, 84th Cong., 1st sess., H. Doc. 93; President Eisenhower's message in *Public Papers of Dwight D. Eisenhower, 1955* (Washington, D.C., 1959), 275–80.

22. Rose, *Interstate*, 69–94; Davies, *The Age of Asphalt*, 20–23; George Fallon and Hale Boggs, *Appropriations for Construction of Highways*, 84th Cong., 1st sess., H. Report 1336, 1955.

23. "New Mexico's Interstate Highways," (New Mexico State Highway Department, Santa Fe, 1958); "The Interstate System in New Mexico: A Progress Report, 1956–1961," (New Mexico State Highway Department, Santa Fe, 1962); *Arizona Daily Star*, May 16, 1955; *Arizona Daily Sun*, January 4, 1960; Governor Johnson's comments in Johnson to Jack Monler, April 24, 1956 SLRM Papers, Box 66089, File 14; Good Roads Association Monthly Newsletter, July 18, 1956, ibid.; Knowlton, *Highway Development in Utah*, 575–80.

24. Black, "San Juan County Roads and Resources," 248–50; Knowlton, *Highway Development in Utah*, 578–79; *Moab Times Independent*, April 23, 1959; L. F. Wylie, "Roads to Scenic Treasures," *Reclamation Era* (1958): 57–59; R. W. Cook to Senator Anderson, February 15, 1957, CPA Papers, Box 65, File 611; Beers statement entitled, "The Key to Durango's Future," in "Durango Chamber of Commerce Minutes, 1956–1958."

25. Rasor address before Uranium Ore Producers Association, May 12, 1956, AEC Records, File 42; Jesse Johnson's comments cited in U.S. Congress, Senate, *Hearings, Federal Highway Act of 1954*, 284–85; Johnson to Grand Junction Chamber of Commerce, February 27, 1957, AEC Records, File 42.

26. *Coconino Sun*, August 31, 1957; Hatfield Chilson, Assistant Secretary of the Interior to Governor McNichols, November 27, 1956, SLRM Papers, Box 27115, File 26; Chairman Paul Jones to Senator Anderson, July 22, 1957, CPA Papers, Box 65, File 611.

27. Anderson to Fields, January 30, 1957; Cook to Anderson, February 15, 1957; Anderson to Emmons, January 30, 1957; Emmons to Anderson, February 21, 1957; CPA Papers, Box 65, File 611.

28. *Albuquerque Journal*, April 4, 1958; *Arizona Daily Star*, December 8, 1960;

Richard Allan Baker, *Conservation Politics: The Senate Career of Clinton P. Anderson* (Albuquerque, 1985), 1–36, 130; Carl Hayden to Paul Jones, August 19, 1957, CPA Papers, Box 65, File 611. Other western politicians who held important positions in Congress at this time were Senator Dennis Chavez of New Mexico, chairman of the Public Works Committee; Senators Gordon Allott of Colorado and Frank Moss of Utah, both on the Interior Committee; and Colorado Congressman Wayne Aspinall, chairman of the House Interior Committee.

29. R. J. Tier, "Secondary Roads," in *Proceedings of the 1959 Highway Engineering Conference* (New Mexico Highway Department, 1959), 10–12; Udall to Burke Peterson, Engineering Corporation of America, April 7, 1959, SLU Papers, Box 51, File 1; Udall's speech, December 9, 1959, in SLU Papers, Box 51, File 10; *Arizona Daily Sun*, January 18, 1962; *Denver Post*, September 17, 1962.

30. Secretary Udall's dedication speech in SLU Papers, Box 104, File 2; *Denver Post*, September 17, 1962; *Arizona Republic*, September 2, 1962.

31. Stewart L. Udall, *The Quiet Crisis* (New York, 1963).

CHAPTER FIVE

1. Secretary Udall's quote as cited in George B. Hartzog, Jr., "The Golden Circle Concept," in SLU Papers, Box 156, File 4; Weldon F. Heald, "Bold Plan to Save the Canyonlands," *Desert Magazine* (April 1962): 17–21; *Salt Lake Tribune*, August 24, 1961.

2. Congressman Taylor's comments cited in Alfred Runte, *National Parks: The American Experience* (Lincoln, 1979), 93–105; Roderick Nash, *Wilderness and the American Mind* (New Haven, 1967); Frederick Jackson Turner's seminal essay in *The Turner Thesis: Concerning the Role of the Frontier in American History*, ed. and intro. George Rogers Taylor (Lexington, MA, 1972), 3–18; Conrad L. Wirth, *Parks, Politics, and the People* (Norman, 1980), 17–18.

3. Earl Pomeroy, *In Search of the Golden West: The Tourist in Western America* (New York, 1957), 3–29; on the "See America First" campaign, consult Runte, *National Parks*, 70–71, 82–105; John A. Jakle, *The Tourist: Travel in Twentieth-Century North America* (Lincoln, 1985), 53–83; Congressman Farris's comments cited in U.S. Department of the Interior, National Park Service, *Proceedings of the National Parks Conference*, January 2–6, 1917 (Washington, D.C., 1917), 20.

4. Runte, *National Parks*, 74; Wirth, *Parks, Politics, and the People*, 42–43; John Ise, *Our National Park Policy: A Critical History* (Baltimore, 1961), 163–65; Ricardo Torres-Reyes, *Mesa Verde National Park: An Administrative History, 1906–1970* (Washington, D.C., 1970), 1–3, 373; Duane A. Smith, *Mesa Verde National Park: Shadows of the Centuries* (Lawrence, 1988), 55–66.

5. Ise, *Our National Park Policy*, 230–33; Pomeroy, *In Search of the Golden West*, 129–30; Congressman Hayden's comments cited in *Congressional Record*, March 11, 1924, 68th Cong., 1st sess., 105274.

6. "Fact Sheet: National Parks and Monuments in Utah," in SLU Papers, Box

156, File 1; Hartzog, "The Golden Circle Concept," 34; John Wesley Powell, *Report on the Lands of the Arid Region of the United States: With a More Detailed Account of the Lands of Utah*, ed. Wallace Stegner (Cambridge, 1962), 119; Faun McKonkie Tanner, *The Far Country: A Regional History of Moab and La Sal, Utah* (Salt Lake City, 1976), 280–89.

7. Edgar L. Hewett, *The Chaco Canyon and Its Monuments* (Albuquerque, 1936), 167–70; John M. Corbett, *Aztec Ruins National Monument* (Washington, D.C., 1963), 61–65; Robert H. Lister and Florence C. Lister, *Aztec Ruins National Monument: Administrative History of an Archeological Preserve* (U.S. Department of the Interior, National Park Service, Southwest Region, 1990).

8. Pomeroy, *In Search of the Golden West*, 64–65; Donald Paul Shock, "The History of Flagstaff" (Master's thesis, Arizona State University, 1950), 134–36; Superintendent Nusbaum's quote cited in Smith, *Shadows of the Centuries: Mesa Verde National Park*, 121; Torres-Reyes, *Mesa Verde National Park*, 363; "1923 Annual Report," National Park Service, Mesa Verde National Park (herafter cited as MVNP), 71; "1928 Annual Report," MVNP, 25; Tanner, *The Far Country*, 288.

9. Wirth, *Parks, Politics, and the People*, 143–50, 226–27; Ise, *Our National Park Policy*, 447–49; Torres-Reyes, *Mesa Verde National Park*, 363; Smith, *Shadows of the Centuries*, 135–48.

10. Ise, *Our National Park Policy*, 455–58; Bernard DeVoto, "Let's Close the National Parks," *Harper's Magazine* 207 (October 1953): 49–52; Charles Stevenson, "The Shocking Truth About Our National Parks," *Reader's Digest* (January 1955): 45–50.

11. Demaray succeeded Newton Drury as Director of the National Park Service for a brief eight-month period until his retirement in December 1951. See United States Department of the Interior, National Park Service, *Historic Listing of National Park Service Officials* (Washington: GPO, 1991), 9; Wirth, *Parks, Politics, and the People*, 5–64.

12. Ise, *Our National Park Policy*, 547–48; Wirth, *Parks, Politics, and the People*, 75–90; President Eisenhower's State of the Union Address in *The Public Papers of the President, Dwight D. Eisenhower, 1956* (Washington, D.C., 1958), 1–27.

13. Wirth, *Parks, Politics, and the People*, 237–84; Conrad Wirth's comments in U.S. Congress, Senate, *Hearings before the Senate Committee on Appropriations*, 84th Cong., 2d sess., H.R. 9390, 1956, 272–73; for budgetary breakdowns, ibid., 292–307.

14. "Outdoor Recreation for America" (Outdoor Recreation Resources Review Commission Report, Washington, D.C., 1962), 25–34; Jakle, *The Tourist*, 185–98; "Report of Winter and Summer Visitors in Arizona" (Tucson: University of Arizona, Bureau of Business Research, 1956); *Public Use of the National Parks: A Statistical Report* (Washington, D.C., 1964), 41–45; Stephen C. Jett, *Tourism in the Navajo Country: Resources and Planning* (Window Rock, AZ, 1966), 33–35.

15. *Coconino Sun*, December 24, 1955, December 1, May 19, 1956; *Arizona Daily Star*, September 22, 1957, January 1, 1961; Jakle, *The Tourist*, 185–89; Jett, *Tourism*

in the Navajo Country, 34–42; Smith, *Shadows of the Centuries*, 149–66; "The Arizona Snow Bowl Makes Flagstaff a Winter Sports Capital" in *Profile of a Beautiful City* (Flagstaff Chamber of Co,mmerce, 1971), 12; 1960 Olympics Committee of Flagstaff to Avery Brundage, January 31, 1956, in CTH Papers, Box 184, File 30.

16. Jett, *Tourism in the Navajo Country*, 9–10, 41–47; before and after World War II, Hollywood directors popularized Monument Valley and other scenic Four Corners areas on film. Some of the more notable westerns produced between 1930 and 1960 included *Stagecoach* (1933), *Ticket to Tomahawk* (1949), *Across the Wide Missouri* (1950), *The Naked Spur* (1952), *Night Passage* (1956), and *How the West Was Won* (1962). On the creation of national monuments on the reservation see Hal K. Rothman, *Navajo National Monument: A Place and Its People* (U.S. Department of the Interior, National Park Service, Southwest Region, Santa Fe, 1991); statistical breakdown of visitors in *Public Use of the National Parks*, 40–45; *Development Possibilities Along the Navajo Highway No. 1* (Albuquerque, n.d.), 1–8.

17. *Durango Herald News*, May 12, 1953; Smith, *Rocky Mountain Boom Town*, 176–77; Lawrence R. Borne, *Dude Ranching: A Complete History* (Albuquerque, 1983), 6–7, 179–99; Pomeroy, *In Search of the Golden West*, 168–70; Jerome Rodnitsky, "Recapturing the West: The Dude Ranch in American Life," *Arizona and the West* 10 (Summer 1968): 111–26.

18. Smith, *Rocky Mountain Boom Town*, 166–67; *Durango Herald Democrat*, January 10, 1950; Ralph G. Ringgenberg, "An Economic Study of the Durango Trading Area" (University of Colorado, Department of Economics, Boulder, 1965), 50; *Durango Herald News*, September 5, 1961, August 6, August 20, 1963, April 12, 1964; Doris B. Osterwald, *Cinders & Smoke: A Mile by Mile Guide for the Durango to Silverton Narrow Gauge Trip* (Lakewood, CO, 1965), 120–28; Torres-Reyes, *Mesa Verde National Park*, 383–84; Chester Thomas, Staff Meeting Report, December 15, 1959, Mesa Verde National Park, Correspondence File; *Durango Herald News*, August 1, 1959; National Park Service, *National Park Use*, 40–45; Smith, *Shadows of the Centuries*, 174–75.

19. *Durango Herald News*, August 25, 1960, April 12, 1964; Betty Gail Nash quotation as cited in Charlie Langdon, *Durango Ski: People and Seasons at Purgatory* (Durango, 1989), chap. 2; Nick Turner quotation in Smith, *Rocky Mountain Boom Town*, 167; Eugene T. Halaas, "Economic Feasibility Bank of Durango" (University of Denver, Department of Economics, Denver, 1965), 11; Governor John A. Love message to 44th Colorado General Assembly, January 11, 1963, in Arthur M. Wyatt Papers, Fort Lewis College, Center for Southwest Studies, Durango, Box 2, File 1.

20. Governor Burroughs's comments as cited in his speech dated November 17, 1959, in JB Papers, Oil Conservation Committee File; Western Governors' Report of 1958 entitled "The State of the West," a series of essays discussing the economic progress of the various western states, in SLRM Papers, Box 66128, Articles File; *Study of Recreation and Tourism in New Mexico* (Albuquerque, 1960), 1–10.

21. The governor's message to the 26th New Mexico Legislature, January 8, 1963, August 16, 1963, in Governor JMC Papers, Reports to New Mexico Legislature File; "The Climate for Business and Industry in the State of New Mexico" (Southwest Research Institute, San Antonio, 1964), 25–32, in JMC Papers, Department of Development File, 1963–66.

22. On Navajo Dam, see Richard Allan Baker, *Conservation Politics: The Senate Career of Clinton P. Anderson* (Albuquerque, 1985), 75–82, 166–70; Udall's dedication speech in *Albuquerque Journal*, September 16, 1962; park attendance figures in "Annual Report, 1962–63" (New Mexico State Park Recreation Commission, Santa Fe, 1963), 13; Charles Craven to Jack Campbell, January 6, 1963, JMC Papers, All America City File.

23. Secretary Stewart L. Udall to Congressman David S. King, May 4, 1961, Senator Wallace F. Bennett to Udall, June 16, 1961, in SLU Papers, Box 93, File 2.

24. Udall to A. V. Kidder, July 27, 1961, SLU Papers, Box 93, File 2; *Moab Times Independent*, July 6, July 20, 1961; U.S. Congress, Senate, Committee on Interior and Insular Affairs, *Proposed Canyonlands National Park in Utah*, 87th Cong., 2d sess., S. 2387, 1962, 1–5; Baker, *Conservation Politics*, 170–75; Moss to Bennett, July 14, 1961, SLU Papers, Box 156, File 1.

25. *Denver Post*, July 9, 1961; *Moab Times Independent*, August 10, 1961; Governor Clyde to Lowell D. Blanton, August 4, 1961, Udall to Clyde, December 1, 1961, in SLU Papers, Box 156, File 1; *Deseret News*, July 28, 1961.

26. On the issue of Dead Horse State Park, see Senator Wallace F. Bennett's statement in *Proposed Canyonlands National Park in Utah*, 22–48; *Salt Lake Tribune*, May 11, 1963; Senator Moss to Udall, May 19, 1961; R. D. Nielson, State Director, BLM, to Director, BLM, Salt Lake City, July 13, 1961; John M. Sprague, Humble Oil Company, to Udall, June 8, 1961; Udall to Clyde, December 1, 1961; all in SLU Papers, Box 156, File 1.

27. Udall to Clyde, December 1, 1961, Clyde to Udall, December 11, 1961, in SLU Papers, Box 156, File 1; for the recommendation of National Park experts regarding creation of a park, see Lloyd M. Pierson, "The First Canyonlands New Park Studies, 1959 and 1960," in *Canyon Legacy* (Fall 1989): 9–14; summary of Canyonlands proposal in *Proposed Canyonlands National Park in Utah*, 6–9; Udall to Clyde, February 1, 1962, SLU Papers, Box 156, File 1; *Deseret News*, April 9, 1963; *Salt Lake Tribune*, April 10, 1963.

28. U.S. Department of the Interior Press Release, February 2, 1962, in SLU Papers, Box 156, File 1; *New York Times*, February 4, 1962. Kennedy's proposal to promote a "See the United States" campaign in order to increase the role of tourism in the national economy is summarized in his message to Congress on the balance of payments, July 1963, in LBJ Papers, White House Central File (hereafter WHCF), P.L. 88–416.

29. *Proposed Canyonlands National Park in Utah*, 215–16, 271–73, 288–90, 301–03, 306–09; Robert R. Edminister, "An Economic Study of the Proposed Can-

yonlands National Park and Related Recreation Resources" (University of Utah, Bureau of Economic and Business Research, Salt Lake City, 1962), 15–34; Dr. Elroy Nelson's rebuttal to the university study in *Salt Lake Tribune*, April 1, 1962; Paul M. Tilden, "Let's Get Going on the Canyonlands," *National Parks Magazine* 18 (February 1963): 18–23.

30. Baker, *Conservation Politics*, 220–21; Karl S. Landstrom, Director BLM, to Udall, January 3, 1963, SLU Papers, Box 156, File 4; for a summary of the amendments to the Moss bill, see U.S. Congress, Senate, Committee on Interior and Insular Affairs, *Proposed Canyonlands National Park in Utah*, 88th Cong., 1st sess., S. 27, 1963, 1–7; *Salt Lake Tribune*, April 7, 1963.

CHAPTER SIX

1. D. Howe Moffat, address to the Second Annual Rocky Mountain Governors' Conference entitled "Four Corners Economic Development Region," JMM Papers, Archive 386, Box 114.

2. Economic conditions in the Four Corners outlined in Title V of the Public Works and Economic Development Act of 1965, 89th Cong., 1st sess., H.R. 6991; "Four Corners Economic Development Region," 32–33, JMM Papers, Box 114.

3. Political scientist Lynton R. Hayes espouses this same argument. See Lynton R. Hayes, *Energy, Economic Growth, and Regionalism in the West* (Albuquerque, 1980), 54–55.

4. Peter Wiley and Robert Gottlieb, *Empires in the Sun: The Rise of the New American West* (1982; reprint, Tucson, 1985), 132–33, 152–53; JMC Papers, Invitations File; Jack August phone conversation with author, February 14, 1988.

5. Cultural geographers and sociologists have done the best work on geographic determinism and its relationship to regional growth. Some of the more useful works include: Howard W. Odum and Harry Moore, *American Regionalism: A Cultural–Historical Approach to National Integration* (New York, 1938); Wilbur Zelinsky, *The Cultural Geography of the United States* (Englewood Cliffs, 1973); D. W. Meinig, *Imperial Texas: An Interpretive Essay in Cultural Geography* (Austin, 1969); Meinig, "American Wests: Preface to a Geographical Introduction," *Annals of the Association of American Geographers* 62 (June 1972): 159–84. One of the most comprehensive historical overviews of the Four Corners states during the Territorial years is Howard Roberts Lamar, *The Far Southwest, 1846–1912: A Territorial History* (1966; reprint, New York, 1970).

6. Zelinsky, *Cultural Geography*, 129–33; Gastil, *Cultural Regions of the United States* (Seattle, 1975), 243–49.

7. Harvey S. Perloff, with Vera Dodds, *How A Region Grows: Area Development in the U.S. Economy* (Washington, D.C., 1963), 137–140; John Walton Caughey, *The American West: Frontier and Region* (Los Angeles, 1969); "Initial Action Plan," Four Corners Regional Planning Commission (FCRPC), 16–20, DFC Papers, FCRPC file; Moffat, "Four Corners Economic Development Region," JMM Pa-

pers, Box 114; Carl Abbot, "The Metropolitan Region: Western Cities in the New Urban Era," in *The Twentieth Century West: Historical Interpretations*, ed. Gerald D. Nash and Richard W. Etulain, 76–87 (Albuquerque, 1989).

8. David C. Lilienthal, *TVA–Democracy on the March* (New York, 1944); William E. Leuchtenburg, *Franklin D. Roosevelt and the New Deal* (New York, 1963); Tugwell's quote as cited in Martha Derthick, *Between State and Nation: Regional Organizations of the United States* (Washington, D.C., 1974), 19; Gordon R. Clapp, "The Tennessee Valley Authority," in Merill Jensen, ed., *Regionalism in America*, 317–29 (Madison, 1951).

9. Gerald D. Nash, *The Great Depression and World War II: Organizing America, 1933–1945* (New York, 1979), 57–58; Richard Lowitt, *The New Deal and the West* (Bloomington, 1984), 218–21, 228; references made to Bernard De Voto, "The West: A Plundered Province," *Harper's Magazine* 169 (August 1934): 355–64.

10. U.S. Congress, House, Committee on Public Works, *Hearings on Public Works and Economic Development Act of 1965*, 89th Cong., 1st sess., 1965, H.R. 6991; Eugene P. Foley, Assistant Secretary of Commerce for Economic Development, "EDA—A Regional Opportunity," JMM Papers, Box 114; Seymour E. Harris, *Economics of the Kennedy Years and a Look Ahead* (New York, 1964), 17–19; Derthick, *Between State and Nation*, 108–11; the six new regions created in addition to the Four Corners were New England, Ozarks, Upper Great Lakes, Coastal Plains, Old West, and Pacific Northwest.

11. *Proceedings: Four Corners–Farmington Industry Opportunity Program* (Farmington Industrial Development Service, Farmington, 1968), 8–12, DFC Papers, FCRPC file; Senator Montoya's comments in a speech before the Governors' Conference on Industrial and Economic Development, JMM Papers, Box 37, File 42; Governor Rampton's quote, JMM Papers, Box 114, Second Annual Rocky Mountain Governor's Conference; for a summary of Johnson's views on "creative federalism," see *Washington Post*, December 31, 1967; Orren Beaty to Dr. Douglas N. Jones, Assistant Secretary for Regional Economic Coordination, Department of Commerce, December 29, 1967, JAL Papers, Box 66196, Four Corners File.

12. Eldon G. Marr, *Population and Employment in the Four Corners Development Region* (University of New Mexico, Bureau of Business Research, Albuquerque, 1968), 1–18. Statistics issued through the Four Corners Regional Planning Commission in September 1967 showed unemployment in Arizona at 4.2 percent, Colorado at 3.2 percent, New Mexico at 5.0 percent, and Utah at 4.7 percent, ("Initial Action Plan," DFC Papers, FCRPC File). See also Richard Allan Baker, *Conservation Politics: The Senate Career of Clinton P. Anderson* (Albuquerque, 1985), 170–75; *San Juan Investigation: Utah and Colorado* (Salt Lake City, 1969), 7–10, 17–18; Dennis "Pete" Byrd interview with Art Gómez, February 10, 1984.

13. Governor Jack Campbell to Frank Ikard, March 9, 1966, JMM Papers, Box 114, File 10.

14. Statistics on oil production during the peak years in New Mexico are found in "Report to the New Mexico Legislature," October 10, 1966, JMC Papers,

Operation Gasbuggy File; historian Duane A. Smith discusses some details of "Operation Gasbuggy" in *Rocky Mountain Boom Town: A History of Durango* (Albuquerque, 1980), 260–63; *Farmington Daily Times*, December 10, 1967; Tom Dugan interview with Art Gómez, August 1, 1985.

15. *Farmington Daily Times*, January 10, 31, 1967; James E. Reeves, Manager, AEC Operations, Nevada, to Governor David F. Cargo, February 23, 1968, DFC Papers, AEC File: Project Gasbuggy; Martin V. Melosi, *Coping with Abundance: Energy and Environment in Industrial America* (Philadelphia, 1985), 262–66; Tom Dugan interview with Art Gómez; for an outstanding analysis of oil politics on a global scale see Yergin, *The Prize*.

16. Ralph G. Ringgenberg, "An Economic Study of the Durango Trading Area" (University of Colorado, Department of Economics, Boulder, 1965), 50–55; John Ise, *Our National Park Policy: A Critical History* (Baltimore, 1961), 544–46; Alden C. Hayes, "The Wetherill Mesa Project" *Naturalist* 20 (1969): 18–25; "1965 Annual Report," National Park Service, Mesa Verde National Park, 79; George Hertzog, Jr. "Management Considerations," in *Proceedings: Second World Conference on National Parks*, 155–61 (Morges, Switzerland, 1974); *Mesa Verde National Park Master Plan* (Washington, D.C., 1975), 6–10; Duane A. Smith, *Shadows of the Centuries* (Lawrence, 1988), 167–80.

17. Thomas Clifford Moses, "An Institutional and Economic Analysis of the Arizona Timber Industry" (Ph.D. diss., University of Arizona, 1981), 15–17, 50–55, 58–60, 76–80; *Annual Report 1969* (Phoenix: Southwest Industries, 1970), 1–9.

18. Moses, "The Arizona Timber Industry," 76–80; Brewer's quote as cited in *Annual Report 1969*, 8; "History of Southwest Forest Industries," in *1983 Corporate Fact Book*, (Phoenix: Southwest Forest Industries, 1983) 30–32; *Flagstaff Federal Sustained Yield Unit* (Washington, D.C., 1969), 7–12.

19. *Annual Report 1967* (Phoenix: Southwest Forest Industries, 1968), 2; *Annual Report 1968* (Phoenix: Southwest Forest Industries, 1969), 2–6; Moses, "The Arizona Timber Industry," 45–48; *Flagstaff Federal Sustained Yield Unit*, 21–27.

20. "Flagstaff: An Arizona Area Resource Study" (Arizona State Employment Service, Phoenix, 1969), 7–19; "Flagstaff: Arizona Community Prospectus" (Arizona Office of Economic Planning Development, Phoenix, 1974), 2–6.

21. Beaty's appointment as federal cochairman in JMM Papers, Box 38, File 77; "Initial Action Plan," 1–4, DFC Papers, FCRPC File; FCRPC newsletter, September 19, 1967, DFC Papers, FCPRC File; *Santa Fe New Mexican*, March 16, 1969; Governor Love's comments in "Minutes of the Executive Meeting Rocky Mountain States Federation, March 18, 1968," JAL Papers, Box 66969, RMSF File.

22. "Initial Action Plan," 16–21, DFC Papers, FCRPC file; "Four Corners Regional Planning Commission: Establishment and History," *Proceedings: Four Corners–Farmington Industry Opportunity Program* (Farmington: Farmington Industrial Development Service, 1968), 10–14.

23. "Initial Action Plan," 21–25, DFC Papers, FCRPC file; *Four Corners Re-*

gional Planning Commission: Annual Report (Farmington: Four Corners Regional Commission, 1968), 5–8; *Development Possibilities Along the Navajo Highway No. 1* (Albuquerque, n.d.).

24. J. E. Neihart, President, Flagstaff Chamber of Commerce, January 4, 1968; J. Lawrence Walkup, President, Northern Arizona University, Flagstaff, to Governor John Love, January 9, 1968; Tommy Neal, State Representative, Durango, to Orren Beaty, December 14, 1967; Fred V. Kroeger to Governor John Love, October 11, 1967, all in JAL Papers, Box 66196, FCRPC file; Governor David F. Cargo to Mike Valentine, Manager, Durango Chamber of Commerce, October 10, 1967, DFC Papers, FCRPC file; on the selection of Farmington as the FCRPC headquarters, see *Farmington Daily Times*, January 15, 1968.

25. Senator Joseph Montoya's comments in *Albuquerque Journal*, April 18, 1969; *Farmington Daily Times*, April 20, 1969; L. Ralph Mecham's rebuttal, U.S. Congress, Senate, Committee on Public Works, *Hearings on the Evaluation of Economic Development Programs*, October 1, 7, 1969, 91st Cong., 1st sess., 174–80 [hereafter cited as *Evaluation Hearings*]; David Cargo comments as cited in *Grand Junction Daily Sentinel*, October 8, 1969.

26. *Annual Report 1968* (Four Corners Regional Planning Commission, Farmington, 1968), 10–13; *Annual Report 1969* (FCRPC, Farmington, 1969), 5, 13–18; *Annual Report 1970* (FCRPC, Farmington, 1970); "Four Corners Regional Planning Commission: Summary of Expenditures, 1969," JMM Papers, Box 46, file 1; *Evaluation Hearings*, 180–81.

27. *Annual Report 1970* (FCRPC, Farmington, 1970), 14–16; "Summary of Expenditures," JMM Papers, Box 46, file 1; *Santa Fe New Mexican*, April 18, 1969; *Evaluation Hearings*, 182–85; *Albuquerque Journal*, March 8, 1970; State Representative Tommy Neal to Governor David Cargo, April 15, 1970, DFC Papers, FCRPC file.

28. In June 1973 Congress renewed authorization of the Title V commissions for one year. President Nixon signed the bill, although he made clear his belief that support of the Title V commissions should be a state responsibility (Derthick, *Between State and Nation*, 4, n. 6.)

CHAPTER SEVEN

1. Governor Rampton's speech in JMC Papers, Western Governors Conference file, 1–5; for President Johnson's statement on the need to decrease American travel expenditures abroad, see his "Discover America" speech, August 3, 1964, LBJ Papers, File WHCF, P.L. 88-416.

2. Rampton's comments to the governors of the Four Corners are found in JMC Papers, Western Governors Conference File; for similar views on the need for interstate cooperation in tourism development, see Emanuel A. Floor, "Travel and the West: A View of 1975," JMC Papers, Western Governors Conference File.

3. Richard Allan Baker, *Conservation Politics: The Senate Career of Clinton P.*

Anderson (Albuquerque, 1985), 220–21; "Projection of Number of Visits and Tourist Expenditures to the Golden Circle Area: 1961–1987" (University of Utah, Bureau of Business and Economic Research, 1962), 1–33, 98, 153; *San Juan Investigation: Utah and Colorado* (Salt Lake City, 1969), 17–21, 69; *Public Use, Tabulation of Visitors to Areas Administered by the National Park Service* (Washington, D.C., 1961), 74–75.

4. Duane A. Smith, *Mesa Verde National Park: Shadows of the Centuries* (Lawrence, 1988), 167–80; Ricardo Torres-Reyes, *Mesa Verde National Park: An Administrative History, 1906–1970* (Washington, D.C., 1970), 383–84; "Superintendent's 1979 Report," Mesa Verde National Park, 2; Smith, *Shadows of the Centuries*, 183, 194–96.

5. Doris B. Osterwald, *Cinders & Smoke: A Mile by Mile Guide for the Durango to Silverton Narrow Gauge Trip* (Lakewood, CO, 1965), 116–29; Eugene T. Halaas, "Economic Feasibility of the Bank of Durango," (University of Denver, Department of Economics, 1965), 23; *Durango Herald*, May 26, 1970; "Here Is Durango" (Durango Chamber of Commerce Report, 1968), 13–28; special issue on the proposed comprehensive plan entitled "Durango: Shaping An Urban Area" in *Durango Herald*, August 15, 1971.

6. Chet Anderson, "Feasibility Report: Purgatory Winter Sports Area" (U.S. Department of Agriculture, U.S. Forest Service, San Juan Forest, District 2, 1964); *Durango Herald*, January 25, 1965.

7. Charlie Langdon, *Durango Ski: People and Seasons at Purgatory* (Durango: 1989), chap. 2; *Durango Herald*, January 25, 1965.

8. Robert Beers cited in Langdon, *Durango Ski*, chap. 7; Forest Service agreement with Durango Ski Corporation, "Minutes: Durango Chamber of Commerce," February 3, 1965; *Durango Herald*, December 4, 1965; skier statistics for years 1965 to 1985 in "Purgatory Ski Resort: Summary of Skier Visits and Adult Ticket Prices," Purgatory Ski Corporation, 1986; "Minutes: Durango Chamber of Commerce," February 1, 1966; "Purgatory Ski Area," brochure, JAL Papers, Box 66194, Colorado Ski File; *Durango Herald*, December 31, 1965; Mike Elliott, Purgatory Ski Corporation, interview with Art Gómez, June 3, 1987.

9. President Johnson's views on year-round tourism are outlined in his "See the United States" speech of August 3, 1964, LBJ Papers, WHCF, P.L. 88–416; Baker, *Conservation Politics*, 124–25; Vice President Humphrey's statement, February 1, 1966, JMC Papers, Tourist Division File; organizational history of "Ski Colorado Country–U.S.A.," JAL Papers, Box 66194, Ski Organization File; Colorado's bid for the 1976 Winter Olympics, JAL Papers, Box 66195, Olympics File; Calvin Rampton to John Love, December 19, 1967, JAL Papers, Box 66195, Olympics File; "Skiing Colorado Business Survey" (Colorado National Bank, Denver, 1964), 1–5.

10. "Summary of Skier Visits, 1965–1970," Purgatory Ski Corporation, 1986; *Durango Herald*, June 17, 1970; "Minutes: Durango Chamber of Commerce,"

March 25, 1970; Gene M. Gressley, "James G. Blaine, 'Alferd' E. Packer, and Western Particularism," *Historian* 44 (May 1982): 370–71.

11. "Environmental Statement: Coconino National Forest and Arizona Snow Bowl Ski Area Proposal" (U.S. Department of Agriculture, Forest Service, Region 3, Flagstaff, Arizona, 1978), 6–28; Diane M. Notarianna, "The San Francisco Peaks Controversy: Application of the Segmentary-Opposition Model to Intercultural Conflict" (Master's thesis, Northern Arizona University, 1985), 4–12; *Arizona Daily Sun*, October 7, 1971; "Snow Bowl Survey," *Northern Arizona Economic Review* (Winter 1977): 1–4; "Flagstaff: Profile of a Beautiful City" (Flagstaff Chamber of Commerce, 1971), 12; visitor statistics for Purgatory Ski Resort for the same period totaled 520,577 skiers ("Summary of Skier Visits," Purgatory Ski Corporation, 1986); Mike Elliott interview with Art Gómez; Gene M. Gressley, "Regionalism and the Twentieth-Century West," in *The American West: New Perspectives, New Dimensions*, ed. Jerome O. Steffen, 197–234 (Norman, 1979).

12. Stephen C. Jett, *Tourism in the Navajo Country: Resources and Planning* (Window Rock, Az., 1966), 9–12; Ansel Franklin Hall, *General Report on the Rainbow Bridge–Monument Valley Expedition of 1933* (Berkeley, 1934), 1–36; "The Golden Circle Concept," SLU Papers, Box 156, File 4; "National Park Service Visitors: Arizona, 1970–75" (U.S. Department of the Interior, National Park Service, Southwest Regional Office, Santa Fe, 1976), 138; other significant visitor increases in Arizona included Canyon de Chelly National Monument, 146.3 percent, Petrified Forest National Monument, 79 percent, Sunset Crater National Monument, 27.2 percent, Walnut Canyon National Monument, 38.8 percent, and Wupatki National Monument, 26.5 percent (Jett, *Tourism in the Navajo Country*, 36).

13. Total visitations to Arizona parks and monuments from 1970 to 1975 equalled 73.9 million visitors ("NPS Visitors to Arizona," 140); "Arizona Tourism and Travel Industry" (Arizona State University, Bureau of Business and Economic Research, Tempe, 1976), 1–5, 51–61, 101–38, 156–60.

14. *Farmington Daily Times*, June 8, 1969; for a brief history on the political developments concerning the creation of Navajo Dam, see Baker, *Conservation Politics*, 64–75, 166, 230–37; the emergence of the New Mexico ski industry is discussed in Lee D. Miller, "Skiing in New Mexico is Big Business," *New Mexico Magazine* 42 (January 1964): 6–9; Jim Boyer, "Ski Boom," *New Mexico Magazine* 46 (January 1965): 11–15, 39; Governor Campbell's "Inaugural address," January 1, 1965, JMC Papers, Inauguration File; *Preliminary Report, Economy, Population, Land Use, Major Thoroughfares and Central Business District: Farmington, New Mexico* (St. Louis, 1967), 24–26; Senator Montoya's dedication speech entitled "Highway 64: The Golden Avenue," September 7, 1967, JMM Papers, Box 38, File 45.

15. Campbell's report, entitled "New Mexico Moves Forward," October 1, 1966, JMC Papers, New Mexico Legislature File; Robert Brierly to Governor Jack Campbell, July 26, 1966, JMC Papers, Ski Industry File; for former governor

Bolack's comments, see "New Mexico Moves Forward" speech, October 1, 1966, JMC Papers, New Mexico Legislature File; "Welcome to Farmington," Farmington Chamber of Commerce, 1971; "Fabulous Farmington, New Mexico," *Farmington Four Corners Magazine* 1 (September 1976): 3–5.

CHAPTER EIGHT

1. Gerald D. Nash, *The American West Transformed: The Impact of the Second World War* (Bloomington, 1985), 201.

2. On Purgatory's multimillion dollar expansion program and national poster campaign, see *Durango Herald*, November 20, 1983.

3. Former Durango city manager Mike Valentine, telephone interview with Art Gómez, Santa Fe, New Mexico, July 14, 1987.

4. Gressley, "Western Particularism," 370–71; Mike Elliott interview with Art Gómez.

5. *Durango Herald*, July 23, 1985, November 3, 1986; Tom Dugan interview with Art Gómez. It should be noted, however, that at present a mass migration of southern Californians to the interior states of Arizona, New Mexico, Colorado, and Utah has stimulated a significant upward trend in the local economies of the Four Corners' municipalities.

Bibliography

MANUSCRIPTS

Atomic Energy Commission. Papers. Regional Operations Office. Grand Junction, CO.

Anderson, Clinton P. Papers. Manuscript Division, Library of Congress. Washington, D.C.

Arizona Timber and Lumber Company. Papers. University of Northern Arizona Library, Flagstaff, AZ.

Burroughs, John. Papers. New Mexico State Records Center and Archives, Santa Fe, NM.

Campbell, Jack M. Papers. New Mexico State Records Center and Archives, Santa Fe, NM.

Garnsey, Morris E. Papers. University of Colorado Library, Boulder, CO.

Hayden, Carl T. Papers. Arizona State University Library, Phoenix, AZ.

Johnson, Lyndon B. Papers. Lyndon Baines Johnson Presidential Library, Austin, TX.

Love, John A. Papers. Colorado Archives and Public Records, Denver, CO.

McNichols, Stephen L. R. Papers. Colorado Archives and Public Records, Denver, CO.

Mechem, Edwin L. Papers. New Mexico State Records Center and Archives, Santa Fe, NM.

Mesa Verde National Park. Correspondence File. Mesa Verde, CO.

Montoya, Joseph M. Papers. University of New Mexico Library, Albuquerque, NM.

Saginaw and Manistee Lumber Company. Papers. University of Northern Arizona Library, Flagstaff, AZ.

Udall, Stewart L. Papers. University of Arizona Library, Tucson, AZ.

Wyatt, Arthur M. Papers. Fort Lewis College Library, Durango, CO.

UNPUBLISHED MATERIAL

Chenoweth, William L. "Historical Review of Uranium-Vanadium Production in the Eastern Carrizo Mountains, San Juan County, New Mexico, and Apache County Arizona." New Mexico Bureau of Mines and Mineral Resources Report, Santa Fe, 1984.

_____. "Early Vanadium-Uranium Mining in Monument Valley, Apache, and Navajo Counties, Arizona, and San Juan County, Utah." Department of Energy (DOE) Report, Grand Junction, 1984.

Crampton, L. J. "The Economic Potential of Western Colorado." University of Colorado, Bureau of Business Research, 1953.

Edminister, Robert R. "An Economic Study of the Proposed Canyonlands National Park and Related Recreation Resources." University of Utah, Bureau of Business and Economic Research, Salt Lake City, 1962.

Haalas, Eugene T. "The Impact of Fort Lewis College on the Durango Economy." University of Denver, Department of Economics, 1965.

_____. "Economic Feasibility of the Bank of Durango." University of Denver, Department of Economics, 1965.

Johnson, Jesse C. "Summary Report Domestic Uranium Procurement Program." Atomic Energy Commission (AEC) Report, Grand Junction, 1954.

_____. "The Outlook for Uranium." AEC Report, Grand Junction, 1962.

Kirkpatrick, Robert K. "Field Survey of Monticello (Dry Valley) District, Green River Desert Area, Utah-Colorado: Union Mines Development Corporation." AEC Report, Grand Junction, 1944.

Kroeger, A. L. "A Report on That Portion of the Durango, Colorado, Coal Field Comprising the La Plata River Watershed." Fort Lewis College Library, Durango, n.d.

LaBoone, Kenneth J. "The Arizona Lumber and Timber Company, 1881–1981." Master's thesis, Northern Arizona University, 1981.

Lauen, Roger Joseph. "Community Change." Ph.D. dissertation, University of Colorado, 1973.

Livingston, C. W. "Report on the West Paradox District, Dolores Plateau Area, Utah-Colorado: Union Mines Development Corporation." AEC Report, Grand Junction, 1946.

Matheny, Robert L. "The History of Lumbering in Arizona before World War II." Ph.D. dissertation, University of Arizona, 1975.

McCleneghan, Thomas J. "Flagstaff, Arizona: Planning for the Future." Arizona State University, Bureau of Business and Public Research, 1959.

Moses, Thomas Clifford. "An Institutional and Economic Analysis of the Arizona Timber Industry." Ph.D. dissertation, University of Arizona, 1981.

Notarianna, Diane M. "The San Francisco Peaks Controversy: Application of the Segmentary-Opposition Model to an Intercultural Conflict." Master's thesis, Northern Arizona University, 1985.

O'Rear, Neilsen B. "Summary and Chronology of the Domestic Uranium Program." AEC Report, Grand Junction, 1966.

Palmer, John Franklin. "Mormon Settlements in the San Juan Basin of Colorado and New Mexico." Master's thesis, Brigham Young University, 1967.

Ringgenberg, Ralph G. "An Economic Study of the Durango Trading Area." University of Colorado, Department of Economics, 1965.

Scarborough, Robert B. "Radioactive Occurrences and Uranium Production in Arizona: Final Report." AEC Report, Grand Junction, 1981.

Shock, Donald Paul. "The History of Flagstaff." Master's thesis, Arizona State University, 1950.

Shumway, Gary Lee. "A History of the Uranium Industry on the Colorado Plateau." Ph.D. dissertation, University of Southern California, 1970.

"Summary U.S. Atomic Energy Commission Access Roads Program." AEC Report, Grand Junction, 1960.

"Uranium Exploration on the Colorado Plateau." AEC Interim Staff Report, Grand Junction, Colorado, 1951.

Weber, Benjamin N. "Geology and Ore Resources of the Uranium-Vanadium Depositional Province of the Colorado Plateau Region: United Mines Development Corporation Final Report." AEC Report, Grand Junction, 1947.

Ximenes, Vicente T. "The Economic Significance of the Natural Gas Industry in New Mexico." Master's thesis, University of New Mexico, 1953.

GOVERNMENT DOCUMENTS

Albrethsen, Holger Jr., and Frank E. McGinley. *Summary History of Domestic Uranium Procurement Under U.S. Atomic Energy Commission Contracts: Final Report.* U.S. Department of Energy. Grand Junction, Colorado, 1982.

Anderson, Chet. "Feasibility Report: Purgatory Winter Sports Area." U.S. Department of Agriculture, Forest Service, San Juan Forest District 2, 1964.

Before the Petroleum Administrator for War, Application of the Pacific War Emergency Pipelines, Inc., A Compendium. Washington, D.C.: GPO, 1944.

Fallon, George, and Hale Boggs. *Appropriations for Construction of Highways.* 84th Cong., 1st sess., H. Report 1336. Washington, D.C.: GPO, 1955.

Ives, John C. *Report Upon the Colorado River of the West.* 36th Cong., 1st sess., S. Exec. Doc. 90. Washington D.C.: GPO, 1859.

Macomb, John N. *Report of the Exploring Expeditions from Santa Fe, New Mexico to the Junction of the Grand and Green Rivers of the Great Colorado of the West in 1859.* Washington, D.C.: GPO, 1876.

Outdoor Recreation Resources Review Commission. "Outdoor Recreation for
    America." Washington, D.C.: GPO, 1962.

Owen, Wilfred. "Transportation and Public Promotional Policy." In
    Transportation and National Policy. Washington, D.C.: GPO, 1942.

[Owen, Wilfred]. "The Future Development of Highway Transportation."
    Proceed ings of the Twenty-First Annual Meeting. Ed. Roy Crum.
    Washington, D.C.: GPO, 1942.

Simpson, James H. *Journal of a Military Reconnaissance from Santa Fe, New
    Mexico to the Navajo Country Made with the Troops under Command of Brevet
    Lieutenant Colonel John M. Washington, Chief of the Ninth Military
    Department and Governor of New Mexico*. 31st Cong., 1st sess., S. Exec. Doc.
    64. Washington, D.C.: GPO, 1851.

Sitgreaves, Lorenzo. *Report of An Expedition Down the Zuni and Colorado Rivers*.
    32d Cong., 2d sess., S. Exec. Doc. 59. Washington, D.C.: GPO, 1854.

Torres-Reyes, Ricardo. *Mesa Verde National Park: Administrative History,
    1906–1970*. Washington, D.C.: U.S. Department of the Interior, National
    Park Service, 1970.

U.S. Atomic Energy Commission. *Atomic Energy Development, 1947–1948*.
    Washington, D.C.: GPO, 1948.

U.S. Atomic Energy Commission, El Paso Natural Gas Company, and U.S.
    Bureau of Mines "Project Gasbuggy: Possible Use of Nuclear Explosive for
    Stimulation of a Natural Gas Reservoir." Special Report. Grand Junction,
    1965.

U.S. Bureau of Census. *Census of the Population, 1960*. Washington, D.C.: GPO,
    1961.

U.S. Code Congressional Service. *Legislative History, Federal Aid Highway Act of
    1950*. 81st Cong., 2d sess. Washington, D.C.: GPO, 1952.

U.S. Congress. *Congressional Record*. 68th Cong., 1st sess. Washington, D.C.:
    GPO, 1924.

U.S. Congress. *Congressional Record*. 79th Cong., 1st sess. Washington, D.C.:
    GPO, 1945.

U.S. Congress. *Congressional Record*. 78th Cong., 2d sess. Washington, D.C.:
    GPO, 1944.

U.S. Congress. Joint Committee of Atomic Energy. *Problems of the Uranium
    Mining and Milling Industry*. 85th Cong., 2d sess. Washington, D.C.: GPO,
    1958.

U.S. Congress. House. *Report and Audit of the Reconstruction Finance Corporation
    and Affiliated Corporations as of June 30, 1945: Defense Plant Corporation*.
    80th Cong., 1st sess., H. Doc. 474. Washington, D.C.: GPO, 1945.

U.S. Congress. House. Committee on Military Affairs. *Atomic Energy, Hearings
    on H.R. 4280*. 79th Cong., 1st sess. Washington, D.C.: GPO, 1945.

U.S. Congress. House. Committee on Public Works. *Hearings on Public Works and Economic Development Act of 1965.* 89th Cong., 1st sess., H.R. 6991. Washington, D.C.: GPO, 1965.

U.S. Congress. House. *A 10-Year National Highway Program: Report to the President.* 84th Cong., 1st sess., H. Doc. 93. Washington, D.C.: GPO, 1955.

U.S. Congress. Senate. Committee on Public Works. *Hearings on the Evaluation of Economic Development Programs.* 91st Cong., 1st sess. Washington, D.C.: GPO, 1969.

U.S. Congress. Senate. Committee on Military Affairs. *Hearings on Science Legislation.* 79th Cong., 1st sess. Washington, D.C.: GPO, 1945.

U.S. Congress. Senate. Special Committee on Atomic Energy. *Hearings on S. 1717, A Bill for the Development and Control of Atomic Energy.* 79th Cong., 1st sess. Washington, D.C.: GPO, 1946.

U.S. Congress. Senate. Committee on Interior and Insular Affairs. *Hearings on Stockpile and Accessibility of Strategic and Critical Materials to the United States in Time of War.* 83d Cong., 1st and 2d sess. Washington, D.C.: GPO, 1954.

U.S. Congress. Senate. Committee on Public Works. *Federal Aid for Highways.* 80th Cong., 2d sess. Washington, D.C.: GPO, 1948.

U.S. Congress. Senate. Committee on Public Works. *Hearings, Federal Highway Act of 1952.* 82d Cong., 2d sess. Washington, D.C.: GPO, 1952.

U.S. Congress. Senate. Committee on Public Works. *Hearings on Federal Act of 1954.* 83d Cong., 2d sess. Washington, D.C: GPO, 1954.

U.S. Congress. Senate. Committee on Appropriations. *Hearings before the Senate Committee on Appropriations,* 84th Cong., 2d sess. Washington, D.C.: GPO, 1956.

U.S. Congress. Senate. Committee on Interior and Insular Affairs. *Hearings on Proposed Canyonlands National Park in Utah.* 87th Cong., 2d sess., S. 2387. Washington, D.C.: GPO, 1962.

U.S. Congress. Senate. Committee on Interior and Insular Affairs. *Hearings on the Proposed Canyonlands National Park in Utah.* 88th Cong., 1st sess., S. 27. Washington, D.C.: GPO, 1963.

U.S. Department of Agriculture. Forest Service. *Forests and National Prosperity: A Reappraisal of the Forest Situation in the United States.* Washington, D.C.: GPO, 1948.

U.S. Department of Agriculture. Forest Service. *Flagstaff Federal Sustained Yield Unit: Periodic Analysis.* Albuquerque: U.S. Forest Service, Region 3, 1969.

U.S. Department of the Interior. Bureau of Reclamation. *San Juan Investigation: Utah and Colorado.* Salt Lake City: Bureau of Reclamation, Region 4, 1969.

U.S. Department of the Interior. National Park Service. *Mesa Verde National Park Master Plan.* Washington, D.C.: GPO, 1975.

U.S. Department of the Interior. National Park Service. *Proceedings of the National Parks Conference.* Washington, D.C.: GPO, 1917.

U.S. Department of the Interior. National Park Service. *Public Use of the National Parks: A Statistical Report.* Washington: D.C.: GPO, 1964.

U.S. Department of the Interior. National Park Service. *Public Use, Tabulation of Visitors to Areas Administered by the National Park Service.* Washington, D.C.: GPO, 1961.

U.S. Federal Trade Commission. *Reports of the Federal Trade Commission on Natural Gas Pipelines in the U.S.A.* Washington, D.C.: GPO, 1940.

U.S. *Public Papers of President Dwight D. Eisenhower.* Washington, D.C.: GPO, 1955, 1958, 1961.

U.S. *Public Papers of President Harry S. Truman.* Washington, D.C.: GPO, 1949.

PUBLIC DOCUMENTS AND REPORTS

Annual Report. Phoenix: Southwest Forest Industries, 1964, 1967–69.

"Annual Report: 1962–63." Santa Fe: New Mexico State Park and Recreation Commission, 1963.

"Annual Review: San Juan National Forest." Durango: United States Department of Agriculture, Forest Service, San Juan District 2, 1959.

"Arizona Snow Bowl Makes Flagstaff a Winter Sports Capital." Flagstaff: Chamber of Commerce, 1971.

"Arizona Tourism and Travel Industry." Tempe: Arizona State University, Bureau of Business and Economic Research, 1976.

Development Possibilities Along Navajo Highway No. I. Albuquerque: Chambers and Campbell, Inc., n.d.

"Durango Chamber of Commerce: Minutes, 1946–1958." Durango: Fort Lewis College Library.

"Environmental Statement: Coconino National Forest and Arizona Snow Bowl Ski Area Proposal." Flagstaff: U.S. Department of Agriculture, Forest Service, Region 3, 1978.

"Fabulous Farmington, New Mexico: The Energy Capital of the West." Farmington: Chamber of Commerce, 1961.

Farmington, New Mexico: Welcome Guide. San Diego: Hart Enterprises, Inc., 1983.

"Flagstaff: An Arizona Area Resource Study." Phoenix: Arizona Employment Service, 1969.

"Flagstaff: Arizona Community Prospectus." Phoenix: Arizona Office of Economic Planning, 1974.

"Flagstaff: Profile of a Beautiful City." Flagstaff: Chamber of Commerce, 1971.

"Fort Apache Indian Reservation Forest Management Plan." Whiteriver, AZ: U.S. Department of the Interior, Bureau of Indian Affairs, Branch of Forestry, 1985.

Four Corners Regional Planning Commission: Annual Report. Farmington: Four Corners Regional Planning Commission, 1968, 1969, 1970.

Fuel for Fighting Fronts via "Big Inch" and "Little Inch." New York: War
    Emergency Pipelines, Inc., 1944.
"Here is Durango." Durango: Chamber of Commerce, 1968.
"History of Southwest Forest Industries." In *1983 Corporate Fact Book*, 30–35.
    Phoenix: Southwest Forest Industries, 1983.
"Industrial Facts and Figures of Flagstaff, Arizona." Flagstaff: Chamber of
    Commerce, 1957.
"Initial Action Plan." Farmington: Four Corners Regional Planning
    Commission, 1967.
Marr, Eldon G. *Population and Employment in the Four Corners Development
    Region.* Albuquerque: University of New Mexico, Bureau of Business
    Research, 1968.
"National Park Service Visitors: Arizona, 1970–75." Santa Fe: U.S. Department
    of the Interior, National Park Service, Southwest Regional Office, 1976.
"New Mexico's Interstate Highways." Santa Fe: New Mexico State Highway
    Department, 1958.
Population and Employment in the Four Corners Development Region. Albuquerque:
    University of New Mexico, Bureau of Business Research, 1968.
*Preliminary Report, Economy, Population, Land Use, Major Thoroughfares and
    Central Business District: Farmington, New Mexico.* St. Louis: n.p., 1967.
Proceedings: Four Corners-Farmington Industry Opportunity Program. Farmington:
    Farmington Industrial Development Service, 1968.
"Purgatory Summary of Skier Visits and Adult Ticket Prices." Durango, CO:
    Purgatory Ski Corporation, 1986.
"Report of Winter and Summer Visitors in Arizona." Tucson: University of
    Arizona, Bureau of Business Research, 1956.
"Skiing Colorado Business Survey." Denver: Colorado National Bank, 1964.
Study of Reclamation and Tourism in New Mexico. Albuquerque: Kirchner and
    Associates, n.d.
"The Climate for Business and Industry in the State of New Mexico." San
    Antonio: Southwest Research Institute, 1964.
"The Interstate System in New Mexico: A Progress Report, 1956–1961." Santa
    Fe: New Mexico State Highway Department, 1962.
"The Northern Arizona Statistical Abstract." Flagstaff: Northern Arizona
    University, Bureau of Business and Economic Research, 1984.
"Timber Management Plan, San Juan National Forest, Region 2." Denver:
    U.S. Department of Agriculture, Forest Service, 1961.
"Welcome to Farmington." Farmington: Chamber of Commerce, 1971.

BOOKS

Abbott, Carl. *The New Urban America: Growth and Politics in Sunbelt Cities.*
    Chapel Hill: University of North Carolina Press, 1981.

———. *Colorado: A History of the Centennial State*. Boulder: University of Colorado Press, 1976.

Arizona Landmarks. Vol. 1, Book 4. Phoenix: Arizona State Land Department, 1971.

Arrington, J. Leonard. *The Changing Economic Structure of the Mountain West, 1850–1950*. Logan: Utah State University Press, 1963.

———. *Great Basin Kingdom: An Economic History of the Latter-day Saints, 1830–1900*. 1958. Reprint. Lincoln: University of Nebraska Press, 1966.

———, and Anthony T. Cluff. *Federally Financed Industrial Plants Constructed in Utah During World War II*. Logan: Utah State University Press, 1969.

Aviel, David S. *The Politics of Nuclear Power*. Washington: n.p., 1982.

Bailey, Garrick A., and Roberta G. Bailey. *Historic Navajo Occupation of the Northern Chaco Plateau*. Tulsa: University of Tulsa Press, 1982.

Baker, Richard Allan. *Conservation Politics: The Senate Career of Clinton P. Anderson*. Albuquerque: University of New Mexico, 1985.

Between Sacred Mountains: Stories and Lessons from the Land. Chinle, AZ: Rock Point Community School, 1984.

Borne, Lawrence R. *Dude Ranching: A Complete History*. Albuquerque: University of New Mexico Press, 1983.

Brownell, Blaine. *The Urban Ethos in the South, 1920–1930*. Baton Rouge: Louisiana State University Press, 1975.

Caughey, John Walton. *The American West: Frontier and Region*. Los Angeles: Ward Ritchie Press, 1969.

Chappell, Gordon S. *Logging Along the Denver & Rio Grande*. Golden: Colorado Historical Railroad Association, 1971.

Cline, Platt. *They Came to the Mountain: The Story of Flagstaff's Beginnings*. Flagstaff: Northland Press, 1976.

———. *Mountain Campus: The Story of Northern Arizona University*. Flagstaff: Northland Press, 1983.

Corbett, John M. *Aztec Ruins National Monument*. Washington, D.C.: U.S. Department of the Interior, National Park Service, 1963.

Crampton, Gregory. *Standing Up Country: The Canyon Lands of Utah and Arizona*. New York: Alfred A Knopf, 1964.

Davies, Richard O. *The Age of Asphalt: The Automobile, the Freeway, and the Condition of Metropolitan America*. Ed. Harold M. Hyman. New York: J. B. Lippincott Company, 1975.

Del Soto, Steven L. *Science, Politics, and Controversy*. Boulder: University of Colorado Press, 1969.

Derthick, Martha. *Between State and Nation: Regional Organizations of the United States*. Washington, D.C.: The Brookings Institution, 1974.

Dykstra, Robert A. *The Cattle Towns: A Social History of the Kansas Cattle Trading Centers Abilene, Ellsworth, Wichita, Dodge City and Caldwell, 1867–1885*. 1970. Reprint. Lincoln: University of Nebraska Press, 1983.

Eisenhower, Dwight D. *The White House Years: Mandate for Change, 1953–1956.* New York: Doubleday & Company, Inc., 1963.

Foreman, Grant, ed. *A Pathfinder in the Southwest: The Itinerary of Lt. A. W. Whipple during His Explorations for a Railway Route from Ft. Smith to Los Angeles in the Years, 1853–1854.* 1941. Reprint. Norman: University of Oklahoma Press, 1968.

Fradkin, Philip L. *A River No More: The Colorado River and the West.* 1968. Reprint. Tucson: University of Arizona Press, 1984.

Gardner, L. C., Arthur Schlesinger, Jr., and Hans Morganthau. *The Origins of the Cold War.* Waltham, MA: Ginn-Blaisdall, 1970.

Garnsey, Morris E. *America's New Frontier: The Mountain West.* New York: Alfred A. Knopf, 1950.

Gastil, Raymond. *Cultural Regions of the United States.* Seattle: University of Washington Press, 1975.

Goetzmann, William H. *Army Explorations in the American West, 1803–1863.* New Haven: Yale University Press, 1959.

Gressley, Gene M. *Bankers and Cattlemen: Politics, Investors, Operators from 1870 to 1900.* 1966. Reprint. Lincoln: University of Nebraska Press, 1971.

Groueff, Stephane. *Manhattan Project: The Untold Story of the Making of the Atomic Bomb.* Boston: Little Brown and Company, 1967.

Groves, Leslie R. *Now It Can Be Told: The Story of the Manhattan Project.* London: Andre Deutsch, 1963.

Guthrie, John A., and George R. Armstrong. *Western Forest Industry: An Economic Outlook.* Baltimore: Johns Hopkins University Press, 1961.

Hall, Ansel Franklin. *General Report on the Rainbow Bridge–Monument Valley Expedition of 1933.* Berkeley: University of California Press, 1934.

Harris, Seymour E. *Economics of the Kennedy Years and a Look Ahead.* New York: Harper & Row, 1964.

Hayes, Lynton R. *Energy, Economic Growth, and Regionalism in the West.* Albuquerque: University of New Mexico Press, 1983.

Hewett, Edgar L. *The Chaco Canyon and Its Monuments.* Albuquerque: University of New Mexico Press, 1936.

Hewlett, Richard G., and Oscar E. Anderson, Jr. *The New World 1939–1947: A History of the United States Atomic Energy Commission.* University Park, PA: Penn State University Press, 1962.

Ise, John. *Our National Park Policy: A Critical History.* Baltimore: Johns Hopkins University Press, 1961.

Jakle, John A. *The Tourist: Travel in Twentieth-Century North America.* Lincoln: University of Nebraska Press, 1985.

Jett, Stephen C. *Tourism in the Navajo Country: Resources and Planning.* Window Rock, AZ: Navajo Tribal Council, 1966.

Johnson, Arthur M. *Petroleum Pipelines and Public Policy, 1906–1959.* Cambridge: Harvard University Press, 1967.

Kelly, Susan Croce and Quinta Scott. *Route 66: The Highway and Its People*,
    Norman: Oklahoma University Press, 1990.
Kessell, John. *Kiva, Cross, and Crown: The Pecos Indians and New Mexico,
    1540–1840*. 1979. Reprint. Albuquerque: University of New Mexico Press,
    1987.
Knowlton, Ezra C. *History of Highway Development in Utah*. Salt Lake City:
    Utah State Road Commission, 1966.
Langdon, Charlie. *Durango Ski: People and Seasons at Purgatory*. Durango:
    Purgatory Press, 1989.
Lamar, Howard Roberts. *The Far Southwest, 1846–1912: A Territorial History*.
    1966. Reprint. New York: W. W. Norton & Company, Inc., 1970.
Larsen, Lawrence H. *The Urban West at the End of the Frontier*. Lawrence:
    Regents Press of Kansas, 1978.
Leuchtenburg, William E. *Franklin Delano Roosevelt and the New Deal*. New
    York: Harper & Row, 1963.
Lilienthal, David E. *The Journals of David E. Lilienthal*. Vol. I: *TVA— Democracy
    on the March*. New York: Harper & Row, 1964.
———. *The Journals of David E. Lilienthal*. Vol. II: *The Atomic Energy Years,
    1945–1950*. New York: Harper & Row, 1964.
Lister, Robert, and Florence Lister. *Aztec Ruins National Monument:
    Administrative History of an Archeological Preserve*. Santa Fe: National Park
    Service, Southwest Cultural Resources Center, 1990.
Lockwood, Frank C. *The Life of Edward E. Ayer*. Chicago: A. C. McClurg and
    Co., 1929.
Lowitt, Richard. *The New Deal and the West*. Bloomington: University of
    Indiana Press, 1984.
Luckingham, Bradford. *The Urban Southwest: A Profile History of Albuquerque, El
    Paso, Phoenix, and Tucson*. El Paso: Texas Western Press, 1982.
Magan, Frank. *The Pipeliners: The Story of El Paso Natural Gas*. El Paso: Guynes
    Press, 1977.
MacDonald, Eleanor Davenport. *I Remember Old MacDonald's Farmington*. Santa
    Fe: Sleeping Fox Enterprises, 1975.
———, and John Brown Arrington. *The San Juan Basin: My Kingdom Was a
    County*. Denver: Green Mountain Press, 1970.
McNary, James. *This Is My Life*. Albuquerque: University of New Mexico Press,
    1956.
Meinig, D. W. *Imperial Texas: An Interpretive Essay in Cultural Geography*.
    Austin: University of Texas Press, 1969.
Melosi, Martin V. *Coping with Abundance: Energy and Environment in Industrial
    America*. Philadelphia: Temple University Press, 1985.
Miller, David E. *The Route of the Dominguez–Escalante Expedition, 1776–1777*.
    Durango: Four Corners Regional Planning Commission, 1976.

Morgan, Neil. *Westward Tilt: The American West Today*. New York: Random House, 1963.

Nash, Gerald D. *The American West Transformed: The Impact of the Second World War*. Bloomington: Indiana University Press, 1985.

_____. *The American West in the Twentieth Century: A Short History of An Urban Oasis*. 1973. Reprint. Albuquerque: University of New Mexico, Press, 1977.

_____. *United States Oil Policy, 1890–1964: Business and Government in the Twentieth Century*. Pittsburgh: University of Pittsburgh Press, 1968.

_____. *The Great Depression and World War II: Organizing America, 1933–1945*: New York: St. Martin's Press, Inc., 1979.

Nash, Roderick. *Wilderness and the American Mind*. New Haven: Yale University Press, 1967.

Noble, David Grant. *Ancient Ruins of the Southwest*. Flagstaff: Northland Press, 1981.

Odum, Howard W., and Harry Moore. *American Regionalism: A Cultural-Historical Approach in National Integration*. New York: Henry Holt and Company, 1938.

O'Rourke, Paul M. *Frontier in Transition: A History of Southwestern Colorado*. Denver: U.S. Department of the Interior, Bureau of Land Management, 1980.

Osterwald, Doris B. *Cinders & Smoke: A Mile by Mile Guide for the Durango to Silverton Narrow Gauge Trip*. Lakewood, CO: Western Guideways, Ltd., 1965.

Paul, Rodman Wilson. *Mining Frontiers of the Far West, 1848–1880*. 1963. Reprint. Albuquerque: University of New Mexico, 1974.

Perloff, Harvey S., with Vera Dodds. *How A Region Grows: Area Development in the U.S. Economy*. Washington, D.C.: Office of Economic Development, 1963.

Peterson, Charles S. *Take Up Your Mission: Mormon Colonizing Along the Little Colorado River, 1870–1900*. Tucson: University of Arizona Press, 1973.

Pomeroy, Earl. *The Pacific Slope: A History of California, Oregon, Washington, Idaho, Utah and Nevada*. Seattle: University of Washington Press, 1965.

_____. *In Search of the Golden West: The Tourist in Western America*. New York: Alfred A. Knopf, 1957.

Powell, John Wesley. *Report on the Lands of the Arid Region of the United States: With a More Detailed Account of the Lands of Utah*. Ed. Wallace Stegner. Cambridge: Harvard University Press, 1962.

Pyne, Stephen J. *Dutton's Point: An Intellectual History of the Grand Canyon*. Grand Canyon, AZ: Grand Canyon Natural History Association, 1982.

Resource Atlas of Coconino County, Arizona. Flagstaff: Northern Arizona University, Department of Geography, 1981.

Richardson, Elmo. *Dams, Parks and Politics: Resource Development and Preser-*

vation in the Truman–Eisenhower Era. Lexington: University of Kentucky Press, 1973.

Rittenhouse, Jack D. *A Guidebook to Highway 66.* 1946. Reprint. Albuquerque: University of New Mexico Press, 1988.

Robbins, William G. *American Forestry: A History of National, State, and Private Cooperation.* Lincoln: University of Nebraska Press, 1985.

Rose, Mark H. *Interstate: Express Highway Politics, 1941–1956.* Lawrence: The Regents Press of Kansas, 1979.

Rothman, Hal. *Navajo National Monument: A Place and Its People.* Santa Fe: National Park Service, Southwest Cultural Resources Center, 1991.

Runte, Alfred. *National Parks: The American Experience.* Lincoln: University of Nebraska Press, 1979.

Sanders, Elizabeth M. *The Regulation of Natural Gas: Policy and Politics, 1938–1978.* Philadelphia: Temple University Press, 1981.

Smith, Alice Kimball. *A Peril and A Hope: The Scientists' Movement in America, 1945–47.* 1965. Reprint. Cambridge: The M.I.T. Press, 1971.

Smith, Duane A. *Rocky Mountain Boom Town: A History of Durango.* Albuquerque: University of New Mexico Press, 1980.

_____. *Mesa Verde National Park: Shadows of the Centuries.* Lawrence: University of Kansas Press, 1988.

_____. *Sacred Trust: The Birth and Development of Fort Lewis College.* Boulder: University of Colorado Press, 1991.

Smyth, Henry De Wolf. *Atomic Energy for Military Purposes: The Official Report on the Development of the Atomic Bomb under the Auspices of the United States Government, 1940–1945.* Princeton: Princeton University Press, 1947.

Szasz, Ferenc Morton. *The Day the Sun Rose Twice: The Story of the Trinity Site Nuclear Explosion, July 16, 1945.* Albuquerque: University of New Mexico Press, 1984.

Tanner, Faun McConkie. *The Far Country: A Regional History of Moab and La Sal, Utah.* Salt Lake City: Olympus Publishing Company, 1976.

Taylor, George Rogers. *The Turner Thesis: Concerning the Role of the Frontier in American History.* Lexington, MA: D. C. Heath and Company, 1972.

Taylor, Raymond W., and Samuel W. Taylor. *Uranium Fever, or No Talk Under $1 Million.* New York: Macmillan Company, 1970.

Truman, Harry S. *Memoirs.* Vol 1: *The Year of Decisions.* New York: New American Library, 1955.

Udall, Stewart L. *The Quiet Crisis.* New York: Holt, Rinehart & Winston, Inc., 1963.

Wade, Richard C. *The Urban Frontier: The Rise of Western Cities, 1790–1830.* Cambridge: Harvard University Press, 1959.

Walker Henry P., and Don Bufkin, eds. *Historical Atlas of Arizona.* Norman: University of Oklahoma Press, 1979.

Wallis, Michael: *Route 66: The Mother Road*. New York: St. Martin's Press, 1990.

Weber, David. *Richard Kern: Expeditionary Artist in the Far Southwest, 1848–1853*. Albuquerque: University of New Mexico Press, 1985.

Wiley, Peter, and Robert Gottlieb. *Empires in the Sun: The Rise of the New American West*. 1982. Reprint. Tucson: University of Arizona Press, 1985.

Williams, Jerry L., and Paul E. McAllister, eds. *New Mexico in Maps*. 1979. Reprint. Albuquerque: University of New Mexico Press, 1986.

Wirth, Conrad L. *Parks, Politics, and the People*. Norman: University of Oklahoma Press, 1980.

Yazzie, Alfred W. *Navajo Oral Tradition*. Vol II. Rough Rock, AZ: Navajo Resource Center, 1984.

Yergin, Daniel. *The Prize: The Epic Quest for Oil, Money, & Power*. New York: Simon & Schuster, 1992.

Zelinsky, Wilbur. *The Cultural Geography of the United States*. Englewood Cliffs: Prentice-Hall, 1973.

Abbott, Carl. "The Metropolitan Region: Western Cities in the New Urban Frontier." In *The Twentieth Century West: Historical Interpretations*, ed. Gerald D. Nash and Richard W. Etulain, 71–98. Albuquerque: University of New Mexico Press, 1989.

"Among These Basins: A New Chapter in American Oil is Being Written." *Oil and Gas Journal* (October 1953): 158–61, 196–98.

"Arizona: Sun, Room, and Low Taxes." *Fortune Magazine* (March 1958): 14–25.

Arnold, Emery C., and Thomas A. Dugan. "Hogback Discovery in San Juan County Was New Mexico's First Oiler in 1922." *Western Oil Reporter* (August 1971): 17–18.

Bail, E. B. "New Mexico–U.S. 66: Albuquerque's Golden Road." In *Sagebrush Lawyer*, by Arthur Thomas Hannett, 277–88. New York: Pageant Press, 1964.

Barnes, Frank C. "Developments in the San Juan Basin." *Oil and Gas Journal* (June 1949): 60–67.

———. "The San Juan Fulfills Its Promise." *Oil and Gas Journal*, (February 1956): 154–55.

Black, Calvin. "San Juan County Roads and Resources." In *San Juan County, Utah: People, Resources, and History*, ed. Allan Kent Powell, 241–58. Salt Lake City: Utah Historical Society, 1983.

Bilodeau, Gary. "The Good Old Days in the San Juan Basin." *The Pipeliner* 40 (April 1977): 24–27.

Boyer, Jim. "Ski Boom." *New Mexico Magazine* 46 (January 1965): 11–15.

Chenoweth, William L. "Uranium Deposits of the Canyonlands Area." *Four Corners Geological Society Guidebook* 8 (1975): 253–60.

Clapp, Gordon R. "The Tennessee Valley Authority." In *Regionalism in America*, ed. Merrill Jensen, 317–29. Madison: University of Wisconsin Press, 1951.

Cohenour, R. E. "History of Uranium and Development of Colorado Plateau Ores with Notes on Uranium Production in Utah." *Guidebook to the Geology of Utah* (1967): 12–22.

Cooper, Valda. "The Fabulous Four Corners." *New Mexico Magazine* 48 (March 1965): 7–14.

Davis, Ronald L. F. "Western Urban Development: A Critical Analysis." In *The American West: New Perspectives, New Dimensions*, ed. Jerome O. Steffen, 178–84. Norman: Oklahoma University Press, 1979.

De Voto, Bernard. "The West: A Plundered Province." *Harper's Magazine* 169 (August 1934): 355–64.

_____. "The West Against Itself." *Harper's Magazine* 194 (January 1947): 1–13.

_____. "Let's Close the National Parks." *Harper's Magazine* 207 (October 1953): 49–52.

Dugan, Thomas A. "The San Juan Basin: Episodes and Aspirations." *New Mexico Geological Society Guidebook* 28 (1977): 83–89.

Dow, F. B. "The Role of Petroleum Pipelines in the War." *Annals of the American Academy of Political and Social Sciences* 230 (November 1943): 93–100.

"El Paso to Boost Gas Flow Westward." *Oil and Gas Journal* (May 1955): 83–85.

"Fabulous Farmington, New Mexico." *Farmington Four Corners Magazine* 1 (September 1976): 3–10.

Gómez, Arthur R. "The New Natural Resources Colonialism: The Small City in the West." In *Natural Resources in Colorado and Wyoming*, ed. Duane A. Smith, 51–59. Manhattan: Sunflower Press, 1982.

Gressley, Gene M. "James G. Blaine, 'Alferd' E. Packer, and Western Particularism." *Historian* 44 (May 1982): 364–81.

Gunderson, R. J. "Population Changes in Northern Arizona Counties." *Northern Arizona Economic Review* 9 (September 1982): 1–5.

Gutman, Walter K. "Vanadium Corporation: Rich Stake in Uranium Bolsters Its Profits." *Barron's Magazine* (September 1954): 15–16.

Hanson, Pauline. "Southwest Forest Industries." *Arizona Highways* (July 1964): 35–47.

Hayes, Alden C. "The Wetherill Mesa Project." *Naturalist* 20 (1969): 18–25.

Haymond, Jay M. "San Juan County Roads: Arteries to Natural Resources and Survival." In *San Juan County, Utah: People, Resources, and History*, ed. Allan Kent Powell, 227–39. Salt Lake City: Utah State Historical Society, 1983.

Heald, Weldon F. "Bold Plan to Save the Canyonlands," *Desert Magazine* (April 1962): 17–21.

Hertzog, George, Jr. "Management Considerations." In *Proceedings: Second World Conference on National Parks*, 155–61. Morges, Switzerland: n.p., 1974.

Krim, Arthur. "Mapping Route 66: A Cultural Geography." In *Roadside America: The Automobile in Design and Culture*. (Iowa: University of Iowa Press, n.d.)

"Land of Sunshine: The Grand Canyon of the Colorado." *Northern Arizona Pioneers Historical Society*. (1975): 1–8.

Lotchin, Roger W. "The Metropolitan–Military Complex in Comparative Perspective: San Francisco, Los Angeles, and San Diego." *Journal of the West* 18 (July 1979): 19–30.

Matheny, Marvin L. "A History of the Petroleum Industry in the Four Corners Area." *Four Corners Geological Society* (1978): 17–24.

Matheny, Robert L. "Lumbering in the White Mountains of Arizona." *Arizona and the West* 18 (Autumn 1976): 237–56.

Mazuzan, George T. "Conflict of Interest: Promoting and Regulating the Infant Nuclear Power Industry, 1954–1956." *The Historian* 46 (November 1981): 1–14.

McWilliams, Carey. "Introduction." In *Rocky Mountain Cities*, ed. Ray B. West, Jr., 7–28. New York: W. W. Norton, Inc., 1949.

Meinig, D. W. "American Wests: Preface to a Geographical Introduction." *Annals of the Association of American Geographers* 62 (June 1972): 159–84.

Miller, Lee D. "Skiing in New Mexico is Big Business." *New Mexico Magazine* 42 (January 1964): 6–9.

Morrissey, Norman S. "Eight Paradox Strikes is a Perfect '56 Score in Prospect?" *Oil and Gas Journal* (October 1956): 149–50.

Nelson, Elroy. "The Impact of Uranium on the Economy of the State and the Southeastern Utah Area." *Guidebook to the Geology of Utah* (1957): 99–105.

Pierson, Lloyd M. "The First Canyonlands New Park Studies, 1959 and 1960." *Canyon Legacy* 1 (Fall 1989): 9–14.

Pomeroy, Earl. "Toward a Reorientation of Western History: Continuity and Environment." *Mississippi Valley Historical Review* 41 (March 1955): 579–600.

Ralph, Henry D. "FPC Backs Phillips." *Oil and Gas Journal* (September 1953): 67–68.

Reilly, Joe. "Pacific Northwest: Pipeline Rarity." *Oil and Gas Journal* (October 1955): 118–21.

Rodnitsky, Jerome. "Recapturing the West: The Dude Ranch in American Life." *Arizona and the West* 10 (Summer 1968): 111–26.

Schlesinger, Arthur, Sr. "The City in American History." *Mississippi Valley Historical Review* 27 (June 1940): 43–66.

Shumway, Gary L. "Uranium Mining on the Colorado Plateau." In *San Juan County, Utah: People, Resources, and History*, ed. Allan Kent Powell, 265–98. Salt Lake City: Utah State Historical Society, 1983.

"Snow Bowl Survey." *Northern Arizona Economic Review* (Winter 1977): 1–8.

"Southwest Forest Industries: A Fully Integrated Forest Products Company." *Builder Architect Contractor Engineer* 39 (August 1977): 6–9.

Stapp, Robert. "Can They Strike It Rich?" *Rocky Mountain Empire Magazine* (August 1949): 2–6.

Stevenson, Charles. "The Shocking Truth About Our National Parks." *Reader's Digest* (January 1955): 45–50.

Stocking, Marion. "Charlie Steen—Prospector." *Four Corners Geological Society Guidebook* 3 (1975): 51–54.

Tier, R. J. "Secondary Roads." *Proceedings of the 1959 Highway Engineering Conference*. Santa Fe: New Mexico State Highway Department, 1959.

Tilden, Paul M. "Let's Get Going on the Canyonlands." *National Parks Magazine* (February 1963): 18–23.

Tripp, R. Maurice. "The Great American Sport—1955 Version." *Oil and Gas Journal* (April 1955): 161–64.

"Twenty-five Years of Progressive and Diversified Growth." *Builder Architect Contractor Engineer* 39 (August 1977): 12.

Wylie, L. F. "Roads to Scenic Treasures." *Reclamation Era* (1958): 57–60.

NEWSPAPERS

Albuquerque Journal, 1951–1970.
Albuquerque Tribune, 1948–1956.
Arizona Daily Star, 1959–1965.
Arizona Daily Sun, 1946–1971.
Arizona Republic, 1962.
Coconino Sun, 1944–1957.
Denver Post, 1948–1962.
Deseret News, 1960–1961.
Durango Herald Democrat, 1949–1953.
Durango Herald News, 1953–1971, 1988.
Farmington Daily Times, 1949–1969.
Farmington Times Hustler, 1906, 1946–1954.
Grand Junction Daily Sentinel, 1948–1969.
Moab Times Independent, 1948–1961.
New York Herald Tribune, 1954.
New York Times, 1953, 1962.
Rocky Mountain News, 1949, 1957.
Salt Lake Tribune, 1961–1963.
San Juan Valley Sun, 1950.

Santa Fe New Mexican, 1969.
Wall Street Journal, 1962.
Washington Post, 1967.

INTERVIEWS

Arnold, Emery. Interview with Tom Dugan, January 14, 1981. Farmington Public Library, Farmington, New Mexico.

August, Jack, Jr. Telephone interview with Art Gómez, February 14, 1988.

Ballantine, Arthur Atwood. Interview with David McComb, June 10, 1974. Fort Lewis College Library, Durango, Colorado.

Balsley, Howard W. Interview with Nancy Taniguchi, May 7, 1979. Moab Public Library, Moab, Utah.

Bollack, Tom. Interview with Tom Dugan, January 14, 1981. Farmington Public Library, Farmington, New Mexico.

Byrd, Dennis "Pete". Interview with Art Gómez, February 10, 1984. In author's possession, Santa Fe, New Mexico.

Dallas, Wayne. Interview with Tom Dugan, April 10, 1981. Farmington Public Library, Farmington, New Mexico.

Dugan, Tom. Interview with Art Gómez, August 1, 1985. In author's possession, Santa Fe, New Mexico.

Elliott, Mike. Interview with Art Gómez, June 3, 1987. In author's possession, Santa Fe, New Mexico.

Gardenswartz, Lester. Interview with Duane A. Smith, January 14, 1977. Fort Lewis College Library, Durango, Colorado.

Lloyd, Leo W. Interview with Duane A. Smith, November 8, 1976. Fort Lewis College Library, Durango, Colorado.

MacDonald, Eleanor. Interview with Jimmy Miller, December 30, 1980. Farmington Public Library, New Mexico.

Porter, L. D. Interview with Art Gómez, June 28, 1983. Arizona State University Library, Phoenix, Arizona.

Shober Grace, and Charlie Graves. Interview with Art Gómez, December 9, 1986. In author's possession, Santa Fe, New Mexico.

Valentine, Mike. Telephone interview with Art Gómez, July 14, 1987.

Index

Udall-Anderson bill, 116
Union Carbide, 10
Union Mines Development Corporation, 22
U. S. Army Corps of Topographical Engineers, 7
U. S. Bureau of Mines, 64
U. S. Department of Defense and arterial roads, 102
U. S. Forest Service, 44, 67, 68, 111, 123, 137, 177, 179, 180–82
U. S. Highway 50, Utah, 103
U. S. Highway 160, Arizona, 104
U. S. Highway 66, at Flagstaff, 41, 65; generally, 97–98, 104, 106, 107, 111
U. S. Navy Department, 39
U. S. Senate Committee on Public Works, 101, 102, 106
United States Vanadium Company (USVC), 10, 11
University of Colorado, 27
University of New Mexico, 156
University of Utah, 145, 166
Upper Colorado River Storage Project, 140, 185
uraninite, 28, 29
uranium, 10, 11; access roads for, 101, 103; federal procurement of, 21–29, 48–55, 72, 101; map for, 95; prospecting for, 74, 81. *See also by state*
Uranium Institute of America (UIA), 53
Uranium Ore Producers Association, 52
Uranium Reduction Company, 29, 50, 51
urban ethos, 50
urban imperialism, 48
Utah, access roads and highways for, 26, 102, 103, 107, 112; canyon country of, 119; defense arterial

road in, 102; Golden Circle in, 119; parks and monuments in, 125, 130, 140–46, 175, and tourism, 140, 173; petroleum in, 41; politics of, 150; smelters in, 10; uranium in, 49, 51, 54, 156. *See also* Canyonlands National Park; Moab, Utah
Utah Industrial Promotion Commission, 149
Utah State Highway Commission, 103
Ute Reservation, Southern, 40

vanadium, 10, 11, 21
Vanadium Corporation of America (VCA), 10, 11, 21, 27, 29, 47, 48, 51, 55, 71, 103, 104, 105
Veterans' Emergency Housing Program, 43–44
Viles, Dennis, 27, 48, 103–4
Vitro Manufacturing Company, 10
vocational education, regionally funded, 168

Wallace, Henry A., 20
War Department, 19, 21, 100
Washington Post, the, xv
Weidman, John Stanley, 67
West, Ray B., xvii
"West Against Itself, The," De Voto, 31
Western Governor's Report, 139
Western States Tourist Development Task Force, 171
Wetherill, John, 10
Wetherill Mesa Project, 160, 175
Whiting, Jay, 66
Williams, Jack, 151
Wilson, Bates, 92
Wilson, Kenneth, 36
Wilson, Woodrow, 98, 123
Wink, Texas, 33